Questions & Answers
for the PPL Course

Questions & Answers for the PPL Course

Jim Stevens & Jeremy M Pratt

2000 Edition

ISBN 1-874783-61-6

Airplan Flight Equipment

Originally published as The Questions and Answers Book for the Private Pilots Licence
First Edition 1993
Second Edition 1994
Reprinted with revisions 1997

Copyright © 1993/4/7 Airplan Flight Equipment
2nd Edition revisions and Radiotelephony Copyright © 1994 Jeremy M. Pratt
Revisions Copyright © 1997 Jeremy M. Pratt

This New Edition
Copyright © 1999 Jeremy M. Pratt

All rights reserved. No part of this publication may be reproduced, stored in a retrieval system, or transmitted in any form or by any means, electronic, mechanical, photocopy, recording, or otherwise, without the prior written permission of the copyright holder.

Questions and Answers
for the PPL Course

Jim Stevens & Jeremy M Pratt

ISBN 1-874783-61-6

Published by:

Airplan Flight Equipment Ltd

Unit 1a, Ringway Trading Estate, Shadowmoss Road, Manchester M22 5LH
Tel: 0161 499 0023   Fax: 0161 499 0298
www.airplan.u-net.com

Acknowledgments

We would like to thank the following for their help and advice:

AOPA
Adrian Dickinson
Steve Dickinson
Ron Campbell
Premo Lonzardi
Medway Flight Training
David Ogilvy
Martin Robinson
Ian Sixsmith
Rob Taylor @ GDi studio

Section Contents

Aviation Law
Papers 1 – 4

Meteorology
Papers 1 – 10

Navigation
Papers 1 – 10

Aircraft General
Papers 1 – 4

Human Performance and Limitations
Papers 1 – 10

Radiotelephony
Papers 1 – 10

Answers and References

Conduct of the Examination

The examination usually takes place at the Flying Training Organisation (FTO) under the supervision of a CAA authorised examiner.

Candidates are expected to provide their own navigation, writing & calculating equipment. Reference books, notes and electronic calculators are **not** permitted. The exam room will have any relevant posters or publications removed. The candidate would not normally be expected to leave and re-enter the exam room whilst the examination is in progress; so go to the toilet first!

Each exam has a specified time limit which will be strictly observed. The person supervising the exam is not allowed to discuss the examination, interpretation of questions etc. whilst the examination is in progress. The exam question paper should not be marked in any way. Use the back of the answer sheet for any rough workings you want to do.

Once the exam is finished, the authorised examiner will mark the paper. In the event of a pass the examiner will discuss any questions wrongly answered. In the event of a fail, the examiner may indicate general areas of weakness, but will not discuss answers to specific questions.

There are three examination papers for each subject, it is not permitted to take the same paper twice. Should the candidate fail all three papers, arrangements will be made for an examination by a CAA staff examiner.

The candidate should be warned before the exam starts that any infringement of the rules will result in disqualification.

Examination Technique

All the examinations are of the multiple choice type – marks are **not** deducted for an incorrect answer.

Before starting the exam paper read through the instructions carefully. Check the time limit so that you know when the exam will finish.

Unless there are specific instructions otherwise, tackle the questions you are sure you can answer first, and return to difficult questions later. Read each question carefully and be sure you understand exactly what is being asked. There will be only one correct answer, sometimes you can reach this by eliminating the wrong answers.

You are not allowed spare paper, or to mark the examination paper in any way. Do any workings out on the back of the answer sheet.

Generally the exams are not 'time – pressure' type, so you may well finish the paper before the time limit is reached. If this is the case the remaining time is best spent by re-checking the answers you have given. Re-read each question carefully to be sure you have understood it properly and have given the correct answer. Remember that marks are not deducted for an incorrect answer, so if you really cannot select the correct answer for a question it is worth taking a guess.

Although good examination technique will help you make the best of your knowledge, it does not guarantee a pass. The best preparation for the exam is to learn the subject fully. Your FTO will not enter you for an exam unless they feel you know the subject well enough to have a good chance of passing. Even once you have passed an exam, you cannot assume that your knowledge of that subject is complete. You should regularly revise and update each subject to keep your knowledge current.

Use of this Publication

To get the best out of this publication you should tackle each paper in order. After completing a paper mark your answers to assess your result. Review any questions you answered incorrectly to see if there is an area in which your knowledge is weak. If this is the case revise that area before attempting the next paper.

It must be stressed that you should review the whole of an area in which you are failing questions. This publication has been designed to test your complete knowledge of each subject area. It is not possible to pass the exam by learning set answers to set questions.

Initially the time limit should be taken as a guide only. In later papers you should aim to be obtaining a pass mark within the specified time limit.

Remember the surest way to pass the exam is to know the subject thoroughly!

The JAR PPL Theoretical Knowledge Examinations

With the introduction of the training syllabus for the Joint Aviation Requirements (JAR) PPL during 1999, the UK Civil Aviation Authority outlined transitional arrangements for those undertaking a PPL course in AIC 5/1999 (White 345).

In essence, this AIC states that if an applicant has achieved a pass in any one of the existing UK PPL written examinations before 1st July 1999, that applicant can complete the remainder of the UK PPL written examinations. One important proviso is that for passes in the UK PPL written examinations to be valid, the licence application must be received by the CAA Flight Crew Licensing (FCL) department by 30th June 2000. Please note that this information was promulgated in January 1999, and you are advised to contact the FCL department for up-to-date information and confirmation of transitional arrangements.

For applicants who do not qualify for transitional arrangements, the newly introduced JAR PPL theoretical knowledge examinations must be completed. Despite much that has been said and 'rumoured' about these examinations, for the most part they closely follow the format and approach of the preceding UK PPL written examinations. This book has been written for those planning to take those examinations, but it has also been designed to be used by candidates for the JAR PPL theoretical knowledge examinations.

What follows is some general advice on how to use this book to prepare for the JAR examinations, but overall the most simple maxim for passing these, or any other theoretical exam, is:

know your subject!

Examination papers may change or be updated, regulations or procedures may be altered. The only way to be sure of gaining a pass in each subject is a proper study of the subject, a sound understanding of the main points and appropriate revision. With that in mind, here are some guidelines for those taking the JAR PPL theoretical knowledge examinations.

Air Law and Operational Procedures

Questions: 40
Time Allowed: 60 mins
Pass Mark   75%

Of all the examinations, this is the one that has altered most radically from the preceding UK Air law examination. In addition to completing the Air Law question papers within this book after reading PPL2 Air Law; study of the following sections of the PPL Course series is strongly recommended:

PPL1 Flying Training; Ex12&13; Supplement 4 Wake Turbulence

PPL1 Flying Training; Forced Landing Without Power; Ditching

PPL2 Radiotelephony; En-Route Procedures; Air Traffic Services

PPL2 Radiotelephony, En-route Procedures, Radar and Non-Radar Services

PPL2 Radiotelephony; Arrival/Traffic Pattern Procedures; Inbound to an Airfield

PPL2 Radiotelephony, Emergency Procedures, Maintenance of Silence

PPL3 Flight Planning, Meteorology Navigation and Performance Integrated

PPL4 Technical; Loading and Performance; Runway Dimensions

PPL4 Technical, Airworthiness, Aircraft Documents

PPL JAR Supplement; Legislation

Meteorology

Questions: 20
Time Allowed: 60 mins
Pass Mark   75%

Completion of the meteorology examination papers within this book, and consistent attainment of a pass mark of 75% or above, should properly prepare the candidate for this examination.

Navigation

Questions: 25
Time Allowed: 90 mins
Pass Mark   75%

In addition to completing the navigation examination papers within this book, you are strongly recommended to thoroughly revise the following sections of the PPL Course series:

PPL1 Flying Training; Ex14 Solo Flights; Use of the QDM Procedure

PPL1 Flying Training; Ex18 Supplement 1 – ATC Services

PPL2 RT; Pre-flight; Introduction to VHF Radio

PPL JAR Supplement; Exercise 18C Radio Navigation

PPL JAR Supplement; Navigation

Aircraft General & Principles of Flight

Questions: 50
Time Allowed: 120 mins
Pass Mark   75%

In addition to completing the Aircraft General examination papers within this book, you are strongly recommended to additionally revise:

PPL4 Technical; The Airframe

Flight Performance & Planning

Questions: 20
Time Allowed: 60 mins
Pass Mark   75%

As preparation for this paper you should revise those questions of the Aircraft General examination papers within this book that cover weight and balance, performance and specific gravity calculations. You should also in particular revise and complete the revision questions of the following sections of the PPL Course series:

PPL4 Technical; Stability and Control; Stability in Pitch

PPL4 Technical; Climbing

PPL4 Technical; Descending

PPL4 Technical; Loading and Performance

Human Performance & Limitations

Questions: 20
Time Allowed: 30 mins
Pass Mark   75%

Completion of the human performance & limitations examination papers within this book, and consistent attainment of a pass mark of 75% or above, should properly prepare the candidate for this examination.

UK Radiotelephony (Communications – PPL)

Questions: 30
Time Allowed: 30 mins
Pass Mark   75%

Completion of the Radio Telephony (RTF) examination papers within this book, and consistent attainment of a pass mark of 75% or above, should properly prepare the candidate for this examination.

PRIVATE PILOT'S LICENCE

Aviation Law, Flight Rules and Procedures (aeroplanes and helicopters)

Time allowed: 40 minutes

Instructions

1 The paper consists of 25 multiple choice questions, each carries 4 marks (total 100 marks). The pass mark is 70% (i.e. 18 questions or more must be answered correctly); marks are not deducted for incorrect answers.

2 Questions relate to UK registered aircraft operating over or in the UK.

3 Be sure to carefully read each question and ensure that you understand it before considering the answer choices. Only one of the answers is complete and correct; the others are either incomplete or based on a misconception.

4 Leave questions that seem difficult at first and return to these when the others have been completed.

5 Indicate the correct answer to each question by placing a tick in the appropriate box of the answer sheet. If you decide to change an answer, completely obliterate the original selection.

6 The back of the answer sheet can be used for working calculations.
DO NOT MARK THE QUESTION PAPER.

Paper 1   Aviation Law

1   For what period of time is the UK PPL valid?
A   13 months
B   5 years
C   Life

2   For a UK PPL to be valid the licence must include a current:
A   Certificate of Experience
B   Certificate of Test, Certificate of Experience, and medical
C   Certificate of Test or Certificate of Experience, and medical

3   A marshaller holding his left arm down and moving the right repeatedly upward and backward is instructing the pilot to:
A   Open up the port engine or turn to starboard
B   Open up the starboard engine or turn to port
C   Proceed to the marshaller on this marshallers right

4   In relation to flight over a congested area, an aircraft may not:
A   Fly below 3000ft
B   Perform aerobatics
C   Practice an engine failure

5   When hiring an aircraft from a Flying Training Organisation (FTO), who is responsible for ensuring that the Certificate of Airworthiness is valid?
A   The Chief Flying Instructor (CFI)
B   The registered aircraft owner or designated aircraft operator
C   The aircraft commander

6   Some UK procedures vary from ICAO procedures. These differences are found in:
A   A schedule of the Air Navigation Order (ANO)
B   The UK Rules of the Air
C   The UK Aeronautical Information Publication (AIP)

7   The holder of a PPL without any instrument qualifications may fly on a Special VFR clearance in a control zone subject to a minimum flight visibility of:
A   5km
B   8km
C   10km

8   To operate an aircraft radio, a radiotelephony licence must be held:
A   And renewed every 12 months
B   Except for a student pilot in the course of his/her training
C   Except by the holder of a valid PPL

9   Approaching an aerodrome non-radio, you receive a flashing red light from the control tower. This means:
A   Give way to other aircraft and continue circling
B   Do not land; wait for permission to land
C   Do not land; aerodrome not available for landing

Paper 1   Aviation Law

10 On a navigation exercise you become lost and are unable to contact the ATSU you planned to call. You should:
A   Select 121.5 MHz and make a MAYDAY call
B   Select 121.5 MHz and make a PAN PAN call
C   Begin circling and wait for assistance

11 A portable telephone on board an aircraft should:
A   Never be used when the aircraft is airborne
B   Be used provided it is a 'digital' model
C   Be left is 'standby' mode an only used to receive incoming calls

12 A white T in the signal area means:

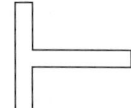

A   Aeroplanes and gliders taking off or landing must do so parallel with the shaft of the T and towards the cross arm
B   The aerodrome has technical facilities for aircraft engineering
C   Approach and take off is particularly susceptible to turbulence

13 Which of the following documents <u>need not</u> be carried in an aircraft during an international private flight?
A   A copy of the aircraft interception procedures
B   Flight crew licences
C   Certificate of Maintenance Review

14 The UK rules of the Air apply to all UK registered aircraft:
A   Wherever they are
B   Only over UK territorial land mass and water
C   Only in controlled airspace

15 In relation to aerobatic manoeuvres:
A   They may not be carried out over a built-up area
B   They may not be carried out below 3000ft amsl
C   They may not be carried out below 3000ft agl

16 You are flying IFR on a north easterly track, the MSA is 3100ft amsl. You should fly at:
A   3100ft Aerodrome QNH
B   5000ft Regional QNH
C   FL50

17 Which of the following must take place from a licensed aerodrome?
A   Flying training for the issue of a PPL
B   Flying training for the issue of an IMC rating
C   All flying training

18 The emergency frequency, 121.5 MHz, may be used for:
A   Distress calls only
B   Practice distress calls only
C   Distress, Urgency and Difficulty (e.g. unsure of position)

14

19 In relation to flight over an open air gathering of 1000 people or more, an aircraft must not fly:
A Below 500ft
B Below 1500ft within 600m of the highest obstacle
C Within 1000m

20 An aircraft is sighted on a conflicting course. Assuming you have right of way, you should:
A Maintain course and speed
B Maintain height, course and speed
C Maintain height and speed

21 If a pilot lands at an aerodrome other than the destination specified in his flight plan, he must ensure that the ATS unit at the original destination is informed within:
A 30 mins. of landing
B 60 mins. of the planned ETA
C 30 mins. of the planned ETA

22 The correct transponder code to indicate a distress situation is:
A 7000
B 7700
C 4321

23 The completion of an aircraft load sheet prior to a public transport flight is the responsibility of:
A The registered aircraft owner
B The aircraft commander
C The person designated by the operator

24 Guidelines regarding charity flights can be expected to be found in:
A A white AIC
B A schedule of the Air Navigation Order
C The UK AIP

25 A UK PPL holder with no instrument flying qualifications may:
A Fly outside controlled airspace in 3km flight visibility
B Fly in class D airspace in 3km flight visibility
C Fly within any control zone when the flight visibility is 5km

Paper 2 Aviation Law

1 A twin engine aircraft with variable pitch (VP) propellers will require:
A 1 logbook
B 3 logbooks
C 5 logbooks

2 Following an engine failure and successful forced landing, you require medical help. To indicate this to search and rescue you should lay out a visual signal in the shape of a letter. Which letter?
A X
B V
C M

3 Flying above the transition altitude, you should work out your cruising level from:
A Heading (True)
B Track (True)
C Track (Magnetic)

4 An anti-collision light may be:
A Any flashing light
B A flashing red, white or green light
C A flashing red or white light, except in the case of a helicopter

5 A flying log book must be retained for what period after the last entry therein?
A 5 years
B 24 months
C 1 year

6 What transponder code should you use in the event of a radio failure?
A 7000
B 7500
C 7600

7 You are in an aircraft on the ground ready to take-off at an aerodrome where take-offs and landings are not confined to the runway. Another aircraft is taking-off ahead, you should:
A Wait until this aircraft has taken-off before lining up
B Keep this aircraft to your left
C Keep to the same side of this aircraft as the circuit direction

8 In flight, in order to overtake a slower aircraft, you should:
A Climb above the other aircraft, and the other aircraft has priority
B Overtake to the right, and you have priority
C Overtake to the right, and the other aircraft has priority

9 In order to report your vertical position as a 'height' the altimeter:
A Is set to QHN and reads distance above mean sea level
B Is set to QNE and reads distance above a specified point on the surface
C Is set to QFE and reads distance above a specified point on the surface

10 Given a QNH of 981hPa/mb and a transitional altitude of 3000ft, assuming 30ft per hPa/mb the transition level would be:
A FL35
B FL40
C FL45

11 If a dumb-bell displayed in the aerodrome signals area has a red letter L superimposed it means:

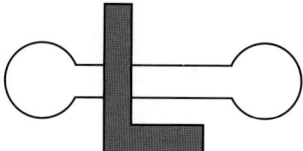

A Light aircraft must not proceed on the area marked with a white L
B Light aircraft are allowed to take-off and land either on a runway or on the area designated by the white L
C Light aircraft must only land on the area designated by a red L

12 One provision of the low flying rules (rule 5) is a requirement to fly not less than 1500' above the highest fixed object within 600m over a congested area. One exemption to this provision is provided for aircraft:
A Taking off and landing at any aerodrome
B Taking off and landing at a licensed aerodrome
C Whilst performing aerobatics

13 At a civilian aerodrome, identification beacons flash two letter morse groups in:
A Green, every 10 seconds
B Green, every 12 seconds
C Green, every 15 seconds

14 A PPL whose licence does not include an Instrument Rating or IMC rating, when flying outside controlled airspace, must comply with a minimum flight visibility of:
A 3km
B 5km
C 10km

15 You are looking for information on operational matters such as ATC services and requirements. What colour AICs would you expect to use?
A White
B Yellow
C Green

16 Taxying to the holding point before entering the active runway, you see several sets of markings. Which do you stop at?
A A solid yellow line
B A ladder-style marking in yellow
C Two continuous, and two broken, lines in yellow

17 As a PPL holder, you are not permitted to do any:
A Public Transport
B Glider towing
C Parachute dropping

18 Before flight, passengers must be briefed on the position and use of emergency exits, safety harnesses and other safety equipment carried. This safety briefing is the responsibility of:
A The aircraft operator
B The registered aircraft owner
C The aircraft commander

Paper 2 Aviation Law

19 A transponder code of 7600 indicates:
A An aircraft with a communications failure
B An aircraft entering UK airspace from an adjacent region where transponder operation is not required
C An aircraft perforrming aerobatics

20 Outside controlled airspace, the semi-circular rule applies:
A At and above FL245
B Above FL245
C At and above 24,500ft QNH

21 During pre-flight preparation, the aircraft commander must:
A Sign the Certificate of Maintenance Review
B Cross-check the aircraft serial number against the Certificate of Airworthiness
C Ensure that the aircraft carries sufficient fuel and oil for the flight

22 Two flying machines of the same class are converging at the same altitude. What initial action should be taken by the commander of the aircraft which has the other to its right?
A Maintain heading and speed
B Climb or descend to pass over or under the other aircraft
C Give way to the other aircraft to avoid passing over, under or ahead of it

23 Which of the following must be carried on a private flight within UK airspace?
A Certificate of Airworthiness, Certificate of Registration, Flight crew licenses
B Certificate of Airworthiness, Certificate of Registration, Flight crew licenses, Technical log
C None of the above

24 A pilot intends to fly a four seat aircraft with three passengers, two of whom are under the age of 18. If the costs are to be shared, what is the minimum proportion that the pilot must pay?
A 25%
B 50%
C 75%

25 A flying machine flown at night that is required to display only a single red light will be:
A An airship
B A glider or free balloon
C A gyrocopter

Paper 3   Aviation Law

1. With regard to the Air Navigation (General) Regulations, which of the following can a pilot carry out in certain circumstances?
A. Replacement of safety belts or safety harnesses
B. Rib stitching of fabric not covering a control surface
C. Replacement of a landing wheel unit

2. A rectangular red/yellow chequered board on the side of an ATC tower means:
A. A right hand circuit is in force
B. Aircraft may move on the manoeuvring area and apron only with the permission of ATC
C. The area beyond this point is unfit for aircraft movement

3. On flying machines and airships, the green and red lights show through _____ degrees from dead ahead. The white tail light shows through _____ degrees either side of dead astern. The missing numbers are:
A. 110, 70
B. 220, 140
C. 100, 90

4. Which of the following is true of an in-flight situation?
A. Gliders must give way to airships and balloons
B. Balloons must give way to airships
C. Airships must give way to gliders and balloons

5. If illness persists, you should inform the authority in writing:
A. On the first day of illness
B. On the seventh day of illness
C. On the twenty-first day of illness

6. If you suffer injury affecting your capacity as flight crew:
A. You need not inform the CAA
B. You must inform the CAA as soon as possible
C. You should inform the CAA immediately

7. If a required light fails in flight (other than an anti-collision light when flying by day) and cannot be repaired or replaced at once, the aircraft:
A. Should land as soon as is safe to do so unless ATC authorises continuation of the flight
B. Must land at the nearest available aerodrome
C. Can continue to its destination, and replace the faulty lights on arrival

8. If you inadvertently enter an area notified as restricted or prohibited, you should:
A. Continue on course, and try to make contact with the appropriate ATC
B. Leave the area as quickly as possible, not descending whilst in the area
C. Leave by the shortest route making height changes as is necessary for the continuation of your flight

9. The transponder conspicuity code is:
A. 7000
B. 7777
C. 7700

Paper 3 Aviation Law

10 When is the only time that you turn to the left when approaching another moving aircraft?
A In the hangar
B In the air
C On the ground

11 Aeronautical Information Circulars dealing with safety matters are:
A White
B Pink
C Green

12 You hear the following words on the radio from another aircraft:
"Pan Pan, Pan Pan, Pan Pan"
Which of the following statements is true?
A The aircraft is threatened by grave and imminent danger and requires immediate assistance
B There is an urgency situation regarding the aircraft itself, or something or somebody in sight of the aircraft
C The aircraft has suffered a complete radio failure

13 The identification beacon at a civil aerodrome will show:
A A two letter morse group in green
B A two letter morse group in red
C An alternating white and green light

14 When two aircraft are approaching 'head on' on the ground:
A Each shall alter course to the right
B Each shall alter course to the left
C The smaller aircraft gives way by altering course to the right

15 A free balloon flying at night, is required to show the following:
A A steady red light suspended between 5 to 10 metres below the basket
B A steady red light suspended between 5 to 10 feet below the basket
C The same lights as an aircraft

16 A glider flying at night shall show the same lights as powered light aircraft or:
A A steady red light showing in all directions
B A steady white light showing in all directions
C A flashing red light showing in all directions

17 When landings are not confined to a runway the commander of an aeroplane that is landing shall land to:
A The right of an aircraft ahead and clear the landing area to the left
B Left of the aircraft ahead and clear the landing area to the right
C Left of the aircraft ahead and clear the landing area to the left

18 When several aircraft are making an approach to land, the one at the lowest altitude shall have the right of way unless:
A The lowest aircraft has cut in front of the other traffic
B ATC has announced a different priority of landing
C Any of the above apply

Paper 3   Aviation Law

19 Pilot's licence privileges are detailed in:
A The AIP
B The ANO
C The Rules of the Air

20 A pilot's flying logbook must be kept:
A With the pilot at all times when acting as an aircraft commander
B With the aircraft documents for an international flight
C For at least two years after the date of the last entry

21 An aircraft taxiing shall give way to:
A All motor vehicles
B A motor vehicle towing another aircraft
C None of the above

22 In order to comply with VFR outside controlled airspace, below 3000' amsl at an IAS of 130 kts, a fixed wing aircraft must:
A Remain 1000' horizontally from cloud
B Remain 1000' vertically from cloud
C Remain clear of cloud

23 In order to comply with licence privileges outside controlled airspace, below 3000' amsl at an IAS of 130kts, a PPL holder without instrument qualification flying a fixed wing aircraft, must:
A Have a flight visibility of at least 1500m
B Have a flight visibility of at least 5km
C Have a flight visibility of at least 3km

24 A white cross displayed at the end of a runway means that:
A The runway should be used in an emergency only
B The runway is not usable
C The runway may be used with caution

25 When operating under a SVFR clearance:
A The aircraft commander must obey the 1500' rule at all times
B The aircraft commander may be required to disregard the 1500' rule
C The responsibility of keeping the aircraft clear of built up areas rests solely with ATC

Paper 4   Aviation Law

1. A VFR full flight plan should be filed:
A. 30 minutes before departure
B. 60 minutes before clearance to start up or taxi is requested
C. 60 minutes before the ETD

2. As a PPL you intend to make a private flight, carrying passengers, and share the cost between those onboard. You may advertise this flight:
A. Only in the local press
B. Only within a flying club if you will be flying one of that club's aeroplanes
C. Only within a flying club at the airfield where the flight will take place

3. If, having filed a flight plan, the aircraft lands at an aerodrome other than the planned destination aerodrome:
A. ATC are responsible for informing the planned destination aerodrome
B. The aircraft commander is responsible for informing the planned destination aerodrome within 30 minutes of landing
C. The aircraft commander is responsible for informing the planned destination aerodrome within 30 minutes of his planned ETA at that aerodrome

4. A ground marker comprising a baseboard supporting a slatted vertical board, both striped orange/white/orange indicates:
A. The boundary of a runway, taxiway or apron on grass airfield
B. The boundary of any part of a runway, taxiway or apron which is unfit for aircraft movment
C. The boundary of an aircraft parking area on a grass airfield

5. "Land after" procedure will only be used at civil aerodromes when the runway is long enough and:
A. The second aircraft is able to keep the the first aircraft in sight at all times
B. It is in daylight hours
C. Both a and b above

6. A white letter L indicates a part of the manoeuvring area to be used:
A. Only for aircraft less than 5700kg
B. Only for aircraft less than 2300kg
C. Only for the taking off and landing of light aircraft

7. You are a PPL without any instrument qualification. You are flying a Cessna 172 (IAS 105 Knots), with a passenger, outside controlled airspace at 2500 feet QNH. What is the minimum flight visibility (i) for you to legally operate in (ii) for VFR flight
A. (i) 3km   (ii) any 'reasonable' visibility
B. (i) 3km   (ii) 1500m
C. (i) 5km   (ii) 5km

8. A continuous red light directed at an aircraft in flight, from ATC, means:
A. Do not land, wait for permission
B. Do not land, aerodrome not available for landing
C. Give way to other aircraft and continue circling

9. An aircraft involved in SAR seen rocking its wings is:
A. Likely to be in turbulent air
B. Directing a surface craft towards an aircraft or surface craft in distress
C. Directing another aircraft towards an aircraft or surface craft in distress

Paper 4   Aviation Law

10   A ground air visual signal in the shape of the letter V means:
A   Assistance is required
B   Medical assistance is required
C   Proceed in the direction indicated by the point of the V

11   It is mandatory to keep a technical log in respect of:
A   All UK registered aircraft only when flying for the purpose of public transport
B   All UK registered aircraft with a C of A either in the transport or aerial work category for all flights
C   All UK registered aircraft with a C of A in the transport or aerial work category only when carrying passengers

12   As a holder of a UK flying licence you must inform the CAA of any illness which prevents you undertaking the duties to which the licence relates after a period of:
A   21 days
B   14 days
C   7 days

13   Which of the following is not required as a personal flying logbook entry?
A   Time of take-off and landing
B   Aircraft registration
C   Details of flight simulator tests

14   A person acting as a member of the crew of any aircraft shall not be permitted to do so if:
A   He/she has consumed any alcohol within the past 8 hours
B   He/she has consumed any alcohol within the past 5 hours
C   If the consumption of alcohol or drugs has impaired his/her ability so to act

15   For the purpose of exercising PPL privileges without a night rating, night is defined as:
A   Dusk to dawn
B   Sunset to sunrise
C   30 minutes after sunset to 30 minutes before sunrise

16   A powered aircraft may not fly over a congested area below the following defined limits:
A   1500 feet above the highest fixed obstacle within 1000 feet of the aircraft
B   1500 feet above the highest fixed obstacle within 600 metres of the aircraft
C   1500 feet above the highest fixed obstacle within 600 feet of the aircraft

17   An aircraft may not fly over a gathering of 1000 or more people who are witnessing or participating in any organised event within:
A   1000 metres
B   2000 metres
C   500 metres

18   A white dumbell with black stripes across each disc at right angles to the shaft indicates:
A   All movements are confined to paved areas
B   Take-off and landing is confined to the paved areas but aircraft may taxi on the grass
C   Aircraft may take-off and land on the grass if they wish

19   A red square with a yellow diagonal inside the signal square indicates:
A   Landing is prohibited
B   The state of the manoeuvring area is poor
C   Aircraft may only land on paved areas

Paper 4   Aviation Law

20   A continuous red light directed at an aircraft on the ground means:
A   The aircraft must stop
B   The aircraft must return to the parking bay
C   The aircraft may continue to the hold but must not take-off

21   A PPL holder who does not hold a Radiotelephony Licence:
A   Must not operate an aircraft radio
B   May use the radio provided two pilots are carried, one of whom holds a Radio Licence
C   Can use the radio but only for local flying

22   You are flying at night and observe the green navigation light of another aircraft on a constant relative bearing of 330°:
A   There is no risk of collision
B   There is a risk of collision, you have the right of way, but be prepared to alter course if the other aircraft fails to give way
C   There is risk of collision, alter course to the left to pass behind the other aircraft

23   When operating under a Radar Information Service (RIS), you are given warning of conflicting traffic. Responsibility for avoiding a collision rests with:
A   The Air Traffic Controller
B   The Aircraft Commander
C   Both equally

24   Which of the following Flight Levels would be appropriate for flight under IFR outside controlled airspace on a track of 005° (T), variation 11° E (below FL 245):
A   55
B   60
C   65

25   An aircraft with a valid Certificate of Airworthiness also has a weight schedule produced. This weight schedule must be kept for:
A   Six months after a subsequent weighing
B   Thirteen months after a subsequent weighing
C   Until the aircraft is scrapped, written-off or removed from the UK register

PRIVATE PILOT'S LICENCE

Meteorology

Time allowed: 60 minutes

Instructions

1 The paper consists of 20 multiple choice questions, each carries 5 marks (total 100 marks). The pass mark is 70% (i.e. 14 questions or more must be answered correctly); marks are not deducted for incorrect answers.

2 Be sure to read each question carefully and ensure that you understand it before considering the answer choices. Only one of the answers is complete and correct; the others are either incomplete, based on a misconception or inaccurate.

4 Leave questions that seem difficult at first and return to these when the others have been completed.

5 Indicate the correct answer to each question by placing a tick in the appropriate box of the answer sheet. If you decide to change an answer, completely obliterate the original selection.

6 The back of the answer sheet can be used for working calculations.
DO NOT MARK THE QUESTION PAPER.

Paper 1   Meteorology

1 If you are flying into an area of low pressure, what drift would you expect to experience in the northern hemisphere?
A Starboard
B None
C Port

2 The observed temperature at the surface is +11°C. This can be described as:
A ISA
B ISA +4
C ISA -4

3 Which of the following conditions is most favourable for the formation of carburettor icing if an aircraft is descending with glide power?

	Relative Humidity	Ambient temp
A	25%	+25°C
B	40%	+30°C
C	30%	-10°C

4 At an inland airfield in central southern England at 2300 hours which of the following sets of conditions is most likely to lead to the formation of radiation fog?

	w/v	Cloud Cover	Temperature	Dew Point
A	10kts	BKN ST	+12°C	+11°C
B	10kts	NIL	+15°C	+12°C
C	3kts	FEW CI	+8°C	+7°C

5 In contrast to brief showers, prolonged precipitation preceding a front is most likely to be related to:
A Stratiform cloud with moderate turbulence
B Cumuloform cloud with little or no turbulence
C Shallow stratiform clouds with little or no turbulence

Refer to Appendix A
Appendix A is a cross section through a 'typical' warm sector depression
Draw in the expected cloud types and precipitation.

6 What cloud type would you expect in I 6, and what visibility and precipitation?
A Cumulus, Good Visibility, Showers
B Stratus, Poor Visibility, Drizzle
C Stratocumulus, Good Visibility, Heavy Showers

7 What cloud type would you expect in L 2?
A Ci
B Cu
C As

8 In the UK, away from exposed coasts, convection thunderstorms are most likely in:
A Warm spells during the winter
B The late evening with westerly winds in summer
C The mid-afternoon in summer

Paper 1 Meteorology

9 The weather most likely as a warm front passes is:
A Slight showers, moderate continuous drizzle
B Moderate continuous rain, intermittent slight drizzle
C Moderate continuous rain, rain showers

10 What is the cloud-type sequence most likely to be associated with the passage of a cold front?
A Cu/Cb, Ns + low St
B St Cu/Cb, + BKN St
C Cu/Cb, Isol Cu

11 Cloud bases in TAFs & METARS are given in:
A Heights above mean sea level
B Heights above the 1013mb/hPa pressure level
C Heights above airfield elevation

12 Which of the following processes can produce both fog and cloud?
A Divergence
B Advection
C Convection

13 The wind which results from air cooling on the side of a valley is known as:
A A katabatic wind
B A valley wind
C An anabatic wind

14 When flying in a sub-zero 0°C airmass, into which rain is falling, which of the following is most likely?
A Hoar frost
B Hail
C Rain Ice

15 In which of the following situations is carburettor icing most likely to be serious over NW Europe?
A Summer, warm air mass, descent power
B Summer, warm, Cruise power
C Winter, cold, Descent power

16 The lowest layer of the atmosphere is:
A The Stratosphere
B The Troposphere
C The Mesophere

Refer to Appendix B

17 What would you expect the 2000' wind at EBBR to be?
A 170/25
B 120/25
C 145/30

18 What would you expect the surface temperature at 55N 05E to be (assuming no cloud)?
A +17°C
B +12°F
C +17°F

Paper 1								Meteorology

Refer to AppendixC

19 At what time UTC would you expect the cold front reach the Isle of Wight (the front has 40nm to travel)?
A	16:00
B	17:30
C	19:00

20 What are the worst conditions of turbulence forecast in zone 2?
A	Light
B	Severe
C	Moderate

Paper 1 Appendix A   Meteorology

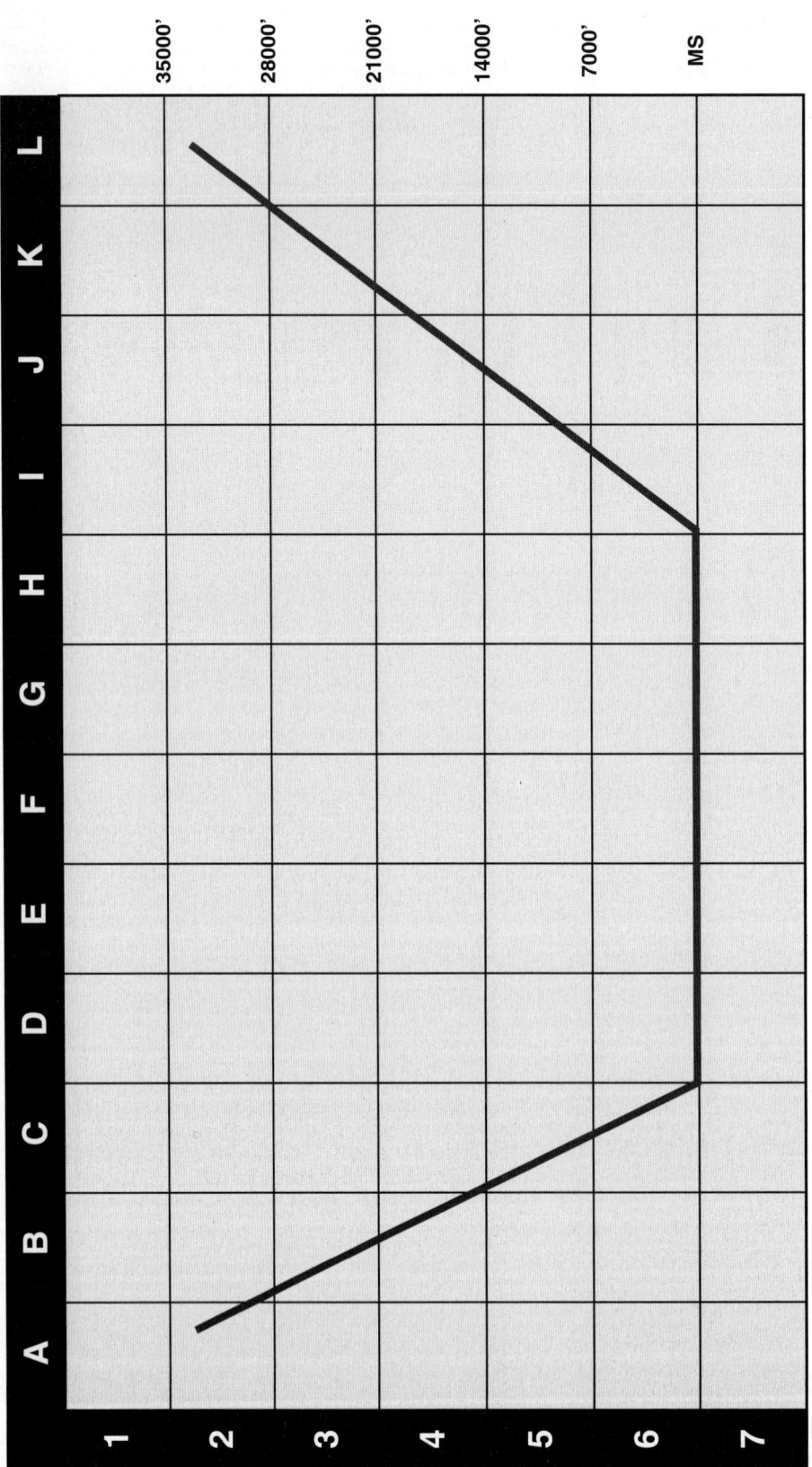

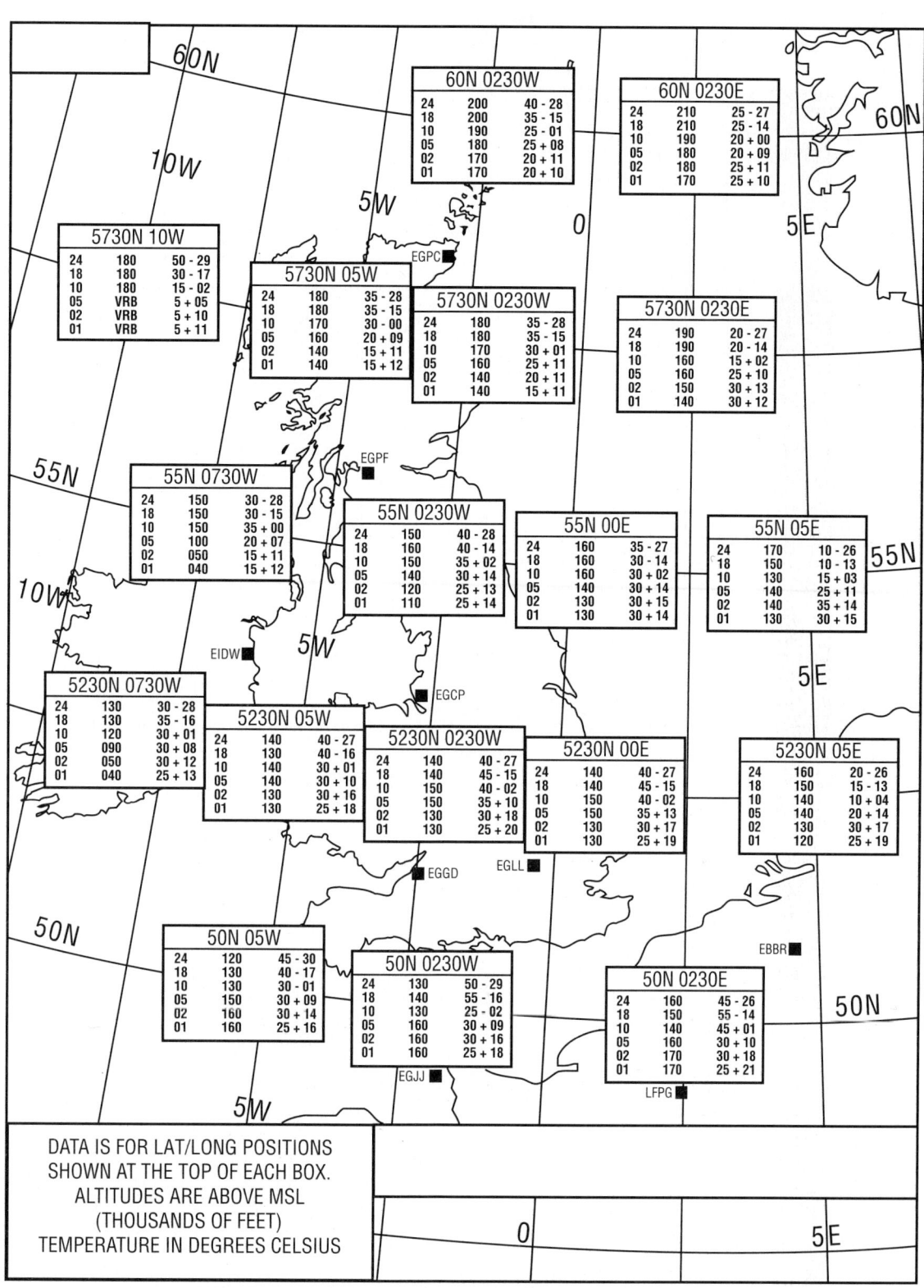

Paper 1 Appendix C — Meteorology

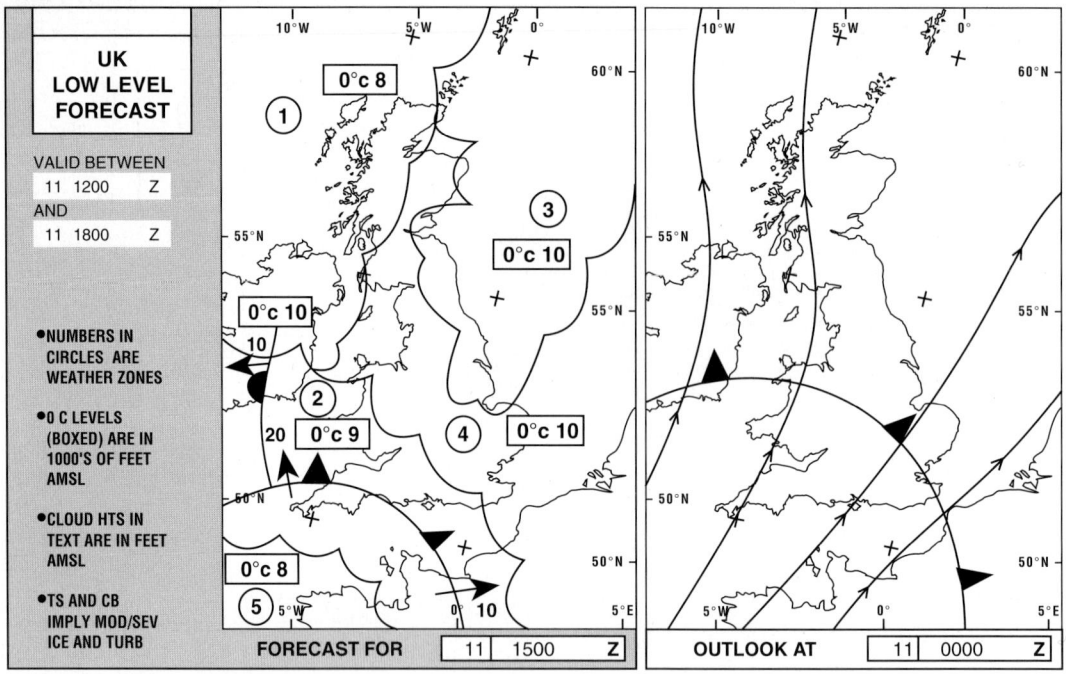

ZONE 1	GEN	8KM	NIL/RAIN	6/8ST 1000/1500 6-8/8LYR 2500/12000
	OCNL	4000M	RAIN	6/8ST 500/1500 8/8LYR 15000/19000
ZONE 2	GEN	10KM	NIL/RAIN	3-5/8SC 2000/4000 6/8LYR 8000/16000
	OCNL	4000M	RAIN	6/8ST 600/1500 8/8LYR 4000/20000
	ISOL	2000M	HEAVY RAIN/TS	5/8ST 400/1500 8/8LYR NS 3000/20000 + EMBD CB 5000/36000 WITH SEV TURB AND ICE.
ZONE 3	GEN	3000M	MIST/DZ	8/8STSC 500/2500
	OCNL	0300M	FOG/DZ	8/8STSC 000/3000 3/8AC 7000/14000
ZONE 4	GEN	12KM	NIL	4-6/8AC 10000/14000
	LOC N	4000M	HAZE	4-6/8AC 10000/14000
	LOC S	8KM	NIL/RAIN	6/8AC 10000/16000 SOME MTW ACTIVITY OVER ENGLAND AND WALES. MAX VSP 350 FPM AT 090.
ZONE 5	GEN	30KM	NIL	4-6/8CUSC 2500/5000
	OCNL	6KM	RAIN SH	5/8CU 2000/12000
	ISOL	4000M	HEAVY SH/TS	CB 1000/30000

OUTLOOK: UNTIL 11/0000Z:

Paper 2   Meteorology

1. You are flying to an airfield on the east coast to arrive in the early afternoon and you suspect a sea breeze will be blowing when you arrive, what is the most likely direction of the surface wind just after the sea breeze has reached the airfield?
A. 350°
B. 100°
C. 260°

2. The rate of fall of pressure with height is:
A. Greater in cold air than warm
B. Greater in warm air than cold
C. Inversely proportional to temp

3. The average change of pressure with height in the lower atmosphere is:
A. 1mb/30ft
B. 1mb/20ft
C. 1mb/50ft

4. A body of air over the ocean is referred to as:
A. Polar air
B. Oceanic air
C. Maritime air

5. Over which of the following surface types would you expect the greatest diurnal range of temperature to occur:
A. An extensive forest area
B. A desert area
C. An ocean

6. A VOLMET broadcast is:
A. A recorded broadcast of the METAR for a specific airfield
B. A special ATC broadcast, to all aircraft on frequency, of a significant change in weather conditions
C. A recorded broadcast of METARs for about 10 airfields

7. An inversion means that the temperature... as height increases
A. Increases
B. Decreases
C. Remains constant

8. A line on a chart joining places of equal sea level pressure is called an:
A. Isogonal
B. Agonic line
C. Isobar

9. An aircraft, flying so that the altimeter indicates 2500ft with the current regional QNH set in the subscale, is flying towards an area of lower pressure. If the pilot fails to revise the sub-scale setting as the QNH changes, then the aircraft will:
A. Gradually climb
B. Gradually descend
C. Maintain 2500ft AMSL

33

10 The temperature at sea level in the ISA is:
A +12.5°C
B +25°C
C +15°C

11 A wind whose direction has changed clockwise in direction can be said to have:
A Reduced
B Backed
C Veered

12 The wind that flows along straight, parallel, isobars is called the:
A Gradient Wind
B Geostrophic Wind
C Isobaric Wind

13 If the wind at altitude is 240/35, the most likely wind on the surface at an inland airfield is:
A 270/40
B 220/20
C 220/40

14 "Lumpy" or "heaped" cloud can be classified as:
A Stratus
B Cumulus
C Cirrus

15 As a parcel of air cools, its ability to hold water vapour:
A Decreases
B Increases
C Remains unaltered

16 Turbulence at low level is more likely to be associated with:
A Steady drizzle
B An anticyclone over the ocean
C A temperature inversion

Refer to Appendix B

17 The abbreviation BKN means
A 1-4 oktas cloud cover
B 3-7 oktas cloud cover
C 5-7 oktas cloud cover

18 In the warnings for zone 4, the following is indicated:
A Mountain wave activity, maximum vertical speed 350 feet per minute at 900ft
B Mountain wave activity, maximum vertical speed 350 feet per minute at 0900 hours
C Mountain wave activity, vertical speed exceeding 350 feet per minute at FL90

19 In zone 5, the forecast cloud includes:
A 5 oktas of cumulus between 20000 and 12000 feet
B Cumulonimbus between 10000 and 30000 feet
C 3-7 oktas of cumulus and stratocumulus between 2500 and 5000 feet

Paper 2 Meteorology

Refer to Appendix A

20 The forecast 2000' wind at EGLL is most likely to be:
- **A** 130/25
- **B** 130/20
- **C** 140/30

Paper 2 Appendix A — Meteorology

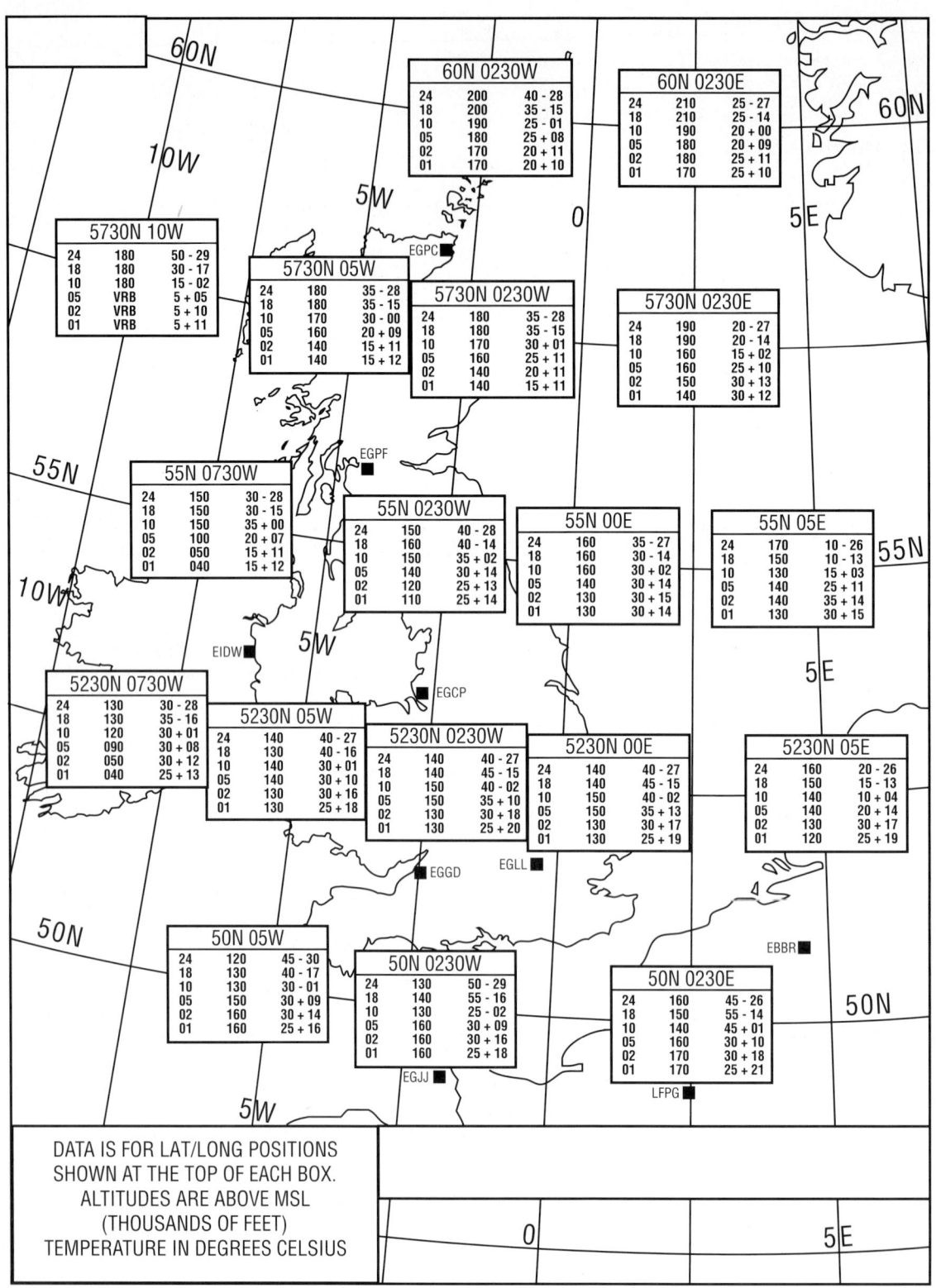

Paper 2 Appendix B — Meteorology

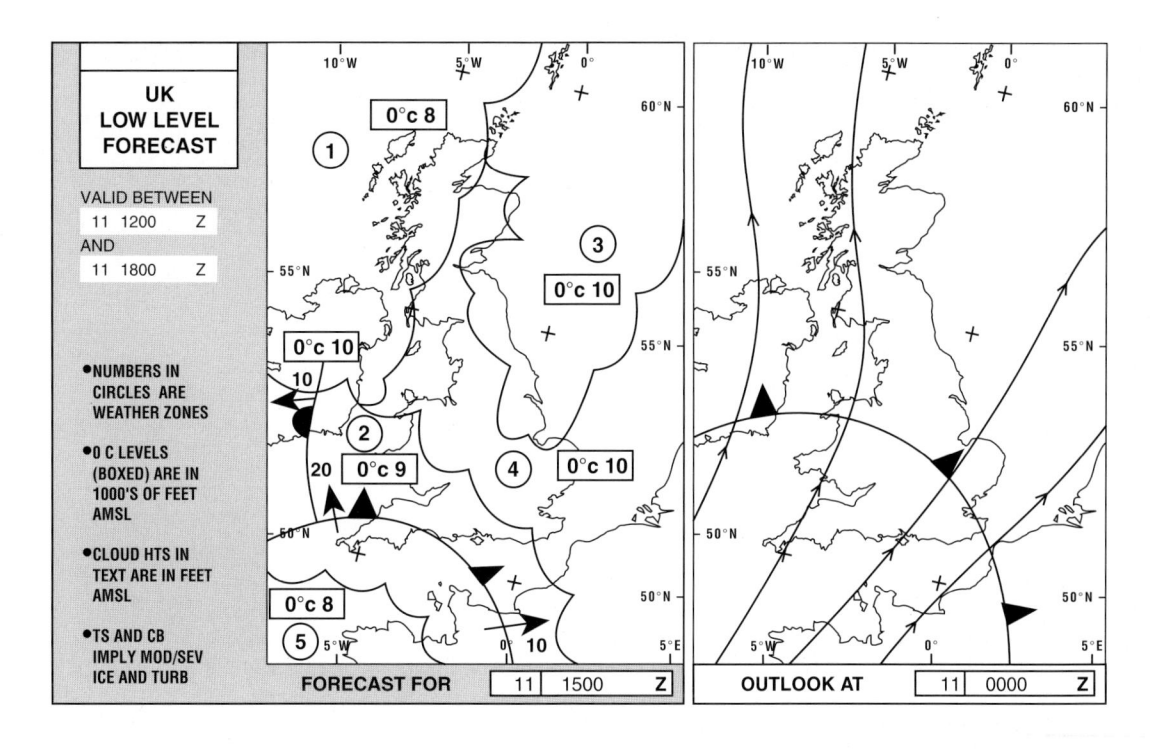

UK LOW LEVEL FORECAST

VALID BETWEEN 11 1200 Z AND 11 1800 Z

- NUMBERS IN CIRCLES ARE WEATHER ZONES
- 0 C LEVELS (BOXED) ARE IN 1000'S OF FEET AMSL
- CLOUD HTS IN TEXT ARE IN FEET AMSL
- TS AND CB IMPLY MOD/SEV ICE AND TURB

FORECAST FOR 11 1500 Z

OUTLOOK AT 11 0000 Z

Zone		Vis	Weather	Cloud
ZONE 1	GEN	8KM	NIL/RAIN	6/8ST 1000/1500 6-8/8LYR 2500/12000
	OCNL	4000M	RAIN	6/8ST 500/1500 8/8LYR 15000/19000
ZONE 2	GEN	10KM	NIL/RAIN	3-5/8SC 2000/4000 6/8LYR 8000/16000
	OCNL	4000M	RAIN	6/8ST 600/1500 8/8LYR 4000/20000
	ISOL	2000M	HEAVY RAIN/TS	5/8ST 400/1500 8/8LYR NS 3000/20000 + EMBD CB 5000/36000 WITH SEV TURB AND ICE.
ZONE 3	GEN	3000M	MIST/DZ	8/8STSC 500/2500
	OCNL	0300M	FOG/DZ	8/8STSC 000/3000 3/8AC 7000/14000
ZONE 4	GEN	12KM	NIL	4-6/8AC 10000/14000
	LOC N	4000M	HAZE	4-6/8AC 10000/14000
	LOC S	8KM	NIL/RAIN	6/8AC 10000/16000 SOME MTW ACTIVITY OVER ENGLAND AND WALES. MAX VSP 350 FPM AT 090.
ZONE 5	GEN	30KM	NIL	4-6/8CUSC 2500/5000
	OCNL	6KM	RAIN SH	5/8CU 2000/12000
	ISOL	4000M	HEAVY SH/TS	CB 1000/30000

OUTLOOK: UNTIL 11/0000Z:

Paper 3   Meteorology

1   There is a natural tendency for air to flow from areas of _____ pressure to _____ pressure
A   High/high
B   High/low
C   Low/high

2   The pressure at sea level in the ISA is:
A   1012.35 mb
B   1025.13 mb
C   1013.25 hPa

3   The lapse rate for a dry parcel of air is:
A   3°C/1000ft
B   1.5°C/1000ft
C   1.98°C/1000ft

4   In the northern hemisphere the coriolis effect deflects air to:
A   The right
B   The left
C   Does not deflect the air at all

5   Select the true statement concerning isobars and wind flow patterns around high and low pressure systems that are shown on a pressure chart:
A   Surface winds flow perpendicular to the isobars
B   When the isobars are far apart, crests of standing waves may be marked by lenticular clouds
C   When the isobars are close together, the pressure gradient force is stronger, and wind velocities are higher

6   With respect to high or low pressure systems:
A   A high pressure area or ridge is an area of rising air
B   A high pressure area or ridge is an area of descending air
C   A low pressure area or trough is an area of descending air

7   What are the most common characteristics of a cold air mass moving over a warm surface?
A   Cumuloform clouds, turbulence, and good visibility
B   Cumuloform clouds, turbulence, and poor visibility
C   Stratiform clouds, smooth air, and poor visibility

8   What is the term used to describe streamers of precipitation trailing beneath clouds, but evaporating before reaching the ground:
A   Foehn
B   Virga
C   Dissipation trails

9   Cloud formed by turbulence and mixing is called:
A   Stratus
B   Roll cloud
C   Turbulence cloud

10   Which weather phenomenon signals the beginning of the mature stage of a thunderstorm:
A   The appearance of an anvil top
B   Growth rate of cloud is maximum
C   The start of precipitation

Paper 3 Meteorology

11 The following symbol means:
A Moderate turbulence
B Moderate icing
C Severe line squall

12 Which of the following are not essential factors for thunderstorm development?
A High temperature
B An unstable atmosphere
C A supply of moist air

13 In the northern hemisphere an aircraft flying directly from low to high pressure would expect to experience:
A No drift
B Starboard drift
C Port drift

14 If a cold front moves at 30 knots, you could expect the warm front to be moving at:
A 20 knots
B 30 knots
C 40 knots

15 Given a surface temperature of +10°C, and a dew point of +5°C, at what height might you expect cumulus clouds to form?
A 2000ft
B 4000ft
C 1000ft

16 Which of the following is the correct decode the following METAR for Amsterdam:
EHAM 12/0600 02025KT 3000 RA BKN005 OVC015 11/10 Q1012
A Amsterdam: Observation at 0600Z, wind 020° at 25 knots, visibility 3000 metres in rain, cloud broken Stratus with base 500ft. agl and 8 oktas Nimbostratus base 1500ft. agl Temperature +11°C Dew point +10°C QNH 1012mb
B Amsterdam: Observation at 0600 UTC, wind 020° at 25 knots visibility 3000m with 6.1mm of rain, broken Stratus base 500ft above mean sea level, overcast Nimbostratus base 1500ft above mean sea level temperature +11°c Dew point +10°c QFE 1012mb
C Amsterdam: period valid between 0600 UTC and 0000 UTC wind 020° at 25kts, visibility 3000m in rain, cloud broken Stratus base 500ft agl, 8 oktas Nimbostratus base 1500ft agl, temperature between +10°c and +11°c QNH 1012mb

Refer to Appendix A

17 What would you expect the forecast 2000ft wind at Lydd (marked) to be?
A 180/40
B 190/25
C 185/33

Refer to Appendix B

18 What is the front to immediately west of the Channel Islands?
A It is a cold Occlusion
B It is a warm Occlusion
C It is a warm front

Paper 3 Meteorology

19 Zone 2, Line 3 cloud and turbulence decode as:
A 8/8 nimbostratus 500 to 1600, moderate turbulence and moderate icing, locally severe icing
B Greater than 5 oktas of nimbostratus 500 to 10000 feet light turbulence and moderate airframe icing, locally severe turbulence
C 8 oktas nimbostratus, base 500 feet, tops 16000 feet with moderate turbulence and icing, locally severe icing

20 Zone 4, Line 2 decodes as:
A Isolated in the north of zone 4, visibility 300 metres in rain and drizzle, 4-7 oktas stratus base 5000 feet tops 12000 feet, 4-7 oktas stratus base 2500 feet tops 16000 feet with moderate turbulence and icing
B Isolated in the north of zone 4, visibility 3000 metres in rain and drizzle, 4-7 oktas stratus base 500 feet tops 1200 feet, 4-7 oktas stratus base 2500 feet tops 16000 feet with moderate turbulence and icing
C Isolated to the north of zone 4, visibility 3000 metres in rain and drizzle, 4-7 oktas stratus base 500 feet tops 1200 feet, 4-7 oktas stratus base 2500 feet tops 16000 feet with moderate turbulence and icing

Paper 3 Appendix A — Meteorology

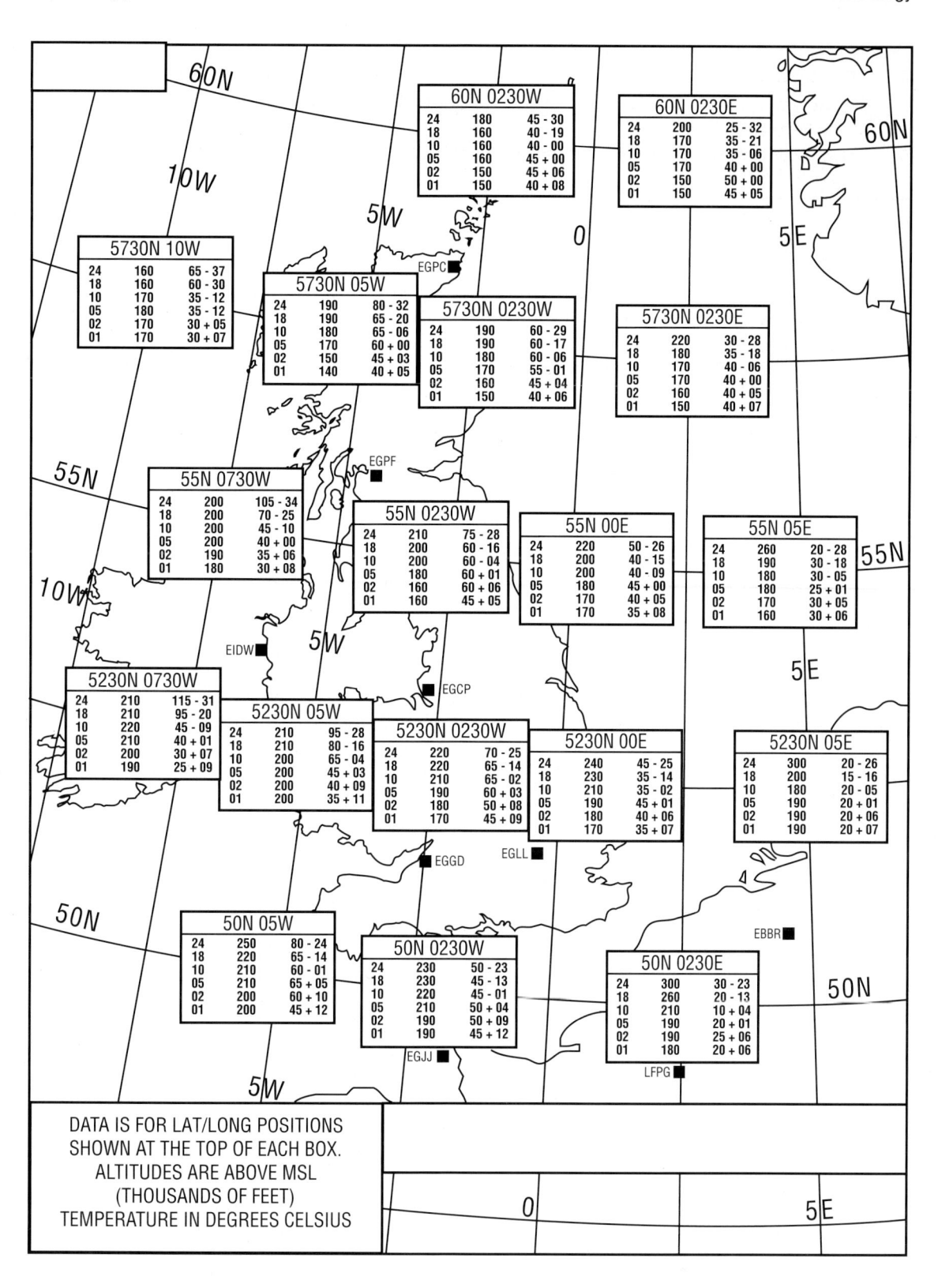

60N 0230W
24	180	45 - 30
18	160	40 - 19
10	160	40 - 00
05	160	45 + 00
02	150	45 + 06
01	150	40 + 08

60N 0230E
24	200	25 - 32
18	170	35 - 21
10	170	35 - 06
05	170	40 + 00
02	150	50 + 00
01	150	45 + 05

5730N 10W
24	160	65 - 37
18	160	60 - 30
10	170	35 - 12
05	180	35 - 12
02	170	30 + 05
01	170	30 + 07

5730N 05W
24	190	80 - 32
18	190	65 - 20
10	180	65 - 06
05	170	60 + 00
02	150	45 + 03
01	140	40 + 05

5730N 0230W
24	190	60 - 29
18	190	60 - 17
10	180	60 - 06
05	170	55 - 01
02	160	45 + 04
01	150	40 + 06

5730N 0230E
24	220	30 - 28
18	180	35 - 18
10	170	40 - 06
05	170	40 + 00
02	160	40 + 05
01	150	40 + 07

55N 0730W
24	200	105 - 34
18	200	70 - 25
10	200	45 - 10
05	200	40 + 00
02	190	35 + 06
01	180	30 + 08

55N 0230W
24	210	75 - 28
18	200	60 - 16
10	200	60 - 04
05	180	60 + 01
02	160	60 + 06
01	160	45 + 05

55N 00E
24	220	50 - 26
18	200	40 - 15
10	200	40 - 09
05	180	45 + 00
02	170	40 + 05
01	170	35 + 08

55N 05E
24	260	20 - 28
18	190	30 - 18
10	180	30 - 05
05	180	25 + 01
02	170	30 + 05
01	160	30 + 06

5230N 0730W
24	210	115 - 31
18	210	95 - 20
10	220	45 - 09
05	210	40 + 01
02	200	30 + 07
01	190	25 + 09

5230N 05W
24	210	95 - 28
18	210	80 - 16
10	200	65 - 04
05	200	45 + 03
02	200	40 + 09
01	200	35 + 11

5230N 0230W
24	220	70 - 25
18	220	65 - 14
10	210	65 - 02
05	190	60 + 03
02	180	50 + 08
01	170	45 + 09

5230N 00E
24	240	45 - 25
18	230	35 - 14
10	210	35 - 02
05	190	45 + 01
02	180	40 + 06
01	170	35 + 07

5230N 05E
24	300	20 - 26
18	200	15 - 16
10	180	20 - 05
05	190	20 + 01
02	190	20 + 06
01	190	20 + 07

50N 05W
24	250	80 - 24
18	220	65 - 14
10	210	60 - 01
05	210	65 + 05
02	200	60 + 10
01	200	45 + 12

50N 0230W
24	230	50 - 23
18	230	45 - 13
10	220	45 - 01
05	210	50 + 04
02	190	50 + 09
01	190	45 + 12

50N 0230E
24	300	30 - 23
18	260	20 - 13
10	210	10 + 04
05	190	20 + 01
02	190	25 + 06
01	180	20 + 06

DATA IS FOR LAT/LONG POSITIONS SHOWN AT THE TOP OF EACH BOX. ALTITUDES ARE ABOVE MSL (THOUSANDS OF FEET) TEMPERATURE IN DEGREES CELSIUS

Paper 3 Appendix B Meteorology

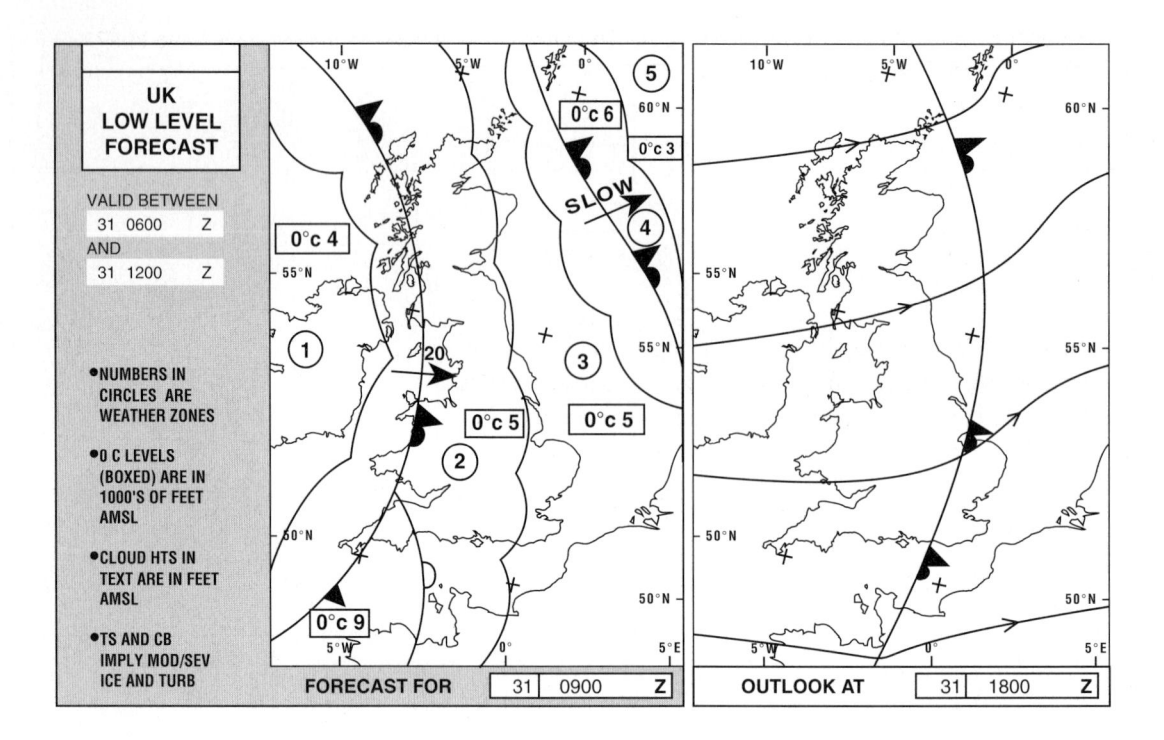

UK LOW LEVEL FORECAST

VALID BETWEEN 31 0600 Z AND 31 1200 Z

- NUMBERS IN CIRCLES ARE WEATHER ZONES
- 0 C LEVELS (BOXED) ARE IN 1000'S OF FEET AMSL
- CLOUD HTS IN TEXT ARE IN FEET AMSL
- TS AND CB IMPLY MOD/SEV ICE AND TURB

FORECAST FOR 31 0900 Z

OUTLOOK AT 31 1800 Z

ZONE 1	GEN	30KM	NIL	6/8CUSC 2000/6000
	ISOL W	8KM	RAIN SH	6/8CU 1500/12000
ZONE 2	GEN	15KM	NIL/RAIN	5/8SC 1500/3500 6-8/8LYR 5000/18000
	WDSPR	6KM	RAIN	6/8ST 800/1500 8/8LYR 2000/20000
	OCNL NEAR FRONTS	3000M	HEAVY RAIN	8/8NS 500/16000 WITH MOD TURB AND ICE. LOC SEV ICE
ZONE 3	GEN	20KM	NIL	2/8SC 4000/7000 2-6/8ACAS 12000/15000
	LOC LAND SE	3000M	MIST	5/8ST 500/1000
ZONE 4	GEN	12KM	NIL/RAIN	6/8STSC 1000/6000 5/8LYR 8000/10000
	ISOL N	3000M	RAIN/DZ	6/8ST 500/1200 6/8LYR 2500/16000 WITH MOD TURB AND ICE
ZONE 5	GEN	15KM	NIL	3/8 10000/12000

OUTLOOK: UNTIL 31/1800Z:

Paper 4 Meteorology

1 When a north-westerly airflow is reaching the UK, which of the following is most likely to be true?
A It is a Tropical Maritime air mass from the Azores
B It is a Polar Continental air mass from Scandinavia
C It is a Polar Maritime airmass from the north Atlantic/Arctic

2 A sea breeze blows:
A From the sea by day
B From the sea by night
C From the land by day

3 As a warm front passes the weather at the surface is most likely to be:
A Isolated slight showers, becoming moderate continuous drizzle
B Moderate continuous rain becoming intermittent slight drizzle
C Moderate continuous rain becoming heavy rain showers

4 The cloud sequence associated with the passage of a 'typical' cold front is:
A CU/CB to Isolated CU/SC
B ST/SC to CU/SC
C NS/ST to AC/AS

5 Moist air is:
A Denser than dry air
B Warmer than dry air
C Less dense than dry air

6 If weather conditions are reported as 'CAVOK', which of the following could not be present:
A Gales
B 1 okta of CB at 9000ft
C Overcast cloud at 5100ft amsl

7 Tropical maritime air typically brings to the south west UK:
A Medium ST cloud and rain, good visibility
B Low ST/SC cloud and drizzle, poor visibility
C Medium CU/SC and showers, good visibility

8 You are flying in a layer of haze, late on a winter afternoon. Which of the following statements is true?
A Flight visibility into sun will be worse
B Flight visibility 'down sun' will be worse
C The position of the sun will not effect flight visibility

9 A SIGMET message is:
A A routine weather report to an aircraft in flight
B A routine weather report from an aircraft in flight
C A warning of reported or forecast hazardous in-flight conditions

10 In relation to mountain wave activity, which of the following cloud types signifies the most turbulent conditions?
A Roll or rotor clouds
B Lenticular clouds
C Stratiform cloud covering the mountain tops

Paper 4 Meteorology

11 Carburettor icing is unlikely:
A   In cloud
B   At temperatures between -10°C and -30°C
C   When the relative humidity is 40%

12 Within a depression two air masses meet so that a warm front is formed. In relation to a 'typical' warm front:
A   Warm air will be replaced by cold air, the frontal slope will be around 1:150
B   Cold air will be replaced by warm air, the frontal slope will be around 1:150
C   Warm air will be replaced by cold air, the frontal slope will be around 1:50

13 An environmental lapse rate is observed to be 2.5°C/1000ft, which of the following is correct:
A   A dry parcel of air would be stable if it was forced to rise
B   A saturated parcel of air would be stable if it was forced to rise
C   A dry parcel of air would be unstable if it was forced to rise

14 As a warm front approaches an stationary observer, the cloud base:
A   Remains the same
B   Lowers
C   Rises

15 The general visibility associated with a cold front _____ the visibility associated with a warm front
A   Is worse than
B   Is the same as
C   Is better than

16 A V-shaped extension of a low pressure area is called a:
A   Ridge
B   Col
C   Trough

Refer to Appendix A

17 What is the likely forecast 2000ft wind at EGPF?
A   155/55
B   160/60
C   155/50

Refer to Appendix B

18 Your fax machine failed to print the cloud type in zone 5. What is the most likely type?
A   Altocumulus
B   Cumulonimbus
C   Nimbostratus

19 What is the altitude of the 0°C isotherm off the southern coast of Cornwall?
A   900ft
B   9000ft
C   900m

20 Zone 3 top line decodes as:
A   3-4 oktas Stratocumulus base 400ft tops 700ft 3-7 oktas Altocumulus or Altostratus 1200ft tops 1500ft
B   3-4 oktas Stratocumulus 4000ft to 2000ft, 3-7 oktas Altocumulus or Altostratus 1200ft/1500ft
C   3-4 oktas Stratocumulus 4000ft to 7000ft 3-7 eights Altocumulus or Altostratus 12000ft to 15000ft

Paper 4 Appendix A — Meteorology

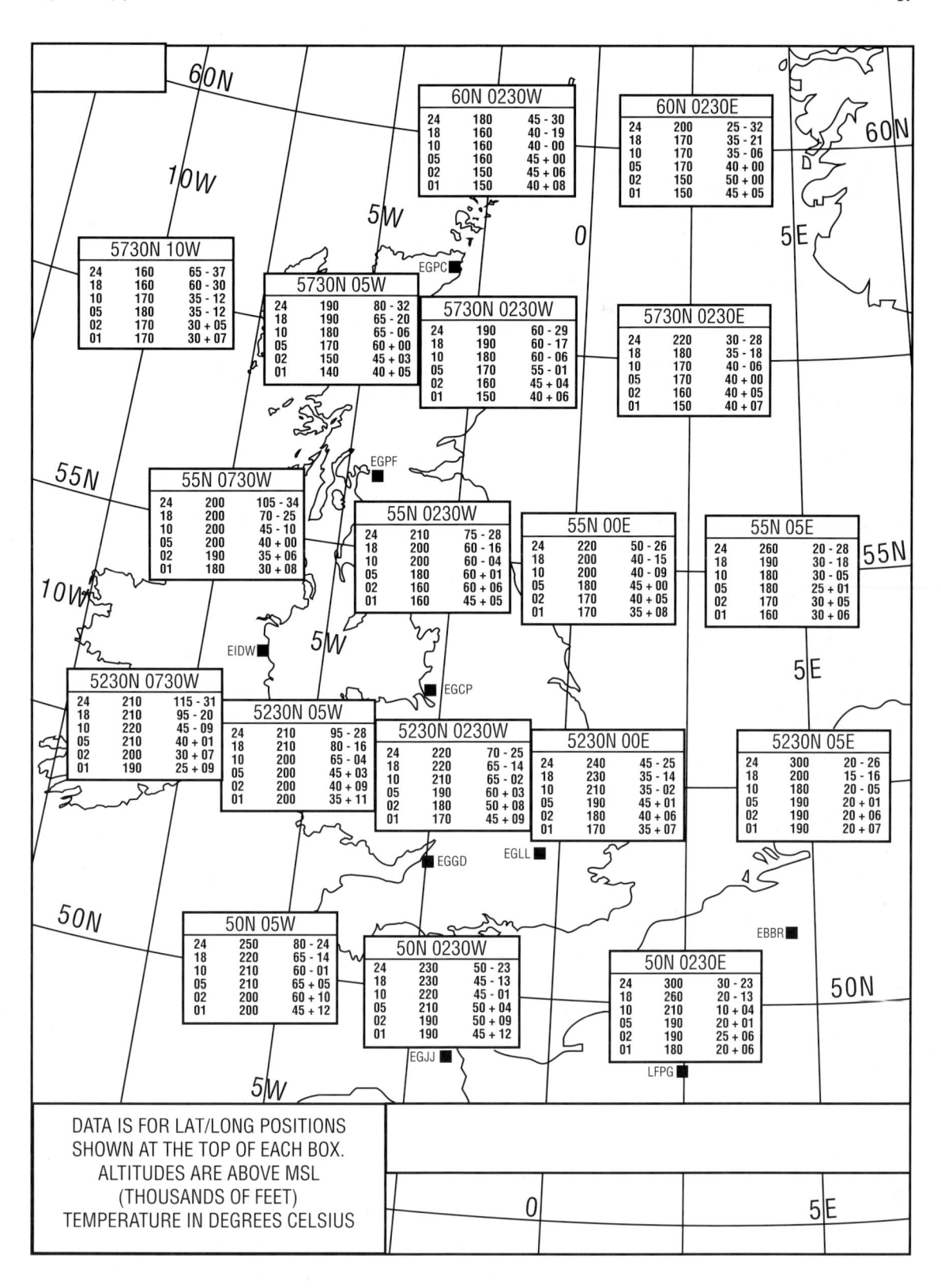

60N 0230W		
24	180	45 - 30
18	160	40 - 19
10	160	40 - 00
05	160	45 + 00
02	150	45 + 06
01	150	40 + 08

60N 0230E		
24	200	25 - 32
18	170	35 - 21
10	170	35 - 06
05	170	40 + 00
02	150	50 + 00
01	150	45 + 05

5730N 10W		
24	160	65 - 37
18	160	60 - 30
10	170	35 - 12
05	180	35 - 12
02	170	30 + 05
01	170	30 + 07

5730N 05W		
24	190	80 - 32
18	190	65 - 20
10	180	65 - 06
05	170	60 + 00
02	150	45 + 03
01	140	40 + 05

5730N 0230W		
24	190	60 - 29
18	190	60 - 17
10	180	60 - 06
05	170	55 - 01
02	160	45 + 04
01	150	40 + 06

5730N 0230E		
24	220	30 - 28
18	180	35 - 18
10	170	40 - 06
05	170	40 + 00
02	160	40 + 05
01	150	40 + 07

55N 0730W		
24	200	105 - 34
18	200	70 - 25
10	200	45 - 10
05	200	40 + 00
02	190	35 + 06
01	180	30 + 08

55N 0230W		
24	210	75 - 28
18	200	60 - 16
10	200	60 - 04
05	180	60 + 01
02	160	60 + 06
01	160	45 + 05

55N 00E		
24	220	50 - 26
18	200	40 - 15
10	200	40 - 09
05	180	45 + 00
02	170	40 + 05
01	170	35 + 08

55N 05E		
24	260	20 - 28
18	190	30 - 18
10	180	30 - 05
05	180	25 + 01
02	170	30 + 05
01	160	30 + 06

5230N 0730W		
24	210	115 - 31
18	210	95 - 20
10	220	45 - 09
05	210	40 + 01
02	200	30 + 07
01	190	25 + 09

5230N 05W		
24	210	95 - 28
18	210	80 - 16
10	200	65 - 04
05	200	45 + 03
02	200	40 + 09
01	200	35 + 11

5230N 0230W		
24	220	70 - 25
18	220	65 - 14
10	210	65 - 02
05	190	60 + 03
02	180	50 + 08
01	170	45 + 09

5230N 00E		
24	240	45 - 25
18	230	35 - 14
10	210	35 - 02
05	190	45 + 01
02	180	40 + 06
01	170	35 + 07

5230N 05E		
24	300	20 - 26
18	200	15 - 16
10	180	20 - 05
05	190	20 + 01
02	190	20 + 06
01	190	20 + 07

50N 05W		
24	250	80 - 24
18	220	65 - 14
10	210	60 - 01
05	210	65 + 05
02	200	60 + 10
01	200	45 + 12

50N 0230W		
24	230	50 - 23
18	230	45 - 13
10	220	45 - 01
05	210	50 + 04
02	190	50 + 09
01	190	45 + 12

50N 0230E		
24	300	30 - 23
18	260	20 - 13
10	210	10 + 04
05	190	20 + 01
02	190	25 + 06
01	180	20 + 06

DATA IS FOR LAT/LONG POSITIONS SHOWN AT THE TOP OF EACH BOX.
ALTITUDES ARE ABOVE MSL
(THOUSANDS OF FEET)
TEMPERATURE IN DEGREES CELSIUS

Paper 4 Appendix B — Meteorology

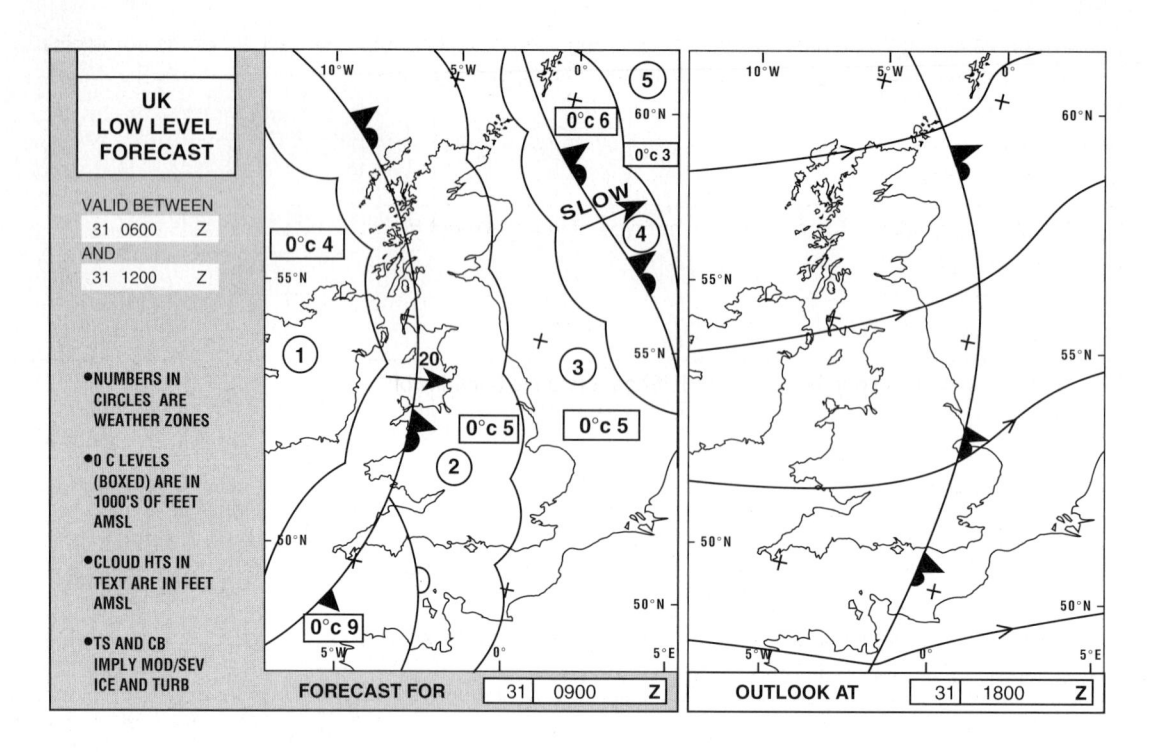

UK LOW LEVEL FORECAST

VALID BETWEEN 31 0600 Z AND 31 1200 Z

- NUMBERS IN CIRCLES ARE WEATHER ZONES
- 0 C LEVELS (BOXED) ARE IN 1000'S OF FEET AMSL
- CLOUD HTS IN TEXT ARE IN FEET AMSL
- TS AND CB IMPLY MOD/SEV ICE AND TURB

FORECAST FOR 31 0900 Z

OUTLOOK AT 31 1800 Z

ZONE 1	GEN	30KM	NIL	6/8CUSC 2000/6000
	ISOL W	8KM	RAIN SH	6/8CU 1500/12000
ZONE 2	GEN	15KM	NIL/RAIN	5/8SC 1500/3500 6-8/8LYR 5000/18000
	WDSPR	6KM	RAIN	6/8ST 800/1500 8/8LYR 2000/20000
	OCNL NEAR FRONTS	3000M	HEAVY RAIN	8/8NS 500/16000 WITH MOD TURB AND ICE. LOC SEV ICE
ZONE 3	GEN	20KM	NIL	2/8SC 4000/7000 2-6/8ACAS 12000/15000
	LOC LAND SE	3000M	MIST	5/8ST 500/1000
ZONE 4	GEN	12KM	NIL/RAIN	6/8STSC 1000/6000 5/8LYR 8000/10000
	ISOL N	3000M	RAIN/DZ	6/8ST 500/1200 6/8LYR 2500/16000 WITH MOD TURB AND ICE
ZONE 5	GEN	15KM	NIL	3/8 10000/12000

OUTLOOK: UNTIL 31/1800Z:

Paper 5 Meteorology

1 A mountain range runs north-south, and a strong wind is blowing from the west. What meteorological phenomena is most likely and where will it be at its most dangerous?
A   Fog; in the valleys
B   Mountain wave activity; to the west of the mountains
C   Mountain wave activity; to the east of the mountains

2 If a stable air mass is forced to rise, what type of cloud is most likely:
A   CU cloud
B   NS cloud
C   TCU cloud

3 A parcel of air is said to be saturated if it has a relative humidity of:
A   50%
B   100%
C   Greater than 90%

4 An aircraft is flying on a constant heading with port drift in the northern hemisphere, maintaining a constant indicated pressure altitude. Which of the following is true?
A   It is likely to be climbing relative to the surface
B   It is likely to be maintaining a constant distance relative to the surface
C   It is likely to be descending relative to the surface

5 Which of the following is most likely to occur after several days of a prolonged winter anticyclone in the UK:
A   Isolated showers with good visibility outside precipitation
B   Clear, stable air and good flying conditions
C   Creation of an inversion with cloud and poor visibility beneath

6 If you stand with your back to the wind in the northern hemisphere, the low pressure will be:
A   On your left
B   On your right
C   Behind you

7 The wind at the surface is 240/15kts, what is it most likely to be at 2000ft?
A   220/25kts
B   260/25kts
C   280/15kts

8 High level cloud will have a base above _____ and is classified _____ .
A   14,000ft/Nimbus
B   16,500ft/Cumuliform
C   16,500ft/Cirriform

9 The force that moves air from high pressure to low pressure is called:
A   Pressure Gradient Force
B   Coriolis Force
C   Isobar Force

10 The temperature at which a parcel of air becomes saturated if it cools is called:
A   The dew point temperature
B   The saturation temperature
C   The condensation temperature

Paper 5　　　　　　　　　　　　　　　　　　　　　　　　　　　　　　　　Meteorology

11 The saturated adiabatic lapse rate (SALR) is approximately:
A   1.5°C/1000m
B   1.98°C/1000ft
C   1.5°C/1000ft

12 Which of the following types of cloud is most likely to be associated with prolonged and continuous moderate rain?
A   Nimbostratus
B   Cumulus
C   Stratus

13 Fog forming over the sea in a 20kt wind is most likely to be:
A   Advection fog
B   Radiation fog
C   Neither, fog cannot form above 12kts windspeed

14 Airframe icing:
A   Cannot occur outside cloud or precipitation
B   Can occur outside cloud or precipitation
C   Can only occur if the Outside Air temperature (OAT) is below freezing (0°C)

15 Polar maritime air is generally:
A   Cold, Moist, Stable
B   Cold, Dry, Unstable
C   Cold, Moist, Unstable

16 The following denotes:

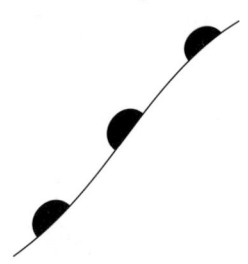

A   A cold front at the surface
B   A warm front at the surface
C   An occluded front at the surface

Refer to Appendix A

17 What would you expect the approximate forecast surface wind at EGGD to be?
A   290/10
B   250/20
C   245/10

Paper 5   Meteorology

Refer to Appendix B

18	The front between Wales and the north east coast is a:
A	Warm occlusion
B	Quasi stationary front at the surface
C	Cold occlusion

19	Assuming a distance of 60nm, at what time will the cold front reach the Isle of Wight?
A	12:00 BST
B	12:00 UTC
C	10:30 UTC

20	In Zone 2 bottom line, the term 'EMBD CB 020/280:
A	May be ignored as the forecast cloud base is below 2000ft
B	Can be seen and avoided
C	Is particularly hazardous

Paper 5 Appendix A — Meteorology

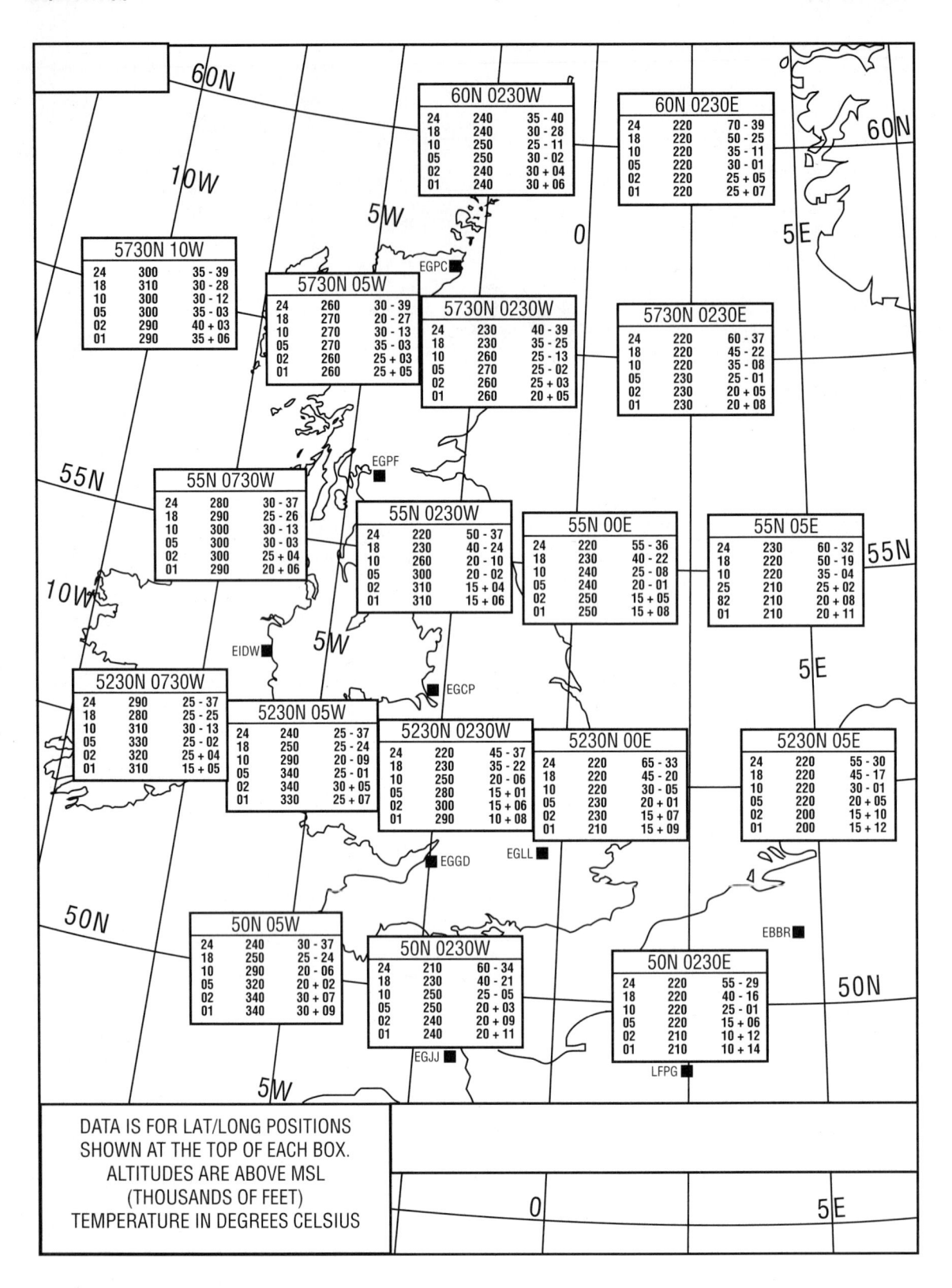

60N 0230W
24	240	35 - 40
18	240	30 - 28
10	250	25 - 11
05	250	30 - 02
02	240	30 + 04
01	240	30 + 06

60N 0230E
24	220	70 - 39
18	220	50 - 25
10	220	35 - 11
05	220	30 - 01
02	220	25 + 05
01	220	25 + 07

5730N 10W
24	300	35 - 39
18	310	30 - 28
10	300	30 - 12
05	300	35 - 03
02	290	40 + 03
01	290	35 + 06

5730N 05W
24	260	30 - 39
18	270	20 - 27
10	270	30 - 13
05	270	35 - 03
02	260	25 + 03
01	260	25 + 05

5730N 0230W
24	230	40 - 39
18	230	35 - 25
10	260	25 - 13
05	270	25 - 02
02	260	25 + 03
01	260	20 + 05

5730N 0230E
24	220	60 - 37
18	220	45 - 22
10	220	35 - 08
05	230	25 - 01
02	230	20 + 05
01	230	20 + 08

55N 0730W
24	280	30 - 37
18	290	25 - 26
10	300	30 - 13
05	300	30 - 03
02	300	25 + 04
01	290	20 + 06

55N 0230W
24	220	50 - 37
18	230	40 - 24
10	260	20 - 10
05	300	20 - 02
02	310	15 + 04
01	310	15 + 06

55N 00E
24	220	55 - 36
18	230	40 - 22
10	240	25 - 08
05	240	20 - 01
02	250	15 + 05
01	250	15 + 08

55N 05E
24	230	60 - 32
18	220	50 - 19
10	220	35 - 04
25	210	25 + 02
82	210	20 + 08
01	210	20 + 11

5230N 0730W
24	290	25 - 37
18	280	25 - 25
10	310	30 - 13
05	330	25 - 02
02	320	25 + 04
01	310	15 + 05

5230N 05W
24	240	25 - 37
18	250	25 - 24
10	290	20 - 09
05	340	25 - 01
02	340	30 + 05
01	330	25 + 07

5230N 0230W
24	220	45 - 37
18	230	35 - 22
10	250	20 - 06
05	280	15 + 01
02	300	15 + 06
01	290	10 + 08

5230N 00E
24	220	65 - 33
18	220	45 - 20
10	220	30 - 05
05	230	20 + 01
02	230	15 + 07
01	210	15 + 09

5230N 05E
24	220	55 - 30
18	220	45 - 17
10	220	30 - 01
05	220	20 + 05
02	200	15 + 10
01	200	15 + 12

50N 05W
24	240	30 - 37
18	250	25 - 24
10	290	20 - 06
05	320	20 + 02
02	340	30 + 07
01	340	30 + 09

50N 0230W
24	210	60 - 34
18	230	40 - 21
10	250	25 - 05
05	250	20 + 03
02	240	20 + 09
01	240	20 + 11

50N 0230E
24	220	55 - 29
18	220	40 - 16
10	220	25 - 01
05	220	15 + 06
02	210	10 + 12
01	210	10 + 14

DATA IS FOR LAT/LONG POSITIONS SHOWN AT THE TOP OF EACH BOX. ALTITUDES ARE ABOVE MSL (THOUSANDS OF FEET) TEMPERATURE IN DEGREES CELSIUS

Paper 5 Appendix B — Meteorology

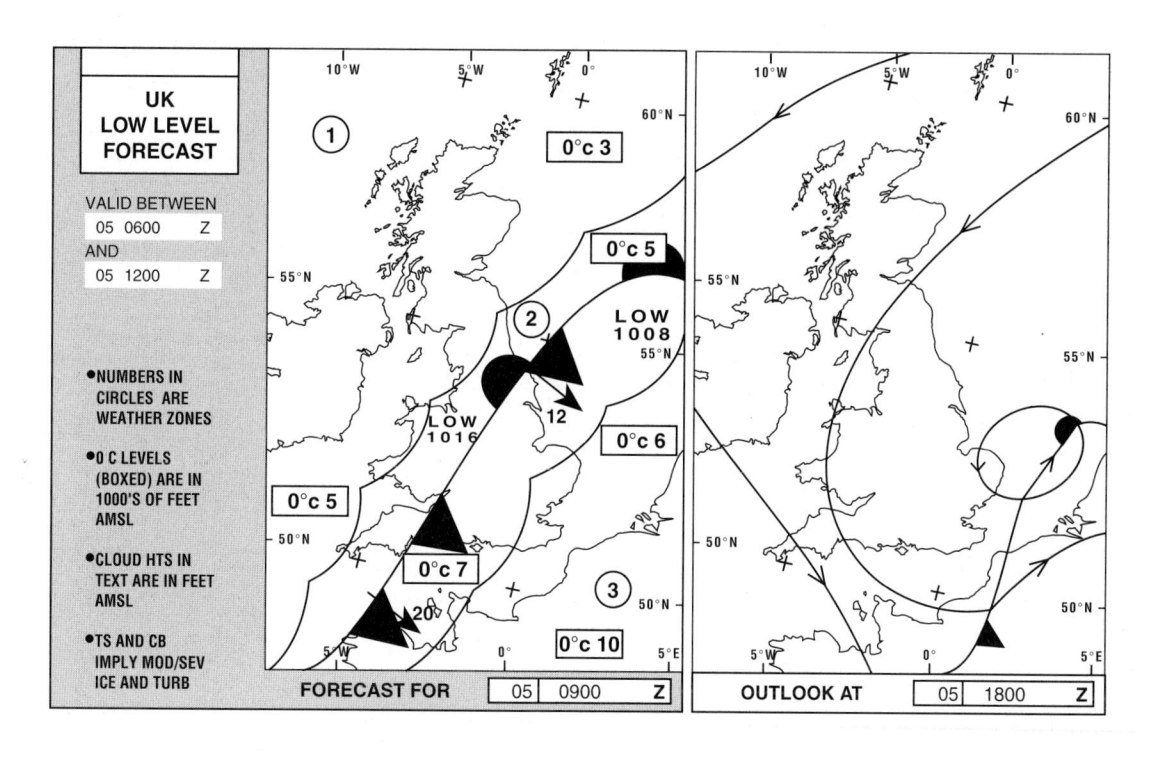

UK LOW LEVEL FORECAST

VALID BETWEEN 05 0600 Z AND 05 1200 Z

- NUMBERS IN CIRCLES ARE WEATHER ZONES
- 0 C LEVELS (BOXED) ARE IN 1000'S OF FEET AMSL
- CLOUD HTS IN TEXT ARE IN FEET AMSL
- TS AND CB IMPLY MOD/SEV ICE AND TURB

FORECAST FOR 05 0900 Z

OUTLOOK AT 05 1800 Z

ZONE 1	GEN	30KM	NIL	4-6/8CUSC 2000/6000
	OCNL	20KM	RAIN SH	6/8CU 1500/10000
	ISOL N	3000M	HEAVY SH /TS/HAIL	CB 800/20000
ZONE 2	GEN	15KM	RAIN	5/8SC 1500/6000 6/8LYR 10000/20000
	OCNL	6KM	RAIN	3-6/8ST 800/1200 8/8LYR 2000/18000 EMBD CU 1500/10000
	ISOL FRONT	2000M	HEAVY RAIN/TS	5/8ST 300/1200 8/8NS 1500/18000 EMBD CB 2000/28000
ZONE 3	GEN	30KM	NIL	2-5/8SC 2000/5000
	OCNL NW	20KM	NIL/RAIN	5/8STSC 1500/5000 5/8AC 12000/18000
	LOC LAND	5000M	HAZE	

OUTLOOK: UNTIL 05/1900Z:

51

Paper 6 Meteorology

1 Which of the following is most likely to occur after passage of a cold front?
A A fall in pressure, a fall in temperature and dew point
B A rise in pressure, a fall in temperature and dew point
C A fall in pressure, a fall in temperature and a rise in dew point

2 Air density generally _____ as altitude increases:
A Increases
B Decreases
C Stays the same

3 You are flying at a constant indicated altitude of 2000ft with a QNH set of 1015mb. After a long flight with constant starboard drift and without up-dating the pressure setting, a new QNH of 998mb is passed to you. When this is set on the altimeter what is the new indicated altitude likely to be (assume 1mb = 30 feet)?
A 1490 feet
B 2490 feet
C 2000 feet

4 An inversion means that the temperature _____ as altitude increases:
A Decreases
B Increases
C Stays the same

5 The approximate temperature lapse rate in the ISA is ____ degrees C per 1000 feet in altitude increase:
A 3.0°C
B 1.5°C
C 2.0°C

6 What prevents air from flowing directly from high to low pressure areas over western Europe?
A Coriolis force
B Surface friction
C Pressure gradient force

7 The general circulation of air associated with a high pressure area in the northern hemisphere is:
A Inward, downward and counter clockwise
B Outward, upward and clockwise
C Outward, downward and clockwise

8 What does the following SIGWX chart symbol mean?
A Hail
B Severe Line Squall
C Widespread Fog

9 The backing of the surface wind is greater:
A At night
B Over the sea in light winds
C Over the land

10 What determines the structure or type of clouds which will form as a result of air being forced to ascend:
A The stability of the air before lifting occurs
B The method by which air is lifted
C The relative humidity of the air after lifting occurs

Paper 6   Meteorology

11 The presence of standing lenticular Altocumulus clouds is a good indication of:
A Updrafts and downdrafts
B An approaching thunderstorm
C An unstable air mass

12 The hazards that thunderstorms pose to aviation include:
A Windshear, severe turbulence, hail
B Heavy precipitaion, lightning, severe icing
C All of the above

13 The layer of the atmosphere above the tropopause is known as the:
A Troposphere
B Stratosphere
C Mesophere

14 It is October, and an area of high pressure has been established over the UK for several days. Which of the following is most likely to represent the TAF for a Midlands airport?
A 0716 04025KT 7000 BKN013 OVC090=
B 0716 05004KT 0800 FG OVC001 TEMPO 0709 0200 VV//// BECMG 0811 3000 BR OVC005 TEMPO 1116 6000 SCT007=
C 0716 30005KT 9999 SCT035 PROB30 TEMPO 0710 5000 TSRA BKN050CB=

15 The cloud sequence that could be expected during the passage of a 'typical' warm front would be:
A CI, AS, CB, CU
B AS, CI, CS, ST, NS
C CI, CS, AS, NS, ST

16 On a cool and cloudless night with no wind, and the air in contact with the surface cooled to its dew point temperature of -5°C. Which of the following is most likely to form?
A Dew
B Fog
C Frost

Refer to Appendix A

17 What is the 2000' wind at EBBR?
A 260/25 gusting to 37
B 280/15
C 265/20

Refer to Appendix B

18 What is the lowest forecast visibility in zone 3?
A 1500m
B 200m or less
C 5km

19 With reference to zone 3 line 2; which area is being referred to?
A Overall near the front
B Occasionally ahead of the front of the zone 3 boundary
C Occasionally near the front in Zone 3

20 In relation to Zone 1, line 3; 6/8ACAS 10000/18000 means:
A 6 eights Altocumulus/Altostratus base 10000 feet, tops 18000 feet
B 6 tenths Altocumulus/Altostratus base 10000 feet, tops 18000 feet
C 6 sixths Altocumulus/Altostratus base 10000 feet, tops 18000 feet

Paper 6 Appendix A — Meteorology

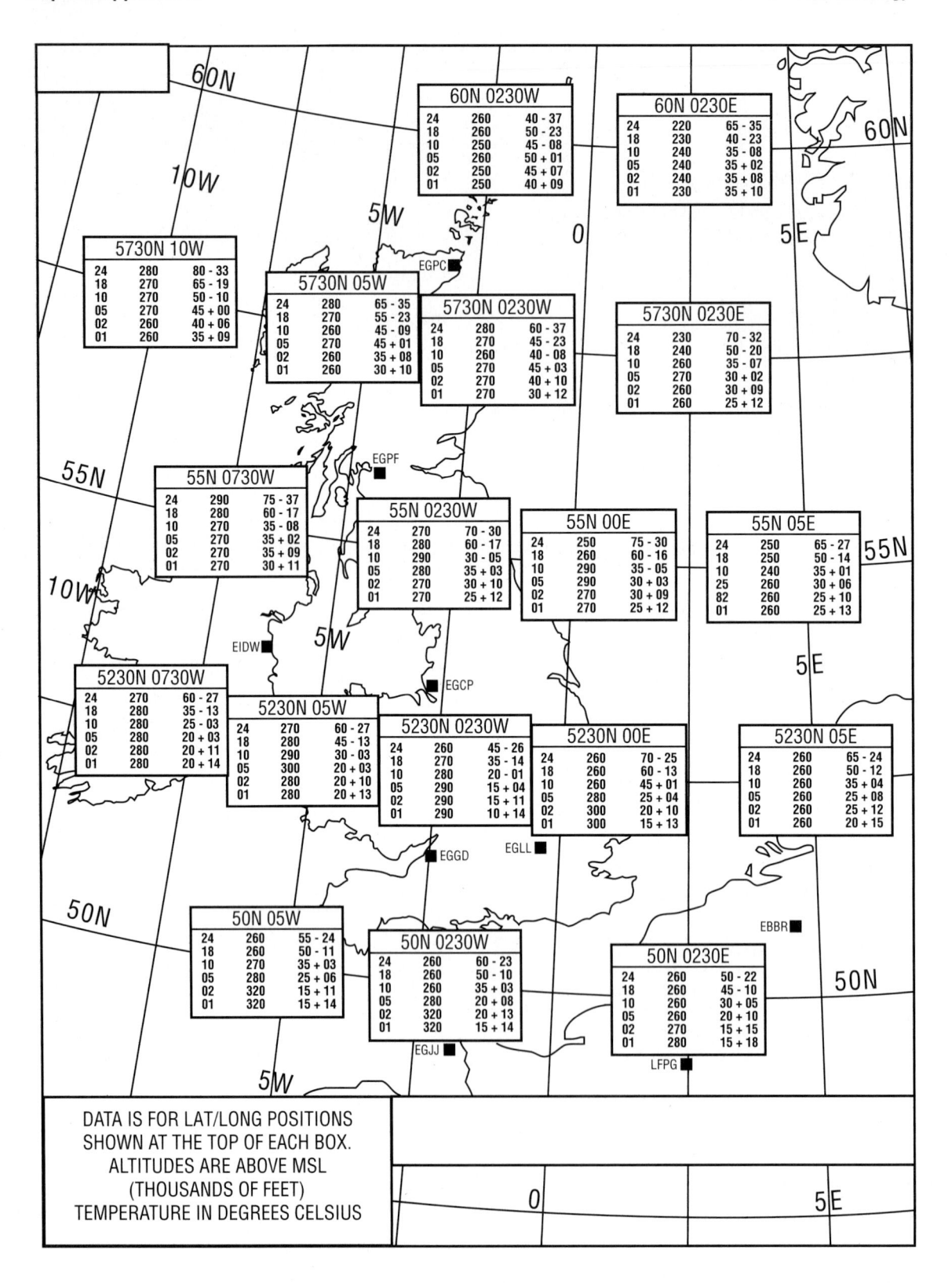

60N 0230W

24	260	40 - 37
18	260	50 - 23
10	250	45 - 08
05	260	50 + 01
02	250	45 + 07
01	250	40 + 09

60N 0230E

24	220	65 - 35
18	230	40 - 23
10	240	35 - 08
05	240	35 + 02
02	240	35 + 08
01	230	35 + 10

5730N 10W

24	280	80 - 33
18	270	65 - 19
10	270	50 - 10
05	270	45 + 00
02	260	40 + 06
01	260	35 + 09

5730N 05W

24	280	65 - 35
18	270	55 - 23
10	260	45 - 09
05	270	45 + 01
02	260	35 + 08
01	260	30 + 10

5730N 0230W

24	280	60 - 37
18	270	45 - 23
10	260	40 - 08
05	270	45 + 03
02	270	40 + 10
01	270	30 + 12

5730N 0230E

24	230	70 - 32
18	240	50 - 20
10	260	35 - 07
05	270	30 + 02
02	260	30 + 09
01	260	25 + 12

55N 0730W

24	290	75 - 37
18	280	60 - 17
10	270	35 - 08
05	270	35 + 02
02	270	35 + 09
01	270	30 + 11

55N 0230W

24	270	70 - 30
18	280	60 - 17
10	290	30 - 05
05	280	35 + 03
02	270	30 + 10
01	270	25 + 12

55N 00E

24	250	75 - 30
18	260	60 - 16
10	290	35 - 05
05	290	30 + 03
02	270	30 + 09
01	270	25 + 12

55N 05E

24	250	65 - 27
18	250	50 - 14
10	240	35 + 01
25	260	30 + 06
82	260	25 + 10
01	260	25 + 13

5230N 0730W

24	270	60 - 27
18	280	35 - 13
10	280	25 - 03
05	280	20 + 03
02	280	20 + 11
01	280	20 + 14

5230N 05W

24	270	60 - 27
18	280	45 - 13
10	290	30 - 03
05	300	20 + 03
02	280	20 + 10
01	280	20 + 13

5230N 0230W

24	270	45 - 26
18	270	35 - 14
10	280	20 - 01
05	290	15 + 04
02	290	15 + 11
01	290	10 + 14

5230N 00E

24	260	70 - 25
18	260	60 - 13
10	260	45 + 01
05	280	25 + 04
02	300	20 + 10
01	300	15 + 13

5230N 05E

24	260	65 - 24
18	260	50 - 12
10	260	35 + 04
05	260	25 + 08
02	260	25 + 12
01	260	20 + 15

50N 05W

24	260	55 - 24
18	260	50 - 11
10	270	35 + 03
05	280	25 + 06
02	320	15 + 11
01	320	15 + 14

50N 0230W

24	260	60 - 23
18	260	50 - 10
10	260	35 + 03
05	280	20 + 08
02	320	20 + 13
01	320	15 + 14

50N 0230E

24	260	50 - 22
18	260	45 - 10
10	260	30 + 05
05	260	20 + 10
02	270	15 + 15
01	280	15 + 18

DATA IS FOR LAT/LONG POSITIONS SHOWN AT THE TOP OF EACH BOX. ALTITUDES ARE ABOVE MSL (THOUSANDS OF FEET) TEMPERATURE IN DEGREES CELSIUS

Paper 6 Appendix B   Meteorology

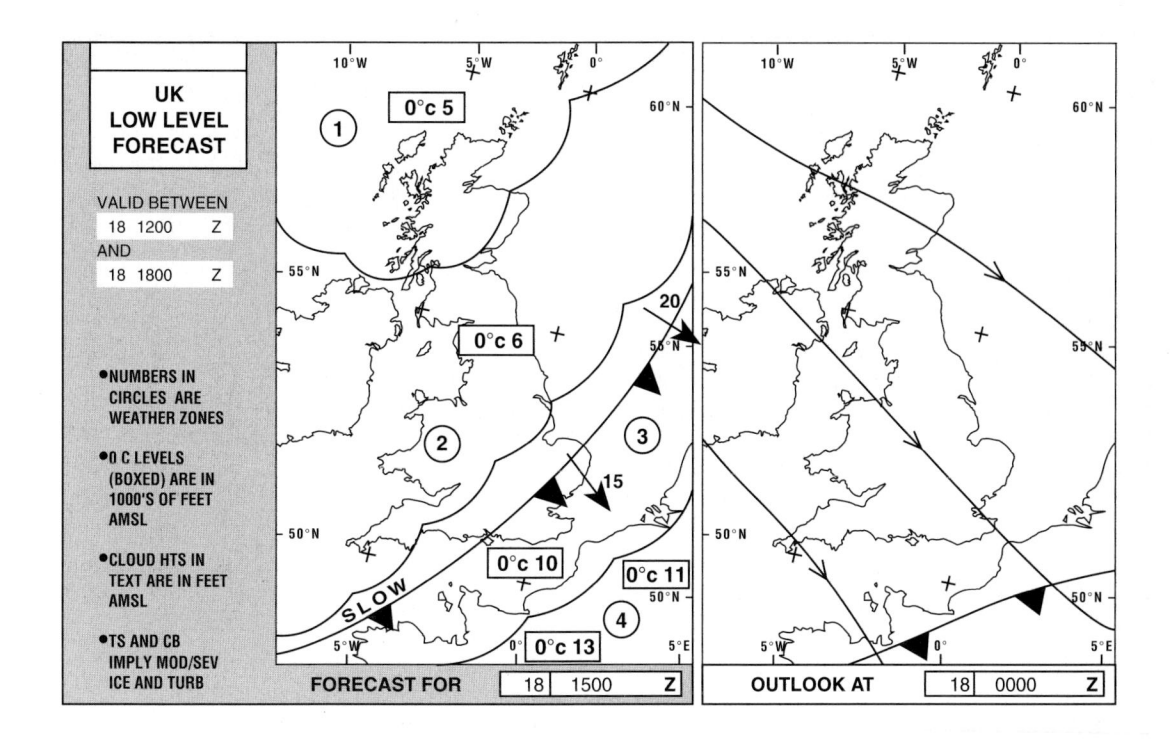

UK LOW LEVEL FORECAST

VALID BETWEEN 18 1200 Z AND 18 1800 Z

- NUMBERS IN CIRCLES ARE WEATHER ZONES
- 0 C LEVELS (BOXED) ARE IN 1000'S OF FEET AMSL
- CLOUD HTS IN TEXT ARE IN FEET AMSL
- TS AND CB IMPLY MOD/SEV ICE AND TURB

FORECAST FOR 18 1500 Z

OUTLOOK AT 18 0000 Z

ZONE 1	GEN	30KM	NIL	3-6/8CUSC 2200/8000
	OCNL	8KM	RAIN SH	6/8CU 1500/12000
	ISOL	3500	TS/HAIL	CB 800/25000 6/8ACAS 10000/18000
ZONE 2	GEN	35KM	NIL	3/8CUSC 3000/6000
	ISOL	10KM	RAIN SH	6/8CU 2000/9000
ZONE 3	GEN	20KM	NIL	5/8SC 2500/6000 2/8AC 12000/14000
	OCNL FRONT	5000M	RAIN/DZ	6-8/8STSC 800/7000 6/8LYR 7000/14000
	ISOL	1500M	MIST/DZ	6-8/8STSC 400/7000 6/8LYR 7000/14000
ZONE 4	GEN	15KM	NIL	5/8SC 3000/5500
	ISOL LAND	5000M	HAZE	1/8CUSC 4000/5500

OUTLOOK: UNTIL 18/0000Z:

Paper 7 Meteorology

1. Which of the following statements is true of advection fog:
A   It can occur over land and sea
B   It usually occurs because of a temperature fall at night
C   It usually occurs when dry air moves over a warm surface

2. A warm front in a 'typical' depression is moving at 20 knots, at what speed (approximately) would you expect the following cold front to be moving:
A   15 knots
B   30 knots
C   10 knots

3. You are flying below 1000ft agl in precipitation ahead of a warm front in winter. The outside air temperature is -2°C. What of the following meteorological phenomena is most likely to affect the aircraft?
A   Rain ice
B   Hail
C   Radiation fog

4. The surface temperature is +20°C, the dewpoint is +5°C. What is the most likely height for the base of convective cloud to form?
A   2500 feet
B   3000 feet
C   6000 feet

5. You depart airfield A where the QNH is 1006mb and fly to airfield B without resetting the altimeter. If airfield B has an elevation of 450ft, what will your altimeter read before resetting, if the airfield B QNH is 1024 (assuming 1mb = 30ft)?
A   90ft
B   -90ft
C   450ft

6. On a cold clear night, ice crystals can form on a surface directly from water vapour. This process is known as:
A   Sublimation or Deposition
B   Supercooling
C   Supersaturation

7. In the northern hemisphere, the surface winds in an anticyclone blow:
A   Clockwise
B   Clockwise except when a front is present
C   Anticlockwise except when a front is present

8. If the temperature at 5000ft is +10°C, this can be said to be:
A   ISA +10
B   ISA +2.5
C   ISA +5

9. A surface wind that has changed in direction from 330 to 270 is said to have:
A   Veered
B   Backed
C   Anti-clocked

Paper 7 Meteorology

10 If you stand facing the wind in the northern hemisphere, an area of low pressure area is:
A To your left
B To your right
C In front of you

11 The great majority of 'weather' is found in:
A The troposphere
B The tropopause
C The stratosphere

Refer to the following diagram, complete the diagram and answer questions 12 to 14.

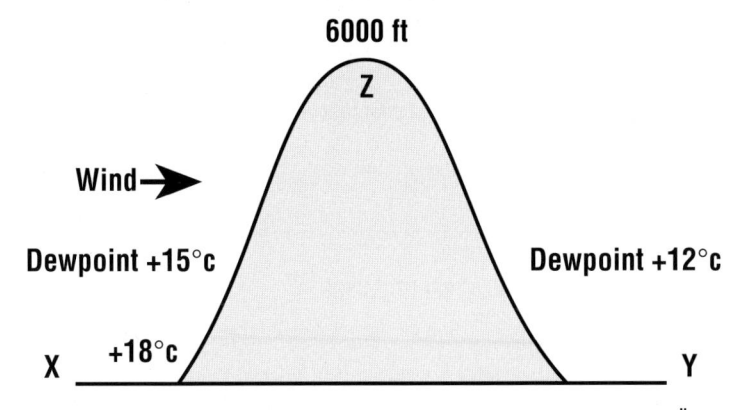

6000 ft
Z
Wind →
Dewpoint +15°c   Dewpoint +12°c
X +18°c   Y

Using the standard lapse rates sketch in the cloud due to the FÖHN wind effect.

12 What will be the temperature at Z?
A 0°C
B +7.5°C
C +6°C

13 What will be the temperature at Y?
A +21°C
B +18°C
C +15°C

14 What are the requirements in terms of humidity and stability of the air mass for a FÖHN wind to occur?
A Moist, stable air mass
B Dry, stable air mass
C Moist, unstable air mass

15 Any precipitation associated with a cold front typically:
A Is steady, prolonged and continues well after the passage of the front
B Is intermittent, becoming more prolonged as the front passes
C Is likely to clear quickly after passage of the front

Refer to Appendix A

16 What is the mean speed of the cold front crossing Cornwall?
A 15mps
B 15kts
C 15mph

Paper 7   Meteorology

17   What type of turbulence and icing is possible in zone 1, line 3?
A   Moderate icing, severe turbulence
B   Moderate icing, moderate turbulence
C   Severe icing, severe turbulence

18   In which zone and specific line might a coastal airfield report the following METAR:
       EG** 18/1020 30020KT 1200 BR BKN005
A   Zone 2 line 3
B   Zone 1 line 3
C   Zone 3 line 4

19   The cloud group in zone 2, line 2 means:
A   Stratus and Stratocumulus base 1000ft amsl, tops 7500ft amsl, with overcast Altocumuluis 8000ft amsl tops XXamsl
B   Stratus and Stratocumulus base 1000ft agl, tops 7500ft agl, with overcast Altocumuluis 8000ft agl tops XXagl
C   Stratus and Stratocumulus base 1000ft agl, tops 7500ft amsl, with overcast Altocumuluis 8000ft agl tops XXamsl

20   In which zone might an airfield report the following METAR:
       EG** 18/0950 27012KT 5000 RADZ BKN015 OVC060 +18/+17 Q1009
A   Zone 1
B   Zone 2
C   Zone 3

Paper 7 Appendix A   Meteorology

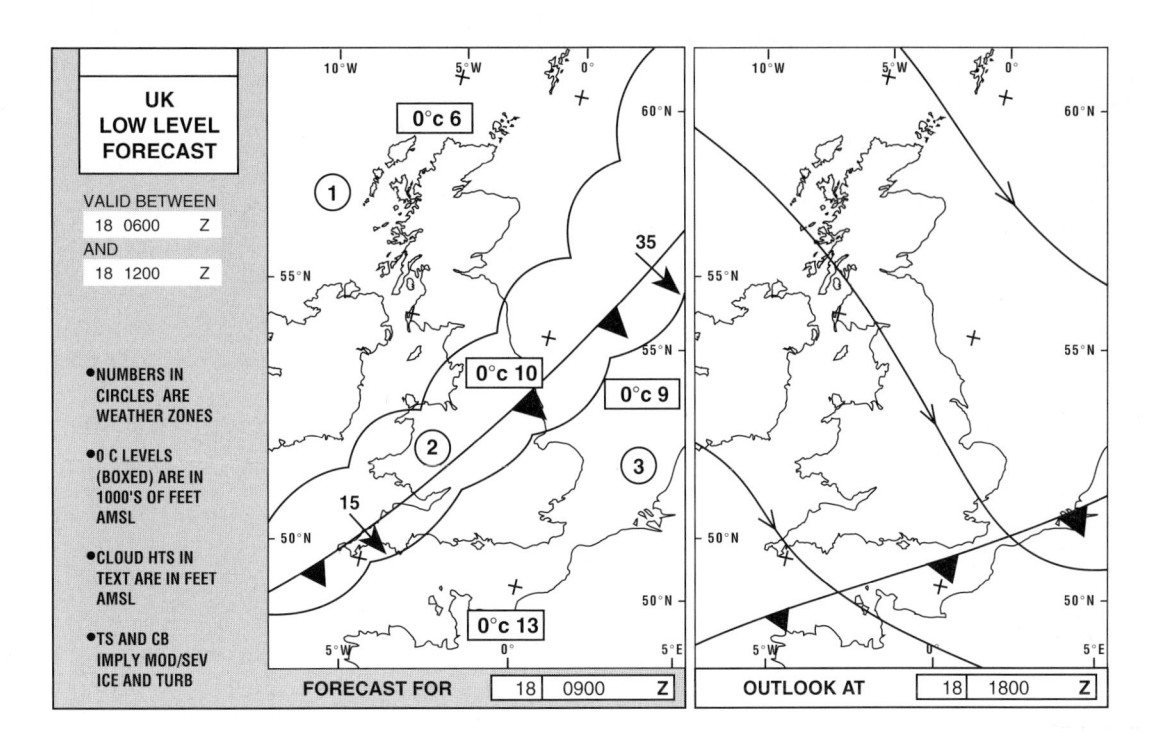

UK LOW LEVEL FORECAST

VALID BETWEEN
18 0600 Z
AND
18 1200 Z

- NUMBERS IN CIRCLES ARE WEATHER ZONES
- 0 C LEVELS (BOXED) ARE IN 1000'S OF FEET AMSL
- CLOUD HTS IN TEXT ARE IN FEET AMSL
- TS AND CB IMPLY MOD/SEV ICE AND TURB

FORECAST FOR 18 0900 Z

OUTLOOK AT 18 1800 Z

ZONE 1	GEN	25KM	NIL	4-6/8CUSC 2500/5000
	OCNL	8KM	RAIN SH	6/8CU 1000/10000
	ISOL N	3500	TS/HAIL	CB 800/25000 6/8AC 10000/18000
ZONE 2	GEN	20KM	NIL	5/8SC 2500/6000 6/8AC 10000/18000
	OCNL	10KM	RAIN	6/8STSC 1000/7500 8/8AC 8000/20000
	ISOL	3000M	HEAVY RAIN	8/8NS 500/16000
	LOC	2000	MIST/DZ	6/8ST 500/1500 6/8LYR 1800/18000
ZONE 3	GEN	25KM	NIL	NIL-2/8SC 3000/4500
	ISOL W	15KM	NIL/RAIN	NIL-2/8SC 3000/4500 5/8AC12000/18000
	ISOL LAND	5000M	HAZE	NIL-2/8ST 800/1500
	OCNL SEA/COT	1500M	MIST	5/8ST 500/1500

OUTLOOK: UNTIL 18/1800Z:

Paper 8 Meteorology

1 The Tropopause is:
A The layer of the atmosphere nearest the earth's surface
B The second layer nearest to the earth's surface
C The boundary between the first and second layers

2 1225 g/m³ relates to :
A The air density at sea level in the ISA
B The air pressure at sea level in the ISA
C The air density at 10000 feet in ISA conditions

3 The surface temperature is +15°C, the base of scattered cumulus cloud is 4000 feet. What is the most likely value for the dew point ?
A +10°C
B - 6°C
C + 6°C

4 The approximate height of the tropopause above mean sea level in the ISA is:
A 65,000ft
B 36,000ft
C 82,000ft

5 The temperature at 10,000ft in the ISA is:
A -5°C
B -10°C
C -15°C

6 An unstable air mass is forced to rise over a mountain range, which of the following is most likely?
A Extensive stratus cloud
B Cumuloform cloud
C Scattered cirrus cloud

7 The dry adiabatic lapse rate (DALR) is:
A 1.98°C/1000ft
B 1.5°C/1000ft
C 3°C/1000ft

8 The observed temperature at the surface is +13°C and at 4000ft it is +16°C. This situation and the result may be:
A An inversion, with better visibility above than below
B An isothermal layer
C A geostrophic layer

9 An aircraft is experiencing contant starboard drift (in the northern hemisphere). If it lands at an aerodrome after a long flight on a constant heading, without resetting the altimeter, which of the following is true?
A The altimeter is likely to over-read
B The altimeter is likely to under-read
C The altimeter is likely to read accurately

Paper 8 Meteorology

10 The force that causes a parcel of air to start moving from an area of high pressure to an area of low pressure, is called:
A The geostrophic force
B The Coriolis force
C The pressure gradient force

11 If the 2000ft wind is 310/35 and the surface wind over land is 280/20, what is the surface wind likely to be over the sea?
A 270/15
B 295/25
C 280/20

12 A strong wind flow over a mountain range which causes strong downdrafts on the lee side may typically be marked by:
A Cirrus clouds
B Lenticular clouds
C Stratus clouds

13 You are approaching an active Cumulonimbus cloud. Which of the following courses of action is valid?
A You can fly around the CB, avoiding it by least 10 miles
B You must land immediately and wait for the CB to pass over
C You can fly under the CB if you can see through to other side

14 At an airfield you ask for a TAF, and are given the following from the fax:
EIDW 0716 12005KT 0100 FG BKN001 BECMG 0810 8000 NSW
Why should you not accept this TAF?
A Because the weather is dreadful
B Because the TAF is not complete
C Because the cloud group has been incorrectly transmitted

15 Orographic clouds form:
A Over the sea during the winter months
B Whenever the eddying motion associated with mechanical turbulence sets off large scale vertical movements
C Over mountain ranges, large hills or sloping planes

16 Which of the following is most likely to "trigger off" a cumulonimbus:
A Convergence in tropical latitudes
B Subsidence in tropical latitudes
C Convection in polar latitudes

17 If maritime air is heated from below as it moves from its source region it will become:
A Stable
B Unstable
C Neutrally stable

18 A CB with anvil signifies that the thunderstorm is in:
A The building stage
B The mature stage
C The dissipating stage

Paper 8 Meteorology

19 Approaching Cirrus cloud may signify:
A An approaching depression
B A valley wind
C Severe turbulence and icing conditions

20 In relation to an occluded front:
A It may occur when the cold front merges into the warm front, combining the cloud and precipitation of both
B It cannot exist outside a depression
C It is likely to be a weak weather feature

Paper 9   Meteorology

1 Which of the following statements best describes the change in pressure with the passage of typical warm and cold fronts:
A After warm front steadily falling, after cold front steady
B After warm front steadies, after cold front rises
C After warm front rises, after cold front falls

2 Clouds formed by convection will usually:
A Be layer clouds
B Have a cloud base within 2000ft of the surface
C Be cumulus type

3 Moist, stable air with a surface temperature of +15°C and a dew point of +7°C is forced to rise over a range of hills with a mean height of 5000ft. What is likely to be the cloud base on the windward side?
A There will be no cloud on the windward side
B 4500ft
C 2000ft

4 If the temperature at 6000 feet is +7°C, in relation to ISA conditions:
A The temperature at 6000 feet is less than ISA
B The temperature at 6000 feet is greater than ISA
C The temperature at 6000 feet is equal to ISA

5 A METAR includes the abbreviation 'CAVOK'. Which of the following might exist at the time of the METAR without invalidating the terms of this abbreviation?
A Total cloud cover at 6000 feet
B 1/8 of CB at 25000
C Visibility of 9999 m

6 Gust fronts are normally associated with:
A Standing waves
B Thunderstorms
C High pressure areas

7 Advection fog is most likely to form when:
A Dry, warm air moves over a cold sea causing evaporation and consequent condensation
B Warm, moist air moves across a sea surface and reaches ambient temperature
C Warm, moist air moves across a cold land surface and is cooled to below its dew point

8 The 0°C level on a SIGWX chart is depicted:
A In hundreds of feet amsl
B In thousands of feet amsl
C In thousands of feet agl

9 With regard to diurnal variation of temperature over land in mid latitudes, is most correct to say:
A Surface temperature is hottest at 1500 UTC, coolest one hour before sunrise
B Surface temperature is hottest at 1500 LMT, coolest at sunrise
C Surface temperature is hottest at noon, coolest at sunset

10 In the ISA, the temperature is assumed to decrease at a rate of:
A 1.98°C per 1000ft
B 1.98°C per 1000m
C 2K per 1000ft

Paper 9 — Meteorology

11 In a TAF the abbreviation BECMG indicates:
A An expected permanent change in forecast conditions
B Becalmed conditions at an offshore installation
C The time of a temporary change in weather conditions

12 When a wind changes direction from southerly to south westerly, it is said to:
A Veer in the northern hemisphere & back in the southern hemisphere
B Back in the northern hemisphere & veer in the southern hemisphere
C Veer in either hemisphere

13 As a cold front passes the pressure:
A Falls
B Rises
C Remains constant

14 An aircraft may accumulate hoar frost:
A Only when the aircraft is on the ground
B Only when the air temperature is below freezing (0°C)
C Only when the airframe temperature is below freezing (0°C)

15 Which is the proper decode the following TAF for Lydd:
EGMD 03/12-21 24015G25KT 6000 BKN035 TEMPO 5000 SHRA BKN020
A Lydd, date 03 period of validity 1200 to 2100 UTC. Surface wind 240 degrees 15 knots going to be 25 knots. Visibility 6000 metres. Cloud 5 to 7 oktas base 3500 feet AMSL, temporarily visibility 5000 metres in rain showers, cloud 5 to 7 oktas base 2000 feet AMSL
B Lydd, date 03 period of validity 1200 to 2100 UTC. Surface wind 240 degrees 15 knots gusting 25 knots. Visibility 6000 metres. Cloud 1 to 4 oktas base 3500 feet agl, temporarily visibility 5000 metres in rain showers, cloud 1 to 4 oktas base 2000 feet agl
C Lydd, date 03 period of validity 1200 to 2100 UTC. Surface wind 240 degrees 15 knots gusting 25 knots. Visibility 6000 metres. Cloud 5 to 7 oktas base 3500 feet agl, temporarily visibility 5000 metres in rain showers, cloud 5 to 7 oktas base 2000 feet agl

16 In a TAF or METAR the code for hail is:
A GR
B HA
C PE

Now Refer to Appendix B

17 Your FAX machine did not print the cloud type zone 2 line 2: what is the most likely answer?
A Sirrus
B Cumulus
C Altostratus

18 The freezing level in zone 4 is:
A 1000ft
B 100ft
C 10,000ft

Paper 9   Meteorology

19 What is the worst forecast weather for the Kent coast at 1600 UTC?

A 20km nil weather, scattered stratocumulus 3000ft amsl to 6000ft amsl

B 800m fog and drizzle, 8/8 stratus/ stratocumulus 200ft/ 5000ft moderate turbulence and ice

C 4000m heavy showers thunderstorms hail cumulonimbus 800ft/20000ft severe icing and turbulence

20 You are planning a flight from Birmingham to Newcastle You are a PPL without an IMC or Instrument Rating and your flight is planned to take place entirely in 'the open FIR' – e.g. Class G airspace – below 3000' AMSL. You will be flying a PA 28 Warrior (IAS 105 knots). Your ETD is 1400Z, with an en-route time of 1:45. Assuming you wish to complete the flight safely and legally, which of the following statements is true:

A There is no doubt that the flight can be safely and legally completed and you should depart on time

B Assuming flight at an altitude to allow adequate terrain clearance, there is the possibility that at times the cloud base will be at, or below, the operating altitude. Provided you avoid the rain showers that accompany this reduction in cloud base, the flight should be able to proceed

C By delaying the departure for two hours the showers will clear the area and, daylight permitting, the flight can proceed

Paper 9 Appendix A — Meteorology

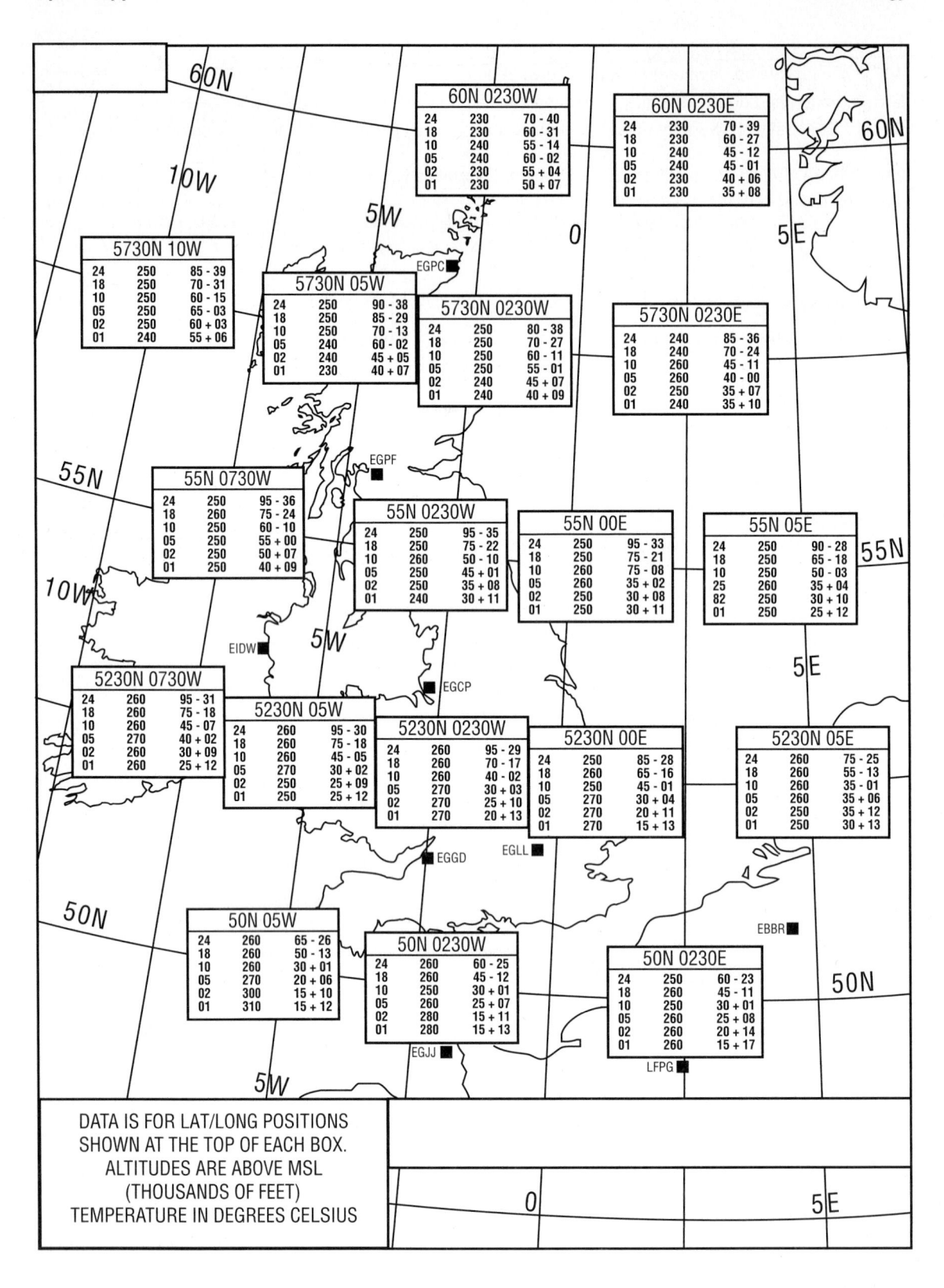

60N 0230W
24	230	70 - 40
18	230	60 - 31
10	240	55 - 14
05	240	60 - 02
02	230	55 + 04
01	230	50 + 07

60N 0230E
24	230	70 - 39
18	230	60 - 27
10	240	45 - 12
05	240	45 - 01
02	230	40 + 06
01	230	35 + 08

5730N 10W
24	250	85 - 39
18	250	70 - 31
10	250	60 - 15
05	250	65 - 03
02	250	60 + 03
01	240	55 + 06

5730N 05W
24	250	90 - 38
18	250	85 - 29
10	250	70 - 13
05	240	60 - 02
02	240	45 + 05
01	230	40 + 07

5730N 0230W
24	250	80 - 38
18	250	70 - 27
10	250	60 - 11
05	250	55 - 01
02	240	45 + 07
01	240	40 + 09

5730N 0230E
24	240	85 - 36
18	240	70 - 24
10	260	45 - 11
05	260	40 - 00
02	250	35 + 07
01	240	35 + 10

55N 0730W
24	250	95 - 36
18	260	75 - 24
10	250	60 - 10
05	250	55 + 00
02	250	50 + 07
01	250	40 + 09

55N 0230W
24	250	95 - 35
18	250	75 - 22
10	260	50 - 10
05	250	45 + 01
02	250	35 + 08
01	240	30 + 11

55N 00E
24	250	95 - 33
18	250	75 - 21
10	260	75 - 08
05	260	35 + 02
02	250	30 + 08
01	250	30 + 11

55N 05E
24	250	90 - 28
18	250	65 - 18
10	250	50 - 03
25	260	35 + 04
82	250	30 + 10
01	250	25 + 12

5230N 0730W
24	260	95 - 31
18	260	75 - 18
10	260	45 - 07
05	270	40 + 02
02	260	30 + 09
01	260	25 + 12

5230N 05W
24	260	95 - 30
18	260	75 - 18
10	260	45 - 05
05	270	30 + 02
02	250	25 + 09
01	250	25 + 12

5230N 0230W
24	260	95 - 29
18	260	70 - 17
10	260	40 - 02
05	270	30 + 03
02	270	25 + 10
01	270	20 + 13

5230N 00E
24	250	85 - 28
18	260	65 - 16
10	250	45 - 01
05	270	30 + 04
02	270	20 + 11
01	270	15 + 13

5230N 05E
24	260	75 - 25
18	260	55 - 13
10	260	35 - 01
05	260	35 + 06
02	250	35 + 12
01	250	30 + 13

50N 05W
24	260	65 - 26
18	260	50 - 13
10	260	30 + 01
05	270	20 + 06
02	300	15 + 10
01	310	15 + 12

50N 0230W
24	260	60 - 25
18	260	45 - 12
10	250	30 + 01
05	260	25 + 07
02	280	15 + 11
01	280	15 + 13

50N 0230E
24	250	60 - 23
18	260	45 - 11
10	250	30 + 01
05	260	25 + 08
02	260	20 + 14
01	260	15 + 17

DATA IS FOR LAT/LONG POSITIONS SHOWN AT THE TOP OF EACH BOX.
ALTITUDES ARE ABOVE MSL (THOUSANDS OF FEET)
TEMPERATURE IN DEGREES CELSIUS

Paper 9 Appendix B — Meteorology

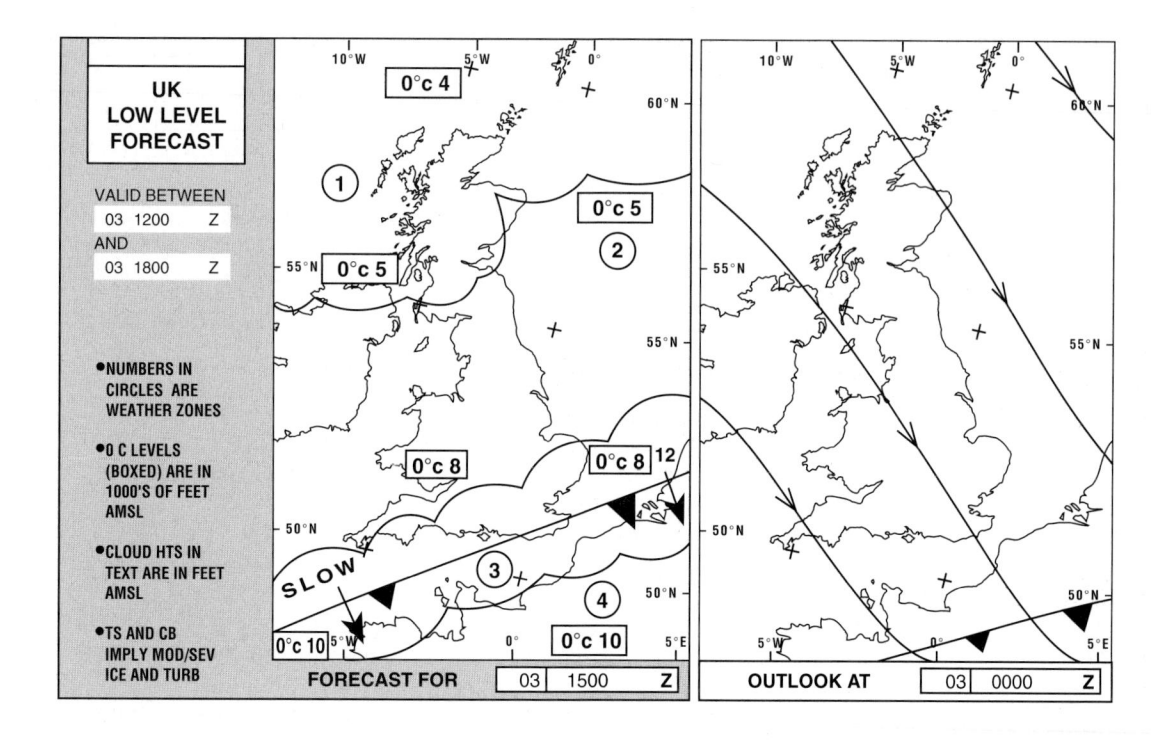

UK LOW LEVEL FORECAST

VALID BETWEEN 03 1200 Z AND 03 1800 Z

- NUMBERS IN CIRCLES ARE WEATHER ZONES
- 0 C LEVELS (BOXED) ARE IN 1000'S OF FEET AMSL
- CLOUD HTS IN TEXT ARE IN FEET AMSL
- TS AND CB IMPLY MOD/SEV ICE AND TURB

FORECAST FOR 03 1500 Z

OUTLOOK AT 03 0000 Z

ZONE 1	GEN	30KM	NIL	3-6/8CUSC 2000/8000
	FRQ	8KM	RAIN SH	6/8CU 1200/14000
	ISOL N	4000M	HEAVY SH /TS/HAIL	CB 800/20000
ZONE 2	GEN	30KM	NIL	3-5/8CU 2500/6000
	OCNL	10KM	RAIN SH	6/8 1500/10000
ZONE 3	GEN	10KM	NIL/RAIN	5/8ST 1200/1500 6-8/8LYR 2000/8000
	OCNL	3500M	RAIN DZ	8/8LYR 600/10000
	LOC	0800M	FOG/DZ	4-6/8STSC 200/5000
	OCNL			MOD TURB AND ICE
ZONE 4	GEN	20KM	NIL/RAIN	NIL-1/8SC 3000/6000

OUTLOOK: UNTIL 03/0000Z:

Paper 10   Meteorology

1 The temperature at sea level in the ISA is equivalent to:
A +25°F
B +15°F
C +59°F

2 A land breeze blows:
A From the sea by day
B From the land by night
C From the land by day

3 In an anticyclone, the air mass tends to:
A Ascend and warm
B Subside and cool
C Subside and warm

4 In a typical depression:
A The warm front moves faster than the cold front
B The warm front moves slower than the cold front
C The cold front moves slower than the warm front

5 A coastal aerodrome has the sea to its southwest. Just after the onset of a sea breeze the runway most likely to be closest to 'into wind' is:
A 22
B 04
C 17

6 For carburettor ice to form, the outside air must be:
A Cold and moist
B Moist
C Below freezing

7 If radiation fog forms on a clear night with light winds, an increase in wind strength from 5 kts to 18 kts:
A Will change radiation fog to advection fog
B Will have no effect
C May cause the fog to lift and become low stratus

8 Which of the following never appear in a TAF?
A Cloud type
B Cloud amount if less than 1/4
C Cloud amount in oktas

Paper 10   Meteorology

9 The following shows:

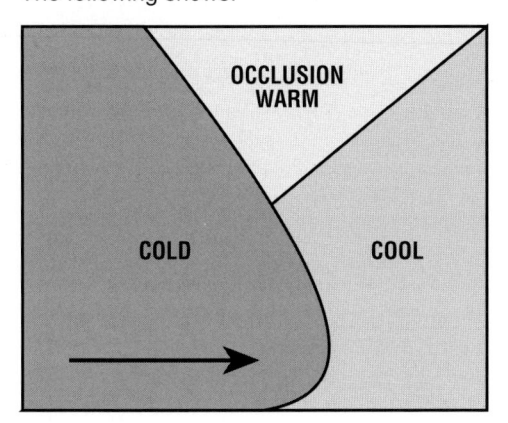

A A cold occlusion
B A cold front
C A warm occlusion

10 The conditions most suitable for the formation of radiation fog are:
A Cloudy night, moist air, small dew point spread
B Cloudless night, dry cool air, moderate winds
C Cloudless night, light winds, moist air

11 Stability of an air mass is likely to be reduced when:
A There is cooling from below
B There is warming from below
C Air is forced to rise

12 When flying towards a depression at a constant indicated altitude, without updating the altimeter subscale setting, the aircraft's actual altitude will be:
A Lower than indicated
B Higher than indicated
C The same as indicated

13 Select the missing word(s).
Radiation fog can _____ in the early morning once the sun rises:
A Form
B Never form or increase
C Never dissipate

14 In the International Standard Atmosphere, mean sea level pressure is:
A 29.92 inches of mercury
B 1225 grams per cubic metre
C 14.7 grams per square inch

Now Refer to Appendix A

15 What is the forecast 2000ft wind at EGGD likely to be?
A 170/30 gusting 39kts
B 200/30
C 185/28

Paper 10 — Meteorology

16 What is the surface temperature likely to be at 55N – 0730W?
A   +9.5°C
B   +12.5°C
C   +14°C

Now Refer to Appendix B

17 Zone 2 shows a:
A   An occluding front
B   A line squall
C   A quasi stationary front

18 What is the lowest visibility forecast in zone 4?
A   8nm
B   20km occasionally 8km
C   20km isolated 8km

19 What is the lowest cloud forecast in zone 1?
A   1500ft amsl
B   2000ft amsl
C   1500ft agl

20 You are planning a flight from Biggin Hill airfield (south of London) to Bembridge on the Isle of Wight. You are a PPL without an IMC or Instrument Rating and your flight is planned to take place entirely in 'the open FIR' – e.g. Class G airspace – below 3000' AMSL. You will be flying a PA 28 Warrior (IAS 105 knots). Your ETD is 1800Z, with an en-route time of 55 minutes. Assuming you wish to complete the flight safely and legally, which of the following statements is true:
A   There is no doubt that the flight can be safely and legally completed and you should depart on time
B   Assuming flight at an altitude to allow adequate terrain clearance, there is the probability that at times the cloud base will be at, or below, the operating altitude. Additionally a front is approaching the route and destination airfield. Cancel the flight
C   By delaying the departure for two hours the front will clear the area and, daylight permitting, the flight can proceed

Paper 10 Appendix A — Meteorology

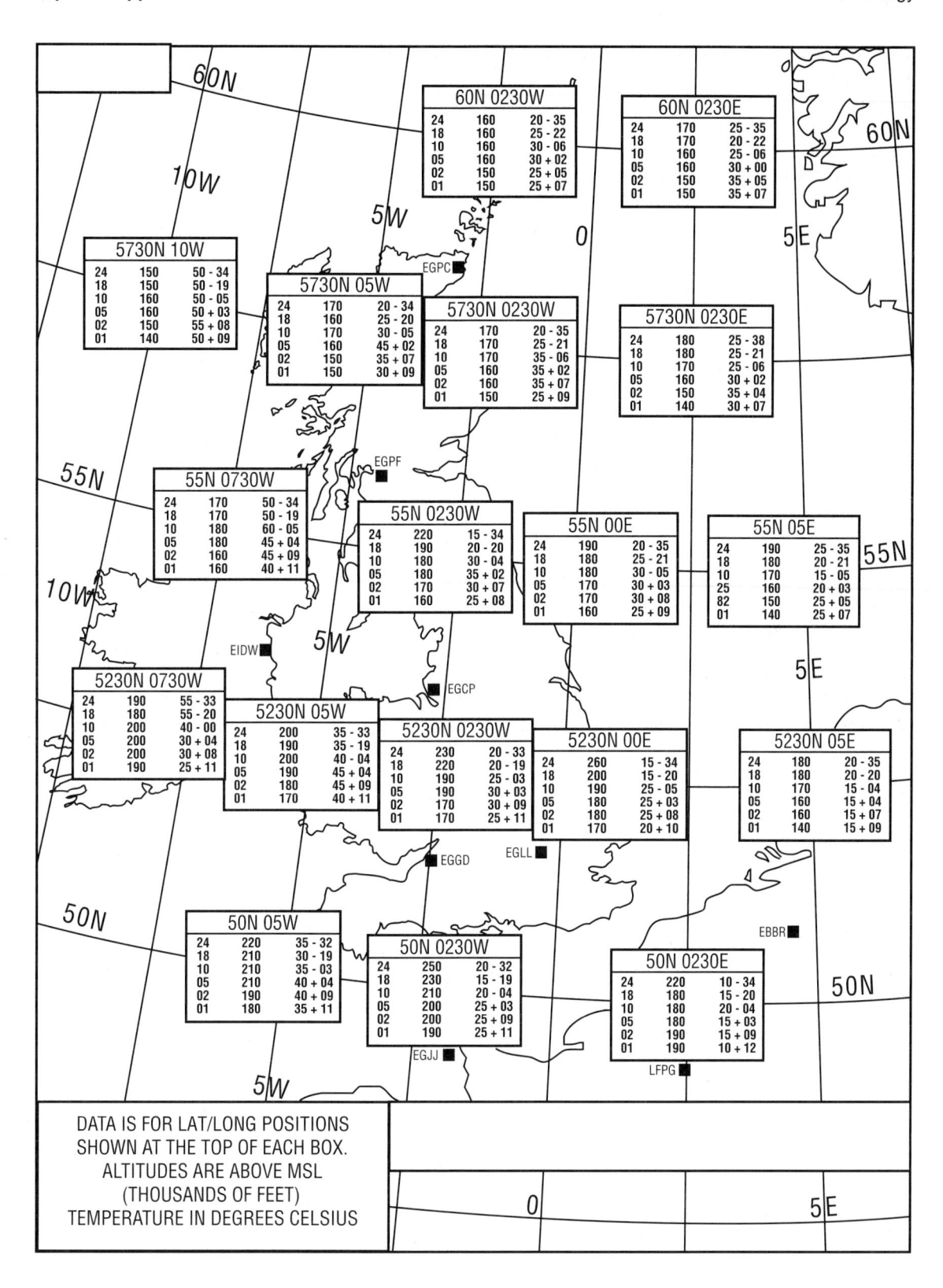

60N 0230W
24	160	20 - 35
18	160	25 - 22
10	160	30 - 06
05	160	30 + 02
02	150	25 + 05
01	150	25 + 07

60N 0230E
24	170	25 - 35
18	170	20 - 22
10	160	25 - 06
05	160	30 + 00
02	150	35 + 05
01	150	35 + 07

5730N 10W
24	150	50 - 34
18	150	50 - 19
10	160	50 - 05
05	160	50 + 03
02	150	55 + 08
01	140	50 + 09

5730N 05W
24	170	20 - 34
18	160	25 - 20
10	170	30 - 05
05	160	45 + 02
02	150	35 + 07
01	150	30 + 09

5730N 0230W
24	170	20 - 35
18	170	25 - 21
10	170	35 - 06
05	160	35 + 03
02	160	35 + 07
01	150	25 + 09

5730N 0230E
24	180	25 - 38
18	180	25 - 21
10	170	25 - 06
05	160	30 + 02
02	150	35 + 04
01	140	30 + 07

55N 0730W
24	170	50 - 34
18	170	50 - 19
10	180	60 - 05
05	180	45 + 04
02	160	45 + 09
01	160	40 + 11

55N 0230W
24	220	15 - 34
18	190	20 - 20
10	180	30 - 04
05	180	35 + 02
02	170	30 + 07
01	160	25 + 08

55N 00E
24	190	20 - 35
18	180	25 - 21
10	180	30 - 05
05	170	30 + 03
02	170	30 + 08
01	160	25 + 09

55N 05E
24	190	25 - 35
18	180	20 - 21
10	170	15 - 05
25	160	20 + 03
82	150	25 + 05
01	140	25 + 07

5230N 0730W
24	190	55 - 33
18	180	55 - 20
10	200	40 - 00
05	200	30 + 04
02	200	30 + 08
01	190	25 + 11

5230N 05W
24	200	35 - 33
18	190	35 - 19
10	200	40 - 04
05	190	45 + 04
02	180	45 + 09
01	170	40 + 11

5230N 0230W
24	230	20 - 33
18	220	20 - 19
10	190	25 - 03
05	190	30 + 03
02	170	30 + 09
01	170	25 + 11

5230N 00E
24	260	15 - 34
18	200	15 - 20
10	190	25 - 05
05	180	25 + 03
02	180	25 + 08
01	170	20 + 10

5230N 05E
24	180	20 - 35
18	180	20 - 20
10	170	15 - 04
05	160	15 + 04
02	160	15 + 07
01	140	15 + 09

50N 05W
24	220	35 - 32
18	210	30 - 19
10	210	35 - 03
05	210	40 + 04
02	190	40 + 09
01	180	35 + 11

50N 0230W
24	250	20 - 32
18	230	15 - 19
10	210	20 - 04
05	200	25 + 03
02	200	25 + 09
01	190	25 + 11

50N 0230E
24	220	10 - 34
18	180	15 - 20
10	180	20 - 04
05	180	15 + 03
02	190	15 + 09
01	190	10 + 12

DATA IS FOR LAT/LONG POSITIONS SHOWN AT THE TOP OF EACH BOX. ALTITUDES ARE ABOVE MSL (THOUSANDS OF FEET) TEMPERATURE IN DEGREES CELSIUS

Paper 10 Appendix B   Meteorology

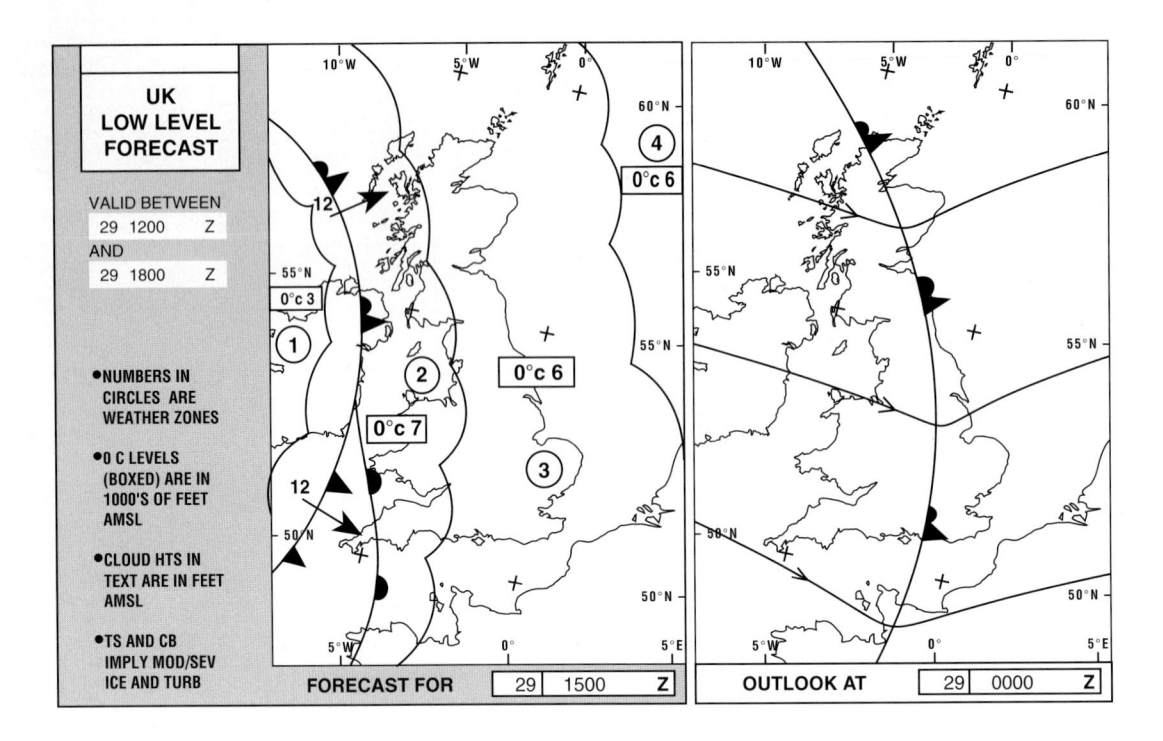

UK LOW LEVEL FORECAST

VALID BETWEEN
29 1200 Z
AND
29 1800 Z

- NUMBERS IN CIRCLES ARE WEATHER ZONES
- 0 C LEVELS (BOXED) ARE IN 1000'S OF FEET AMSL
- CLOUD HTS IN TEXT ARE IN FEET AMSL
- TS AND CB IMPLY MOD/SEV ICE AND TURB

FORECAST FOR 29 1500 Z

OUTLOOK AT 29 0000 Z

ZONE 1	GEN	30KM	NIL	6/8CUSC 2000/8000
	ONCL	8KM	RAIN SH	6/8CUSC 1500/12000
ZONE 2	GEN	14KM	NIL/RAIN	5/8SC 1500/6000 5/8LYR 8000/12000
	OCNL	8KM	RAIN	5/8ST 800/1500 8/8LYR 2000/17000
	ISOL FRONT	5000M	HEAVY RAIN	8/8LYR 500/20000
	ISOL	2000M	RAIN/DZ	8/8LYR 300/6000
ZONE 3	GEN	15KM	NIL	5/8CUSC 3000/6000
	OCNL	6KM	NIL	6/8STSC 1000/7000 6/8LYR 8000/10000
	ISOL	2500M	MIST/DZ	8/8STSC 500/7000
	ISOL SW	8KM	RAIN SH	6/8CUSC 2000/10000
ZONE 4	GEN	20KM	NIL	1/8SC 2500/6000
	ISOL	8KM	HAZE	1/8SC 2500/6000

OUTLOOK: UNTIL 29/0000Z:

PRIVATE PILOT'S LICENCE

Navigation

Time allowed: 1 hour 15 minutes

Instructions

1 The paper consists of 20 multiple choice questions, each carries 5 marks (total 100 marks). The pass mark is 70% (i.e. 14 questions or more must be answered correctly); marks are not deducted for incorrect answers.

2 Be sure to carefully read each question and ensure that you understand it before considering the answer choices. Only one of the answers is complete and correct; the others are either incomplete or based on a misconception.

3 Leave questions that seem difficult at first and return to these when the others have been completed.

4 Indicate the correct answer to each question by placing a tick in the appropriate box of the answer sheet. If you decide to change an answer, completely obliterate the original selection.

5 The back of the answer sheet can be used for working calculations.
DO NOT MARK THE QUESTION PAPER.

Paper 1   Navigation

1   It is planned to carry out a flight from Gloucestershire Airport (N5153.65 W00210.03) to Peterborough (Sibson) (N5233.35 W00023.18). The destination alternate is Peterborough (Conington) (N5228.08 W00015.07). Complete the attached flight plan using a CAA 1:500,000 scale map and then answer the following questions.

1   The direct track from Gloucestershire Airport to Peterborough (Sibson) is:
A   055° (M)
B   060° (T)
C   245° (D)

2   What is the distance from Gloucestershire Airport to Peterborough (Sibson) Aerodrome?
A   74nm
B   80nm
C   76nm

3   The magnetic heading on the diversion leg from the destination to the alternate would be:
A   134°
B   140°
C   144°

4   The groundspeed on the diversion leg from the destination to the alternate would be:
A   97kts
B   99kts
C   92kts

5   You set course overhead Gloucestershire airport at 11:09, what is your ETA for Peterborough (Sibson)?
A   11:55
B   11:44
C   12:01

6   On the initial part of the flight after departing Gloucestershire airport, which ATSU might be able to offer a LARS service, and on what frequency?
A   Gloster VDF 125.65
B   Brize Zone 119.00
C   Brize Radar 134.30

7   To maintain a minimum separation of 500ft below the lowest base of controlled airspace on the flight from Gloucestershire to Peterborough (Sibson), what would be the highest cruising level that could be used?
A   6400ft amsl
B   4000ft amsl
C   FL40

8   If the aircraft's fuel consumption is 15 imp. gals per hour, allowing 4 imp. gals for start, taxy, take-off and climb, and given a requirement to have at least 10 imp. gals on board once overhead Peterborough (Sibson), how what is the minimum on-board fuel required on starting at Gloucestershire?
A   25.5 imp. gal
B   21.5 imp. gal
C   23.5 imp. gal

Paper 1 Navigation

9 Assuming that you depart Gloucestershire with a fuel amount of 35 imp. gals, and the flight proceeds according to the flight plan and the fuel consumption as above, what would be your endurance once overhead Peterborough (Sibson)?
A 1 hour 18 minutes
B 67 minutes
C 123 minutes

10 The route crosses close to area R204/2.2. What is the vertical limit of this area?
A 2200ft amsl
B 2200ft agl
C FL2.2

11 What is the nature of area R204/2.2?
A It is a restricted area, active 135 days per year
B It is a restricted area applying to helicopters only
C It is a restricted area, activated by NOTAM

12 The MEF **28** represents a vertical distance of:
A 2800ft agl
B 2800ft amsl
C 28000ft amsl

13 Which type of airspace boundary is signified by the marking:

───────

A A MATZ
B Class A airspace
C Class D airspace

14 Just to the north of Daventry VOR your route crosses a major road aligned approximately north/south. What is the designator of this road?
A The M1 motorway
B The 'S' dual carriageway
C The M45 motorway

15 What is significant about the obstruction located immediately east of Daventry town (N5212.74 W00109.87)?
A It has cables
B It consists of 369 individual masts
C It is lighted

16 What is the meaning of the chart symbol close to track at Rothwell (west of Kettering)?
A It is a Gas venting site
B It is a cable grounding site
C It is a gliding site

17 Having set course overhead Gloucestershire at 11:09, you are abeam Rothwell at 11:45. What has your average groundspeed been to this point?
A 99 knots
B 112 knots
C 108 knots

Paper 1 Navigation

18 Approaching Peterborough (Sibson), you expect to penetrate the Wittering MATZ. On what frequency would you contact the controlling ATSU?
A   117.60
B   130.20
C   273

19 Based on the relief portrayal of the 1:500,000 scale map, what in theory is the highest possible terrain within 5nm of Peterborough (Sibson)?
A   499ft amsl
B   299ft amsl
C   600ft amsl

20 What is the meaning of the following symbol as found on ICAO charts:

1700 ▲
(650) ▲

A   A mast rising to 1,700ft amsl, which is 650ft in height
B   A mast 1,700ft agl on ground 650ft amsl
C   A mast 650ft high on ground 1,700ft amsl

Paper 1 Appendix A Navigation

Latitude and longitude are given as an aid to identification but where locations and facilities are marked on the chart, their charted positions should be used.

From	To	FL/Alt	Safety Alt ft amsl	Tas kt	W/V	Trk T	Drift	Hdg T	Var	Hdg M	GS kt	Dist nm	Time hr/min
Gloucestershire N5153.65 W00210.03	Peterborough (Sibson) N5233.35 W00023.18	2500	2400	90	240/10				4°W				
											Total		

Alternate

From	To	FL/Alt	Safety Alt						Var				
Peterborough (Sibson) N5233.35 W00023.18	Peterborough (Conington) N5228.08 W00015.07	2500	1800	90	240/10				4°W				

Note: Safety Altitude is derived from the higher of:

1   the highest ground plus 1299ft;

    or

2   the highest structure plus 1000ft; rounded up to the next 100ft, within 5nm of track.

Paper 2 — Navigation

It is planned to carry out a flight from airfield A at (N5200.52 E00013.57) to airfield B at (N5205.13 W00208.15). The destination alternate is airfield C at (N5200.17 W00228.50). Complete the attached flight plan using a CAA 1:500,000 scale map and then answer the following questions.

1	What is the total flight time from airfield A to airfield B?
A	63 minutes
B	48 minutes
C	55 minutes

2	What is the distance from A to B?
A	95nm
B	87nm
C	83nm

3	What is the magnetic track from A to B?
A	277°
B	273°
C	268°

4	What is the groundspeed between A and B?
A	89kts
B	94kts
C	85kts

5	What is the magnetic heading required for the diversion from B to C?
A	239°
B	254°
C	249°

6	Given a fuel consumption of 8.5 imp. gal per hour; allowing 2 imp. gals for start, taxi, take-off and climb plus 2 imp. gals for the approach and landing or missed approach at destination; and requiring a reserve of 5 imp. gals on arriving overhead the destination alternate, what is the minimum fuel required (rounded to the nearest imp. gal)?
A	18 imp. gals
B	21 imp. gals
C	23 imp. gals

7	What altimeter setting would you expect to use when setting out en-route on departure from A?
A	Standard Pressure Setting (QNE)
B	Aerodrome QNH
C	Stansted QFE

8	What is the classification of the lowest controlled airspace above the aircraft as it passes Henlow airfield?
A	Class F
B	Class A (LTMA)
C	Class D (CTA)

Paper 2   Navigation

9 What is the minimum legal altitude for flying directly over the mast which is passed approximately 8nm from the departure airfield, assuming the flight is being conducted under VFR?
A 1351ft amsl
B 1900ft amsl
C 751ft agl

10 Assuming that you will fly no closer than 100ft to the base of controlled airspace, what is the maximum altitude at which you may fly the complete route A to B?
A 2400ft amsl
B 3400ft amsl
C 2900ft amsl

11 Which ATSU, and on what frequency, could you obtain a LARS service for the first part of the flight from A to B?
A Stansted; 120.625
B Luton; 129.55
C Stansted; 116.25

12 If you are unable to contact Turweston, although it is during the notified hours of watch for the ATSU, what should be your lowest legal altitude when passing over the airfield?
A 2500ft amsl
B 3000ft amsl
C 2000ft amsl

13 The map symbol ⊕ VRP ASHBOURNE means:
A A Visual Reference Point, notified in the UK AIP
B A Venting under Reduced Pressure site
C A Variable Routing Procedure, notified in the AD section of the UK AIP

14 You have decided that you need to uplift 25imp. gals for a flight, but the fuel pump reads in litres. How many litres do you ask for?
A 30lt
B 95lt
C 114lt

15 Your destination (B) is non-radio. Approaching the airfield, before you have it in sight, what altimeter setting should you use for the descent to joining level?
A Barnsley QNH
B Chatham QNH
C Cotswold QNH

16 At 20nm from the destination, you are at 5,000ft amsl; you want to descend to 2,000ft QNH on reaching the destination. Given a groundspeed of 100knots in the descent, what will be your minimum rate of descent required?
A 250ft per minute
B 210ft per minute
C 170ft per minute

Paper 2   Navigation

17   On the diversion from B to C, 5nm from C, the route passes south of a spot height of 1114ft. What does the symbol immediately south of this spot height mean?

A   Hang-Gliding
B   Microlight flying
C   Parachuting

18   Convert 39.5US gallons to litres:
A   150lt
B   180lt
C   160lt

19   A danger area is notated D044/3.2. This Danger Area is active up to a level of:
A   3200ft amsl
B   3200ft agl
C   4400ft amsl

20   What type of area is the destination (B) situated within, and what is its vertical limit?
A   Restricted area; 1000ft amsl
B   Gas venting area, 10,000ft amsl
C   HIRTA, 10,000ft amsl

Paper 2 Appendix A   Navigation

Latitude and longitude are given as an aid to identification but where locations and facilities are marked on the chart, their charted positions should be used.

From	To	FL/Alt	Safety Alt ft amsl	Tas kt	W/V	Trk T	Drift	Hdg T	Var	Hdg M	GS kt	Dist nm	Time hr/min
N5200.52 E00013.57	N5205.13 W00208.15			95	190/15							
										Total		

Alternate

From	To			Tas	W/V							
N5205.13 W00208.15	N5200.17 W00228.50			95	210/10							

Note: Safety Altitude is derived from the higher of:

1.   the highest ground plus 1299ft;

      or

2.   the highest structure plus 1000ft; rounded up to the next 100ft, within 5nm of track.

82

Paper 3

Navigation

It is planned to carry out a VFR flight from Chichester/ Goodwood (N5051.55 W00045.55) to Shobdon (N5214.48 W00252.88) via the disused airfield at Grove (N5136.28 W00126.09). Complete the attached flight plan using a CAA 1:500,000 chart and answer questions 1 to 20 below.

1. What is the track (°T) from Goodwood to Grove?
- A 325°(T)
- B 330°(T)
- C 327°(T)

2. What is the distance (nm) from Grove to Shobdon?
- A 68nm
- B 66nm
- C 64.5nm

3. What is the estimated flight time from Goodwood to Shobdon?
- A 103mins
- B 93mins
- C 90mins

4. Using the flight plan time, assuming fuel consumption of 5 imp. gallons/hour plus a reserve of 4 imp. gallons overhead the destination, what is the minimum fuel required?
- A 11.75imp. gallons
- B 11imp. gallons
- C 10.75imp. gallons

5. Based on the answer to question 4, what would be the weight of the minimum fuel required, in lbs, given a specific gravity of 0.72?
- A 77lbs
- B 85lbs
- C 79lbs

6. The surface wind at Chichester/Goodwood is 220/15. Your aircraft has a crosswind limit of 12 knots and you may not accept a tailwind component. Runways 06/24; 10/28 and 14/32 are available. Which runway(s) are within your aircraft's limits?
- A 24
- B 10/28
- C 14/32

You are airborne at 1300 UTC and set heading overhead Goodwood at 1305 UTC.

7. At 1332 you determine your position as 2nm east of the mast at N5118 W00114. Using the groundspeed experienced from overhead Goodwood, what is the revised ETA for Grove?
- A 1345
- B 1349
- C 1352

8. What is the height above sea level of the mast at position N5134 W00131?
- A 1013ft
- B 233ft
- C 993ft

Paper 3 Navigation

9   What ATSU would you call and on what frequency to obtain a Lower Airspace Radar Service in the vicinity of Basingstoke?
A   Odiham; 109.60
B   Farnborough; 125.25
C   Odiham; 125.25

10 Approaching Grove, in order to avoid traffic, you turn onto a compass heading of 270°. Compass deviation is 3° E. What is your true heading assuming variation is 4°W?
A   266°
B   269°
C   271°

11 You are aware that Fairford MATZ is active. What is the latest position at which you should contact the appropriate ATSU before entering the MATZ?
A   Approximately 6nm before reaching Grove
B   Overhead Grove
C   Any point before reaching the MATZ boundary

12 You are overhead Grove at 1345 UTC and your remaining fuel is 12 gallons. Assuming flight plan time from here to Shobdon, with a consumption of 5 gallons/hour, what will be your remaining endurance at Shobdon?
A   1hr 30mins
B   1hr 20mins
C   1hr 40mins

13 Just after setting heading overhead Grove for Shobdon, you ask Brize Radar for the Regional Pressure Settings for the rest of your flight. Which RPS(s) do you require?
A   Portland
B   Chatham
C   Cotswold & Barnsley

14 On the leg from Grove to Shobdon, having held your planned heading, you establish your position as overhead Windrush airfield (N5148 W00144). Assuming no further change of wind velocity, what heading alteration is needed to fly to Shobdon?
A   12° Port
B   12° Starboard
C   15° Port

15 Later in the flight, you find yourself 3nm east of Ledbury (N5202 W00236). What aerial activity might you expect to see in this area?
A   Parachuting
B   Hang-Gliding
C   Microlight Flying

16 On the leg from Grove to Shobdon, assuming a regional QNH of 996mb, what is the correct Flight Level to use?
A   FL35
B   FL40
C   FL45

Paper 3 Navigation

17 You intend to descend from 4000ft amsl to be level at 2300ft amsl once overhead Shobdon, with an average groundspeed in the descent of 100 knots. If you maintain a rate of descent of 500ft per minute in the descent, what is the minimum distance from Shobdon (rounded to the nearest mile) at which you can start the descent?

A 6 miles
B 7 miles
C 8 miles

18 In order to ensure a clearance of 1,000 feet above any high ground/obstacle within 5nm of planned track, what is the minimum altitude at which the whole flight can be made (rounded up to the nearest 100 feet)?

A 2800ft amsl
B 2500ft amsl
C 2600ft amsl

19 What does the symbol ⊞ mean at Shobdon?

A Use only grass runway
B Gliding as an additional activity
C Runway may not be suitable except for emergency use only

20 The light has deteriorated as you approach Shobdon. What visual aid to navigation at Shobdon might help you?

A A flashing white light
B A flashing green light
C A flashing red light

Paper 3 Appendix A　　　　　　　　　　　　　　　　　　　　　　　　　　　　　　　　Navigation

Latitude and longitude are given as an aid to identification but where locations and facilities are marked on the chart, their charted positions should be used.

From	To	FL/Alt	Safety Alt ft amsl	Tas kt	W/V	Trk T	Drift	Hdg T	Var	Hdg M	GS kt	Dist nm	Time hr/min
Goodwood N5051.55 W00045.55	Grove N5136.28 W00126.09	3000		85	250/20								
Grove N5136.28 W00126.09	Shobdon N5214.48 W00252.88	3500		85	270/15								
											Total		

Note: Safety Altitude is derived from the higher of:

1. the highest ground plus 1299ft;

   or

2. the highest structure plus 1000ft; rounded up to the next 100ft, within 5nm of track.

86

Paper 4   Navigation

You planning a VFR cross country flight from Shoreham (N5050.07 W00017.67) to Stapleford (N5139.15 E00009.35) via Canterbury (N5116.73 E00104.73).
Complete the attached flight plan and answer questions 1 to 20 below

1   What is your true track ('T') from Shoreham to Canterbury?
A   061°(T)
B   064°(T)
C   058°(T)

2   What is the distance (nm) from Shoreham to Canterbury?
A   58nm
B   55nm
C   56nm

3   What is the estimated flight time from Shoreham to Canterbury?
A   35mins
B   40mins
C   37mins

4   Using the total flight plan time, an average fuel consumption of 22 litres per hour, plus a reserve of 22 litres overhead the destination, what is the minimum fuel required in imperial gallons?
A   9.9 gallons
B   9.5 gallons
C   9.2 gallons

5   You wish to uplift a total of 65 litres of fuel, which has a Specific Gravity of 0.72. What will be the weight of that fuel in kilograms?
A   104kg
B   47kg
C   53kg

6   The surface wind at Shoreham is reported as 140/15. Your aircraft has a crosswind limit of 12 knots, and you may not accept a tailwind component. Runways 03/21; 07/25; 13/31 are available. Which runway is within your aircraft's limits?
A   13
B   03
C   25

You are airborne at 1100 UTC and set heading overhead Shoreham at 1105 UTC.

7   At 1123 UTC you pinpoint your position as overhead Bewl Water (N5104 E00023). Using the groundspeed experienced from overhead Shoreham, what is the revised ETA for Canterbury?
A   1141 UTC
B   1143 UTC
C   1139 UTC

8   What is the level of the ground (amsl), where a lighted mast is located at (N5117.5 E0059)?
A   300ft
B   381ft
C   336ft

9 What frequency would you select to contact Southend for a QDM?
A   124.60
B   111.35
C   128.95

10 Halfway along track from Canterbury to Stapleford, located at (N5124 E0036), there is a red circle with M in the centre. What does this mean?
A   Marshes
B   Area of intense microlight activity
C   Mining activity

11 What are the significant features of the danger area D146/3 4 miles east of St Mary's Marsh VRP?
A   It is a permanent danger area for which a DAAIS is available
B   It is a danger area active to 300ft amsl
C   It is a danger area activated by NOTAM, which is subject to local bylaws

12 Passing St. Mary's Marsh VRP you have 24 litres of fuel on board. Assuming a fuel consumption of 22 litres per hour, what be the endurance when you arrive overhead Stapleford?
A   53mins
B   50mins
C   55mins

13 Passing the M25 en-route to Stapleford, what is the base of controlled airspace?
A   3500ft amsl
B   2000ft amsl
C   2500ft amsl

14 According to the map, what facility is located on Stapleford airfield?
A   Microlight Activity
B   Customs (24hrs)
C   The LAM VOR/DME

15 Stapleford's runways are 22/04 and 10/28. The reported surface wind is 160/12. What runway(s) would be most suitable to use, given a crosswind limit of12kts and no tailwind component allowed?
A   04
B   10
C   28

16 What would be the crosswind component if you use runway 10?
A   13kts
B   9kts
C   10kts

17 Referring to the UK VFR Flight Guide extract at Appendix B, you should be aware that if you arrive overhead at Stapleford at 1400 UTC, and runway 22L is in use:
A   The LDA for runway 22 is 1077m, you must not overfly the villages of Abridge and Lambourne below 1000ft amsl
B   The LDA for runway 22 is 900m, you must not overfly the villages of Abridge and Lambourne below 1000ft amsl
C   The airfield is open from 0830 UTC to sunset in the winter, departure noise abatement procedures apply to some runways, circuits are left-hand

Paper 4 Navigation

18 In order to ensure a clearance of 1000ft above any high ground/obstacle within 5nm of planned track, what is the minimum altitude at which the whole flight can be made (rounded up to the nearest 100ft).
A 2200ft
B 2000ft
C 1800ft

19 Referring to the UK VFR Flight Guide extract at Appendix B, you will be aware that:
A Power cables up to 210ft agl cross the approach to runway 22L 1nm from the threshold
B Power cables up to 210ft amsl cross the straight-ahead departure 1nm from runway 22L
C You may operate up to two hours outside the published hours without PPR

20 Referring to the UK VFR Flight Guide extract at Appendix B, you will be aware that:
A Stapleford A/G frequency is 115.60
B Stapleford elevation is 185ft amsl
C The LAM VOR/DME transmits on 117.50

Paper 4 Appendix A   Navigation

Latitude and longitude are given as an aid to identification but where locations and facilities are marked on the chart, their charted positions should be used.

From	To	FL/Alt	Safety Alt ft amsl	Tas kt	W/V	Trk T	Drift	Hdg T	Var	Hdg M	GS kt	Dist nm	Time hr/min
Shoreham N5050.07 W00017.67	Canterbury N5116.73 E00104.73	2000		85	175/15								
Canterbury N5116.73 E00104.73	Stapleford N5139.15 E00009.35	2000		85	190/20							Total	

Note: Safety Altitude is derived from the higher of:

1. the highest ground plus 1299ft;

   or

2. the highest structure plus 1000ft, rounded up to the next 100ft, within 5nm of track.

EGSG STAPLEFORD

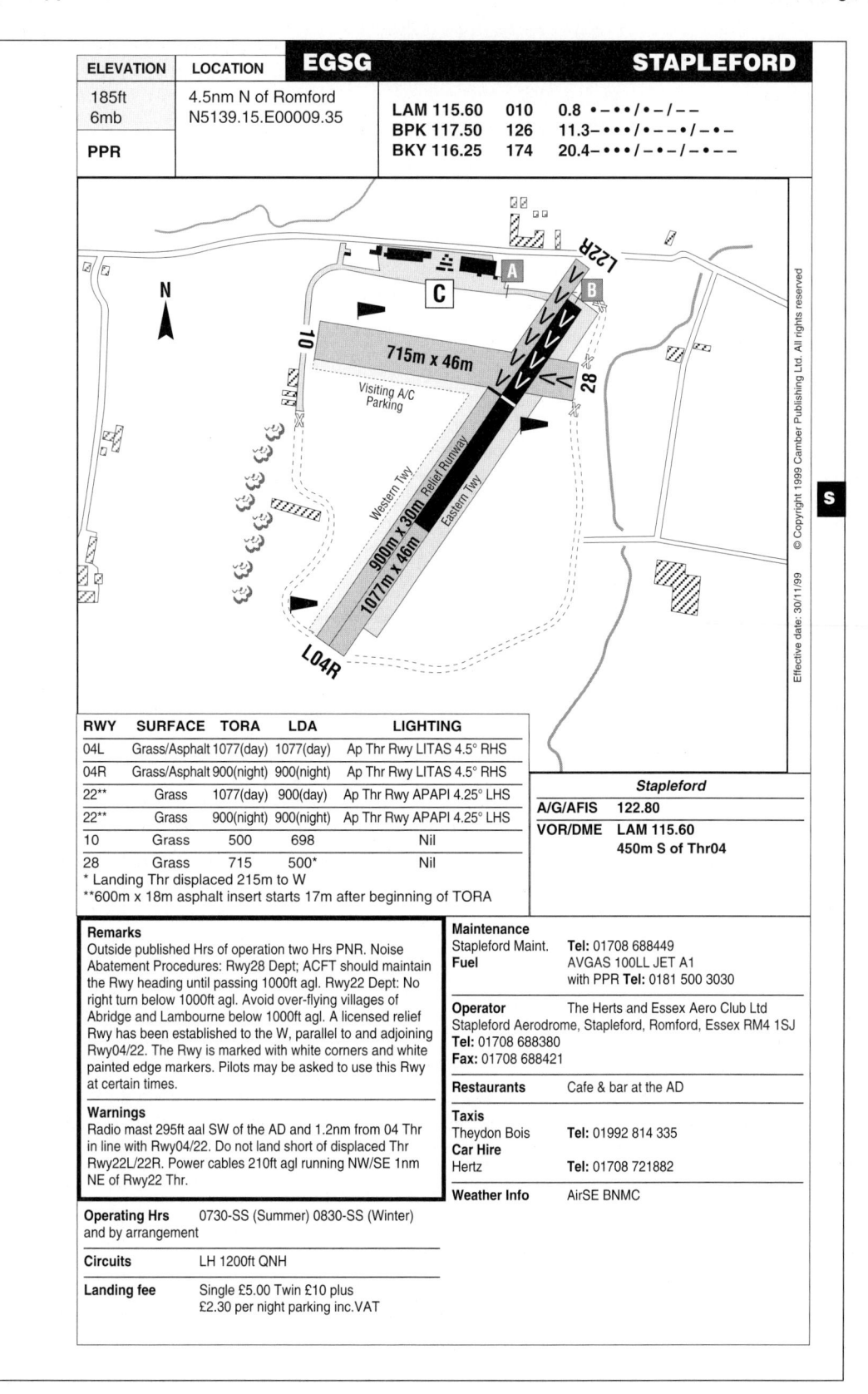

ELEVATION	LOCATION			
185ft 6mb	4.5nm N of Romford N5139.15.E00009.35	LAM 115.60	010	0.8 •–••/•–/––
PPR		BPK 117.50	126	11.3 •–••/•–––/•––
		BKY 116.25	174	20.4 •••/–•–/–•––

RWY	SURFACE	TORA	LDA	LIGHTING
04L	Grass/Asphalt	1077(day)	1077(day)	Ap Thr Rwy LITAS 4.5° RHS
04R	Grass/Asphalt	900(night)	900(night)	Ap Thr Rwy LITAS 4.5° RHS
22**	Grass	1077(day)	900(day)	Ap Thr Rwy APAPI 4.25° LHS
22**	Grass	900(night)	900(night)	Ap Thr Rwy APAPI 4.25° LHS
10	Grass	500	698	Nil
28	Grass	715	500*	Nil

* Landing Thr displaced 215m to W
** 600m x 18m asphalt insert starts 17m after beginning of TORA

Stapleford
A/G/AFIS 122.80
VOR/DME LAM 115.60
450m S of Thr04

Remarks
Outside published Hrs of operation two Hrs PNR. Noise Abatement Procedures: Rwy28 Dept; ACFT should maintain the Rwy heading until passing 1000ft agl. Rwy22 Dept: No right turn below 1000ft agl. Avoid over-flying villages of Abridge and Lambourne below 1000ft agl. A licensed relief Rwy has been established to the W, parallel to and adjoining Rwy04/22. The Rwy is marked with white corners and white painted edge markers. Pilots may be asked to use this Rwy at certain times.

Warnings
Radio mast 295ft aal SW of the AD and 1.2nm from 04 Thr in line with Rwy04/22. Do not land short of displaced Thr Rwy22L/22R. Power cables 210ft agl running NW/SE 1nm NE of Rwy22 Thr.

Maintenance
Stapleford Maint. Tel: 01708 688449
Fuel AVGAS 100LL JET A1
with PPR Tel: 0181 500 3030

Operator The Herts and Essex Aero Club Ltd
Stapleford Aerodrome, Stapleford, Romford, Essex RM4 1SJ
Tel: 01708 688380
Fax: 01708 688421

Restaurants Cafe & bar at the AD

Taxis
Theydon Bois Tel: 01992 814 335
Car Hire
Hertz Tel: 01708 721882

Weather Info AirSE BNMC

Operating Hrs	0730-SS (Summer) 0830-SS (Winter) and by arrangement
Circuits	LH 1200ft QNH
Landing fee	Single £5.00 Twin £10 plus £2.30 per night parking inc.VAT

Paper 5   Navigation

It is intended to fly VFR cross-country from Hucknall airfield (N5300.85 W00113.10) to Manchester Airport (N5321.22 W00216.50) via a turning point at Hawarden airfield (N5310.68 W00258.67).

Complete the attached flight log before answering questions 1 – 20.

1   What is the distance in nautical miles from Hucknall to Hawarden?
A   64nm
B   62nm
C   63.5nm

2   What amount of drift is being experienced on the first leg?
A   3° Port
B   4° Starboard
C   3° Starboard

3   If the average fuel consumption is estimated to be 25 litres/hour and you are required to have 45mins holding reserves plus 30mins diversion fuel; what is the minimum fuel (US gals) you are required to begin the flight with?
A   13 gals
B   16 gals
C   18 gals

4   What is the track (T) from Hucknall to Hawarden?
A   277°
B   279°
C   281°

5   Hucknall airfield's elevation is:
A   459ft
B   515ft
C   281ft

6   Given a QNH of 998mb, what is the correct minimum Flight Level for the leg Hucknall to Hawarden in accordance with the quadrantal rule?
A   FL45
B   FL40
C   FL35

7   With reference to your answer to question 6 above, select the correct statement from those below:
A   You may transit the Manchester CTA at this level, without contacting Manchester, provided you remain VMC
B   You will avoid controlled airspace all the way to Hawarden if you descend to 3400ft amsl
C   Subject to Manchester ATC permission, you may transit the Manchester CTA, VFR, up to 3400ft amsl

8   Your route passes close to a circle named 'Ashcroft'. From the information on the map you know that Ashcroft is:
A   An airfield with limited or no facilities, with an elevation of 149ft amsl
B   A Gas Venting Area up to FL149
C   A VRP, whose radial from Liverpool is 149°(M)

Paper 5　　　　　　　　　　　　　　　　　　　　　　　　　　　　　　Navigation

9 The marked circle centred on (N5316 W0257) just north of Hawarden is:
A An area of intense radio transmissions, 2.2nm in radius
B A restricted area, extending upwards from 2200ft amsl
C A restricted area, extending from the surface to 2200ft amsl

10 What is the airborne time from Hawarden to Manchester?
A 17mins
B 15mins
C 14mins

11 What is the track (T) <u>from</u> Manchester to Hawarden?
A 247°
B 067°
C 065°

12 If you are planning to fly from Hawarden to Manchester at 3000ft amsl which ATSU would you contact?
A Liverpool 119.85
B London FIS 125.475
C Manchester 119.40

13 If the appropriate ATSU is unable to give you a clearance as in question 12 above due to traffic. What would be the most suitable action?
A Continue the flight in VMC, without contacting any ATSU until you approach the Manchester ATZ
B Continue the flight above 3500ft amsl, without contacting any ATSU until you are 10nm from Manchester
C Route towards a suitable VRP, remaining outside controlled airspace, and make a further request for clearance to Manchester when approaching that VRP

14 Overhead Hawarden you estimate fuel remaining at 65 litres. Given a fuel consumption of 25 litres an hour, what will be your estimated remaining fuel endurance on arrival at Manchester?
A 2hours 55mins
B 2hours 20mins
C 2hours 5mins

15 The Manchester TMA extends from:
A SFC – 3500 ALT
B 3500 ALT – above FL 245
C 2500 ALT – 3500 ALT

16 Your route takes you directly over the town of Chester and an obstruction to 371ft. In accordance with the low flying rules in relation to congested areas, your minimum altitude over this area should be:
A 2000ft amsl
B 3000ft amsl
C 1500ft amsl

17 You alter your track to route via the Manchester Low Level Route. To stay within this route you should fly at:
A No more than 1250ft agl
B No more than 1250ft Manchester QNH
C No less than 1250ft Manchester QNH

Paper 5   Navigation

18 You have diverted towards Manchester Barton. According to the map, a specified hazard at Barton is:
A Winch launch cables
B Gliding
C Foot launch hang/para gliding

19 On arrival overhead Barton, the runway is blocked. You estimate that you have 45 litres of fuel aboard, your nearest alternate is 30 minutes flying time away, and you wish to land at either with no less than 15 litres of fuel remaining. How long can you hold before needed to divert, assuming fuel consumption of 25 litres/hour?
A 32 minutes
B 18 minutes
C 48 minutes

20 The map symbol of a blue-lined triangle ▲ indicates a:
A Visual Reference Point (VRP)
B Reporting point
C Special access lane entry/exit

Paper 5 Appendix A   Navigation

Latitude and longitude are given as an aid to identification but where locations and facilities are marked on the chart, their charted positions should be used.

From	To	FL/Alt	Safety Alt ft amsl	Tas kt	W/V	Trk T	Drift	Hdg T	Var	Hdg M	GS kt	Dist nm	Time hr/min
Hucknall N5300.85 W00113.10	Hawarden N5310.68 W00258.67	3000		85	260/15				5W				
Hawarden N5310.68 W00258.67	Manchester N5321.22 W00216.50	2000		90	280/20				5W				
											Total		

Note: Safety Altitude is derived from the higher of:

1. the highest ground plus 1299ft;

   or

2. the highest structure plus 1000ft; rounded up to the next 100ft, within 5nm of track.

95

Paper 6

Navigation

It is planned to carry out a VFR cross-country flight from Skegness (N5310.40 E00020.00) to Netherthorpe (N5319.02 W00111.77) via a turning point at Hucknall airfield (N5300.85 W00113.10). Complete the attached flight plan and then answer questions 1 – 20.

1 What is the distance from Skegness to Hucknall in km?
A 104 km
B 92 km
C 56 km

2 What amount of drift are you experiencing on the first leg?
A 10° Port
B 13° Starboard
C 13° Port

3 What is your magnetic track from Skegness to Hucknall?
A 264°
B 277°
C 259°

4 What is the estimated flight time from Skegness to Hucknall?
A 41mins
B 37.5mins
C 35mins

5 What is your groundspeed from Hucknall to Netherthorpe?
A 66kts
B 130kmh
C 84 mph

6 Assuming a QNH of 995mb, what would be the correct Flight Level in accordance with the quadrantal rule for the route Skegness to Hucknall?
A FL40
B FL30
C FL45

7 Given:
2.5 imp. gals for start, taxy and take-off;
Flight plan time to destination of 1hour 30 minutes, plus a diversion of 25 minutes at an average fuel consumption of 4.7 imp. gals per hour;
2imp. gals for approach and landing;
7imp. gals reserve required overhead diversion;
what is the total fuel (in imp. gals) required for the flight?
A 21 imperial gallons
B 25 imperial gallons
C 27 imperial gallons

8 What is the distance from Hucknall to Netherthorpe to the nearest half nautical mile?
A 17nm
B 18.5nm
C 20nm

Paper 6   Navigation

9   What is your heading (°T) from Hucknall to Netherthorpe?
A   001°
B   004°
C   358°

10   What is the elevation of Netherthorpe above sea level?
A   250ft amsl
B   310ft amsl
C   580ft amsl

11   Directly south of Skegness is an area annotated as 'Gibraltar Point/2'. This is a:
A   WRDA active to 2000ft amsl
B   Gas Venting Area, up to 200ft agl
C   Bird sanctuary, with an effective altitude of 2000ft amsl

12   To receive a Lower Airspace Radar Service (LARS) from Coningsby MATZ, on what frequency should you make your initial call?
A   119.375 MHz
B   111.10 MHz
C   120.80 MHz

13   You intend to operate under the Coningsby MATZ stub. What altimeter setting should you be using?
A   Coningsby QFE
B   Skegness QFE
C   QNH

14   Having set course overhead Skegness at 1014, you are overhead the disused airfield of Digby at 1030. What is your revised ETA for Hucknall?
A   1039
B   1046
C   1052

15   Approximately 3nm west of Newark-on-Trent is area D305/1.5. In relation to this area:
A   It is a permanent danger area, active to FL150
B   It is a danger area activated by NOTAM, active to 3050ft amsl
C   It is a danger area activated by NOTAM, active to 1500ft amsl

16   After the turning point at Hucknall, which ATSU and on what frequency would you contact for a LARS service?
A   Waddington 127.35
B   East Midlands 119.65
C   Lincolnshire AIAA 119.375

17   An MEF of **3**² represents:

A   A Maximum Elevation Figure – this is NOT a safety altitude
B   The Minimum Elevation for Flight
C   A Maximum Elevation Figure – the approved safety altitude in that area

Paper 6 Navigation

18 With regard to the rules concerning flight over congested areas, what would be a sensible minimum planned altitude for overflight of Mansfield (N5308.57 W00111.72)?
A 5000ft amsl
B 2300ft amsl
C 1500ft amsl

19 Convert 258lbs of AVGAS to US gallons at a specific gravity of 0.72:
A 36 US gallons
B 43 US gallons
C 95 US gallons

20 If the entire route from Skegness to Netherthorpe was flown at an altitude of 1800ft amsl:
A The flight would enter the Lincolnshire AIAA and the Coningsby ATZ but not the Coningsby MATZ
B The flight would not enter the Lincolnshire AIAA or the Coningsby MATZ
C The flight would not enter the Lincolnshire AIAA or the Waddington ATZ

Paper 6 Appendix A Navigation

Latitude and longitude are given as an aid to identification but where locations and facilities are marked on the chart, their charted positions should be used.

From	To	FL/Alt	Safety Alt ft amsl	Tas kt	W/V	Trk T	Drift	Hdg T	Var	Hdg M	GS kt	Dist nm	Time hr/min
Skegness N5310.40 E00020.00	Hucknall N5300.85 W00113.10	2000		85	010/20				5W				
Hucknall N5300.85 W00113.10	Netherthorpe N5319.02 W00111.77	2000		85	350/15				5W				
										Total			

Note: Safety Altitude is derived from the higher of:

1 the highest ground plus 1299ft;

or

2 the highest structure plus 1000ft; rounded up to the next 100ft, within 5nm of track.

Paper 7 Navigation

You are to plan a VFR cross-country flight from Bournemouth (N5046.80 W00150.55) to Dunkeswell (N5051.60 W00314.08) then to Bristol (N5122.96 W00243.15).
Complete the attached flight plan and answer questions 1 to 20 below:

1 What is your track (T°) from Bournemouth to Dunkeswell?
A 270°
B 275°
C 273°

2 What is your magnetic heading from Bournemouth to Dunkeswell?
A 269°
B 275°
C 261°

3 What is the estimated flight time from Bournemouth to Dunkeswell?
A 50mins
B 41.5mins
C 40mins

4 Using the planned flight time from Bournemouth to Bristol and assuming a fuel consumption of approximately 5 imp. gals per hour, plus a required reserve of 6 imp. gals overhead Bristol, plus 2 imp. gals for start, taxy and take-off, plus 3 imp. gals for approach and landing, what is the minimum required fuel in litres?
A 61 litres
B 73 litres
C 67 litres

5 Given:
Aircraft empty weight   507kg
Pilot's weight   75kg
Fuel (85 litres at specific gravity 0.72)
Maximum total weight authorised   725kg
What is the maximum payload that can be carried?
A 81kg
B 60kg
C 23kg

6 Bournemouth tower reports the surface wind as 190/12. Your aircraft has a crosswind limit of 10kts and you may not accept a tailwind component. Runways 08/26 and 17/35 are available, which runway would you choose to use?
A 17
B 26
C 35

You are airborne at 0930 UTC and set heading overhead Bournemouth at 0935 UTC.

7 At 0955 you pinpoint your position as being 3nm north of Beaminster (N5049 W0245). Using the revised groundspeed, what is the new ETA for Dunkeswell?
A 1006 UTC
B 1014 UTC
C 1009 UTC

Paper 7   Navigation

8 From the position given above, what heading change is required to reach Dunkeswell?
A 13° port
B 11° starboard
C 7° port

9 In accordance with the low flying rules, in VMC what is the lowest altitude for flight over the mast at (N5148.50 W003.50)?
A 1275ft amsl
B 2025ft amsl
C 3025ft amsl

10 On track from Dunkeswell to Bristol, just south of Taunton on the M5, there is an 'S' in a red circle. What does this mean?
A Motorway service area
B Special police area
C Subterranean cables

11 Approaching Dunkeswell at 2700ft amsl you are unable to contact Dunkeswell, therefore:
A You may enter the Dunkeswell ATZ without contacting Dunkeswell, provided you remain VMC
B You will pass over the Dunkeswell ATZ, there is no need to contact Dunkeswell
C You should alter your route to avoid the Dunkeswell ATZ

12 Radar vectors from Yeovilton take you to overhead Cannington (N5109 W0304), where you are asked to resume your own navigation. What is the required magnetic heading to Bristol?
A 045°
B 034°
C 041°

13 Assuming you maintain this new track, from what altitude does the Bristol CTA commence?
A 1500ft amsl
B 1500ft agl
C Surface

14 On what frequency would you use to contact Bristol for VDF information?
A 380
B 127.35
C 128.55

15 What does the following symbol ⌐ BRISTOL ⌐ mean outlined in magenta?
A Runway length greater than 1850m
B Customs facilities available
C Operated subject to PPR

16 10 miles from the Bristol CTA you wish to descend from 3500ft amsl to 2000ft amsl to be level at the CTA boundary. Given a groundspeed in the descent of 110kts, what is the minimum rate of descent required?
A 280ft per minute
B 220ft per minute
C 165ft per minute

101

Paper 7 Navigation

17 The surface wind at Bristol is given as varying between 240° and 190° at 18 knots. If your aircraft has a maximum demonstrated crosswind component of 15 knots, what is the maximum angle between the wind and runway 27 that will leave the crosswind component within limits?

A 30°
B 50°
C 75°

18 What does the magenta symbol ● mean?
A Bird sanctuary
B High intensity radio transmission area
C Gas venting station

Refer to the UK VFR Flight Guide extract at Appendix B to answer the following two questions:

19 From study of appendix B you know that:
A Runway 27 landing threshold is displaced by about 135m, all aircraft must join final not below 1000ft QFE
B Non-radio aircraft are not accepted, circuit height is 1000ft QFE
C Grass areas are unsuitable for aircraft parking, ground signals are displayed outside the tower

20 From study of appendix B you know that:
A After landing on 27 you may be able to vacate right on taxiway D for the western apron
B After landing on 09 you may be able to vacate left onto taxiway H
C After landing on 09 you may vacate onto taxiway J for the eastern apron

Paper 7 Appendix A Navigation

Latitude and longitude are given as an aid to identification but where locations and facilities are marked on the chart, their charted positions should be used.

From	To	FL/Alt	Safety Alt ft amsl	Tas kt	W/V	Trk T	Drift	Hdg T	Var	Hdg M	GS kt	Dist nm	Time hr/min
Bournemouth N5046.80 W00150.55	Dunkeswell N5051.60 W00314.08	2000		90	220/20				5W				
Dunkeswell N5051.60 W00314.08	Bristol N5122.96 W00243.15	1500		95	260/25				5W				
											Total		

Note: Safety Altitude is derived from the higher of:

1. the highest ground plus 1299ft;

   or

2. the highest structure plus 1000ft, rounded up to the next 100ft, within 5nm of track.

103

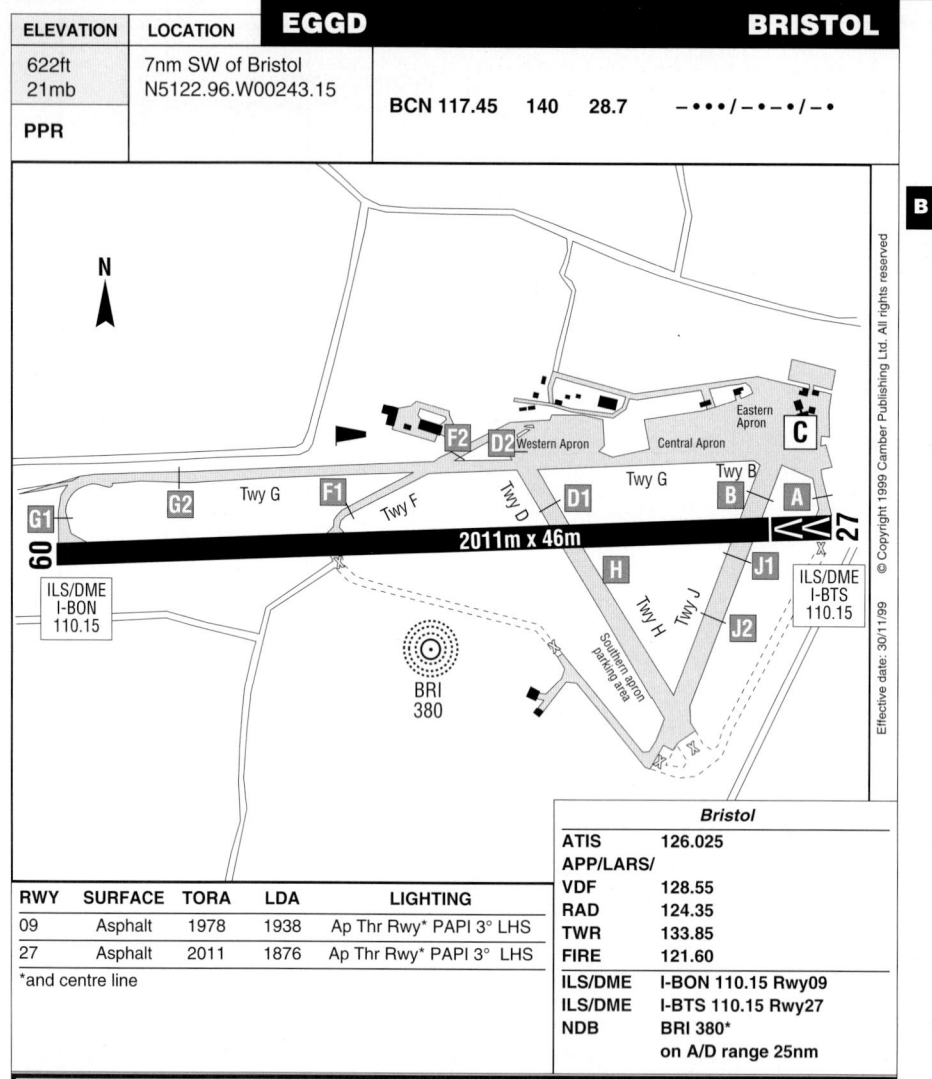

ELEVATION	LOCATION	**EGGD**			**BRISTOL**
622ft 21mb	7nm SW of Bristol N5122.96.W00243.15				
PPR		BCN 117.45	140	28.7	– • • • / – • – • / – •

RWY	SURFACE	TORA	LDA	LIGHTING
09	Asphalt	1978	1938	Ap Thr Rwy* PAPI 3° LHS
27	Asphalt	2011	1876	Ap Thr Rwy* PAPI 3° LHS

*and centre line

	Bristol
ATIS	126.025
APP/LARS/VDF	128.55
RAD	124.35
TWR	133.85
FIRE	121.60
ILS/DME	I-BON 110.15 Rwy09
ILS/DME	I-BTS 110.15 Rwy27
NDB	BRI 380* on A/D range 25nm

Remarks
Non-radio ACFT not accepted. Training is not permitted under any circumstances between the Hrs of 2200-0700 daily. See also 'Booking & Training Procedures'. Propeller driven ACFT of more than 5700kg MTWA must not join the final APProach track to any Rwy at a height of less than 1000ft QFE. Parking and start up procedure for all ACFT on central, western and eastern aprons is under the guidance of the apron marshaller following clearance from ATC. Grass areas are unsuitable for parking of ACFT. Helicopter Operations: A helicopter training area is designated S of Rwy09/27. Handling required for all visiting ACFT Tel: Servisair 01275 472776 Fax: 01275 474514. Bristol Flight Centre Tel: 01275 474501 Fax: 01275 474851.

Warnings
Ground signals not displayed, except light signals. Hot air balloon activity takes place in VMC and daylight Hrs from a site 4.5nm NE of the AD and downwind of the site. Balloons may be observed passing below the CTA or if radio equipped, within the CTR/CTA. Pilots will be notified by ATC of known balloon activity which may affect their flights. Glider and hang glider activity takes place along the Mendip hills, to the south of the AD. ATC will only be notified of such activity when gliders and hang gliders are operating within designated areas within the CTR/CTA and so pilots may not always receive warning of the activity. ACFT using Bristol Airport are to carry 3rd party insurance cover of not less than £500,000. Bird scaring is carried out on a regular basis but birds may not always be detected on the extreme western end of the AD and on the APProaches and Dept tracks of all Rwys. Pilots must conform to the noise abatement techniques laid down for the type of ACFT and operate so as to cause the least disturbance practicable in areas surrounding the airport.

Paper 7 Appendix B | Navigation

Effective date: 30/11/99 © Copyright 1999 Camber Publishing Ltd. All rights reserved

Operating Hrs	H24

Circuits Variable 1000ft QFE for non-jet ACFT
Rwy09 normally RH only but ATC may vary
Rwy27 normally LH

Landing fee On Application

Maintenance
Global Trading **Tel:** 01275 472484
Fuel AVGAS 0800-2000 (Local)
Surcharge APPlies outside these Hrs AVGAS through
Bristol Flight Ctr **Tel:** 01275 474601
AVTUR JET A1 Mon-Fri 0500-0130 Sat-Sun 0500-2300

Operator Bristol Airport Plc
Bristol Airport, Bristol BS19 3DY
Tel: 01275 474444
Fax: 01275 474800 / 474482 (ATC)
Telex: 449295 AIRPORT BRISTOL

Restaurants
Restaurant refreshments and club facilities available
Duty-Free Shop & 24hr (airside) bar

Taxis
Airport Taxis Ltd **Tel:** 01275 474812
Car Hire
Avis **Tel:** 01275 472613
Europcar **Tel:** 01275 474623
Hertz **Tel:** 01275 472807

Weather Info M T9 T18 Fax 252 A VS BCFO

Booking & Training Procedures
A booking system operates for instrument training. Training periods can be booked by Application to ATC. Filing of a flight plan does not constitute a booking and failure to make a booking may result in the ACFT being refused use of the facilities. Pilots are to inform ATC of booking cancellations. Circuit training by non-Bristol based ACFT is only available by prior arrangement with ATC. Booking procedures for all circuit training ACFT may be introduced by ATC during busy periods. Circuit direction for all training ACFT will be varied by ATC for air traffic and noise nuisance avoidance purposes.

CTA/CTR-Class D Airspace
Normal CTA/CTR Class D Airspace rules APPly.

Visual Reference Points (VRPs)

VRP	VOR/NDB	VOR/DME
Bath N5122.70 W00221.42	BCN R126°/LA 244°M	BCN 126°/40nm
Cheddar Reservoir N5116.78 W00248.08	BCN R152°/BRI 212°M	BCN 152°/32nm
Chew Valley N5119.50 W00235.70	BCN R139°/BRI 130°M	BCN 139°/35nm
Churchill N5120.00 W00247.60	BCN R148°/BRI 230°M	BCN 148°/29nm
Clevedon N5126.35 W00251.08	BCN R143°/LA 267°M	BCN 143°/23nm
East Nailsea N5125.80 W00244.10	BCN R137°/BRI 352°M	BCN 137°/26nm
Hanham N5126.93 W00230.95	BCN R125°/BRI 066°M	BCN 125°/32nm
Portishead N5129 70 W00246.42	BCN R132°/BRI 348°M	BCN 132°/23nm
Radstock N5117.53 W00226.92	BCN R135°/LA 236°M	BCN 135°/40nm
Weston-Super-Mare N5120.70 W00258.33	BCN R159°/BRI 262°M	BCN 159°/25nm

Note: ACFT entering the Controlled Airspace via Portishead, Radstock or Cheddar VRP's may be required to hold at East Nailsea, Churchill or Chew Valley VRPs as APPropriate.

Paper 8   Navigation

It is planned to carry out a VFR cross-country flight from Gloucestershire Staverton airport (N5153.65 W00210.03) to Cambridge (N5212.30 E00010.50) via Northampton Sywell (N5218.29 W00047.48).

Complete the attached flight log and then answer questions 1 to 20.

1   What is the true heading from Gloucestershire to Northampton?
A   073°
B   076°
C   079°

2   What is your estimated groundspeed from Gloucestershire to Northampton?
A   103kts
B   105kts
C   100kts

3   What amount of drift are you experiencing on the first leg?
A   10P
B   10S
C   12P

4   On the first leg what is maximum Flight Level you can use for the entire flight, in accordance with the quadrantal rule and remaining outside controlled airspace, given a QNH of 1001mb?
A   FL35
B   FL30
C   Neither of the above

5   What is your estimated enroute airborne time on the first leg?
A   30mins
B   32.5mins
C   36mins

6   Passing Edgehill/Shenington (N5204.91 W00128.48), what hazard(s) should you be aware of:
A   A Gas Venting Area
B   A gliding and microlight site
C   A gliding site with cables to 2500ft agl, and foot launched hang/para gliding

7   You wish to descend from 9000ft to 2000ft in 5 minutes, the required Rate of Descent is :
A   900 feet/minute
B   1200 feet/minute
C   1400 feet/minute

8   What height above ground level are the masts located at (N5212 W0115)?
A   1119ft agl
B   404ft agl
C   715ft agl

106

Paper 8 Navigation

9 Given:

4 US gals required for start, taxy and take-off;

average fuel consumption of 5 US gallons per hour for flight plan time Gloucestershire to Cambridge plus 30 minutes diversion;

plus 3 US gals for approach and landing;

and 8 US gals reserve required overhead the alternate;

what is the minimum fuel required (in litres)?

A 102 litres
B 85 litres
C 22 litres

10 On the first leg, you establish your position as overhead Long Marston (N5208.44 W00145.18). How much and in what direction would you alter heading to regain track at Northampton?

A 17° right
B 27° right
C 20° left

11 What is the magnetic track from Northampton to Cambridge?

A 099°
B 096°
C 103°

12 What is the distance in statute miles from Northampton to Cambridge?

A 66.5
B 36
C 41.5

13 In order to remain outside the Northampton/Sywell Aerodrome Traffic Zone (ATZ) you should?

A Avoid Northampton by a minimum of 5nm
B Fly not below 2000ft aal
C Fly not below 2000ft amsl

14 In VMC, and in accordance with the low flying rules, what would be the minimum level for flight over the mast just north east of Little Staughton (N5214.57 W00021.85)?

A 671ft QNH
B 850ft Little Staughton QFE
C 500ft Little Staughton QFE

15 On the second leg, what is the most appropriate ATSU and contact frequency for a LARS service?

A Mildenhall, 128.90
B Bedford, 124.40
C Cottesmore, 130.20

107

Paper 8 Navigation

16 An aircraft has a maximum total weight authorised of 2440lbs/1106kg. The aircraft loading (without fuel) is:
Basic Aircraft 1515lbs.
Pilot and passengers 600lbs.
Baggage 37lbs.
Ignoring balance and performance considerations, what is the maximum fuel (in US gals) that can be carried without exceeding the maximum total weight authorised, assuming a specific gravity of 0.72?
A 40 US gal
B 46 US gal
C 48 US gal

17 What does the small magenta circle at position (N5319 W0022) represent?
A Gas venting site up to 3500ft amsl
B Gas venting site up to 350ft agl
C Gas venting site 3.5nm diameter

18 Approaching Cambridge in poor lighting conditions, what visual aid at the airfield might help?
A A rotating red and green light
B A flashing red light
C A flashing green light showing the Morse 'Cl'

19 The figure **09** to the north of Cambridge represents:

A The minimum safety altitude for that area
B The height (AGL) of the highest man-made obstruction in that area
C The maximum elevation of known and possible unmarked features in that area

20 By the radius of Cambridge's ATZ (2.5nm), what is the minimum runway length you can expect?
A 1851m
B 1601m
C 1751m

Paper 8 Appendix A   Navigation

Latitude and longitude are given as an aid to identification but where locations and facilities are marked on the chart, their charted positions should be used.

From	To	FL/Alt	Safety Alt ft amsl	Tas kt	W/V	Trk T	Drift	Hdg T	Var	Hdg M	GS kt	Dist nm	Time hr/min
Gloucester Staverton N5153.65 W00210.03	Northampton Sywell N5218.29 W00047.48	3000		92	190/22				5W				
Northampton Sywell N5218.29 W00047.48	Cambridge N5212.30 E00010.50	2000		90	180/18				5W				
										Total			

Note: Safety Altitude is derived from the higher of:

1   the highest ground plus 1299ft;

    or

2   the highest structure plus 1000ft, rounded up to the next 100ft, within 5nm of track.

109

Paper 9 — Navigation

It is planned to carry out a VFR cross-country flight from Bembridge, Isle of Wight (N5040.68 W00106.55) to Blackbushe (N5119.43 W00050.85) via a turning point at Thruxton (N5112.62 W00135.90).

Complete the attached flight log before answering questions 1 – 20.

1 What is the true track from Bembridge to Thruxton?
A 327°
B 330°
C 333°

2 What drift will the aircraft experience on the first leg?
A 10° Starboard
B 10° Port
C 12° Starboard

3 What is the magnetic heading on the first leg?
A 324°
B 341°
C 316°

4 What is the distance in kilometres from Bembridge to Thruxton?
A 68km
B 76km
C 72km

5 What is the estimated enroute flight time from Bembridge to Thruxton?
A 31mins
B 30.5mins
C 29.5mins

6 Assuming a fuel consumption of 6.1 US gals per hour, how much fuel is used on the first leg in pounds, given a specific gravity of 0.81 and the planned enroute time?
A 41lbs
B 34lbs
C 20.2lbs

7 Initial contact to Southampton should be made on what frequency?
A 120.225
B 113.35
C 391.5

8 What is the highest Flight Level useable for the first leg, in accordance with the quadrantal rule, remaining clear of class A airspace?
A FL65
B FL45
C FL85

9 What is the vertical extent of the Southampton CTR?
A 3000ft amsl to FL55
B 2500ft amsl to FL55
C Surface to 2000ft amsl

Paper 9   Navigation

10 To which ATSU, and on what frequency would you call for penetration of the Middle Wallop MATZ?
A   Boscombe Down, 126.7
B   Middle Wallop, 108.2
C   Middle Wallop, 376

11 What is the magnetic track from Thruxton to Blackbushe?
A   072°
B   073°
C   080°

12 What is the anticipated groundspeed on the second leg?
A   100kts
B   97kts
C   104kts

You take-off at 1605 and set course overhead Bembridge at 1610

13 If you are unable to obtain clearance to cross the Southampton CTR, what is the most practical course of action?
A   Maintain radio silence whilst routing over the CTR above FL55
B   Remain clear of the CTR by routing to the south and west, not above 1900ft amsl
C   Remain clear of the CTR by routing to the east and overhead Winchester, not above 1900ft agl

14 At 1626 you are positioned east abeam the Romsey VRP, based on the groundspeed to this point what is your revised ETA for Thruxton?
A   1635 UTC
B   1641 UTC
C   1643 UTC

15 You wish to descend from 8500ft to 2500ft over a distance of 19 nautical miles, at a ground speed of 135 knots. What minimum rate of descent is required?
A   950 feet/min
B   610 feet/min
C   710 feet/min

16 On the second leg, what is the recommended minimum point for contacting the Farnborough MATZ?
A   Overhead Thruxton
B   When 5 minutes from the MATZ boundary
C   When passing Andover

17 Blackbushe are reporting a surface wind variable between 240° and 180° at 15 knots. If your aircraft demonstrated crosswind limit of 12 knots, and runway 26 is in use, in what sector will the crosswind component be outside limits?
A   230° to 210°
B   200° to 180°
C   240° to 200°

111

Paper 9   Navigation

Refer to the UK VFR Flight Guide extract at Appendix B to answer the following questions

18 Assuming that you are flying a single engine aircraft, what circuit direction and height would you expect on runway 26 at Blackbushe?
A Right-hand at 1200ft amsl
B Right-hand at 1200ft agl
C Left-hand at 800ft agl

19 If you planning to land at Blackbushe on a bank holiday Monday you should be aware that:
A The airfield is not available to flights requiring a licenced airfield and fuel may not be available
B Farnborough ATZ will be inactive, so flights may approach south of the Woking-Basingstoke railway line
C The airfield will be closed

20 From Appendix B you can ascertain that:
A Cessna 337 aircraft may not use this airfield, and it is open between 0700 and 1700 in the summer
B The TORA and LDA for runway 26 is 1237m, fuel is available 7 days a week
C All circuits are left-hand at 800ft QFE, there is considerable out-of-hours activity

Paper 9 Appendix A

Navigation

Latitude and longitude are given as an aid to identification but where locations and facilities are marked on the chart, their charted positions should be used.

From	To	FL/Alt	Safety Alt ft amsl	Tas kt	W/V	Trk T	Drift	Hdg T	Var	Hdg M	GS kt	Dist nm	Time hr/min
Bembridge IOW N5040.68 W00106.55	Thruxton N5112.62 W00135.90	3000ft		85	270/18				5W				
Thruxton N5112.62 W00135.90	Blackbushe N5119.43 W00050.85	2500ft		82	290/22				5W				
										Total			

Note: Safety Altitude is derived from the higher of:

1. the highest ground plus 1299ft;

    or

2. the highest structure plus 1000ft, rounded up to the next 100ft, within 5nm of track.

113

Paper 9 Appendix B   Navigation

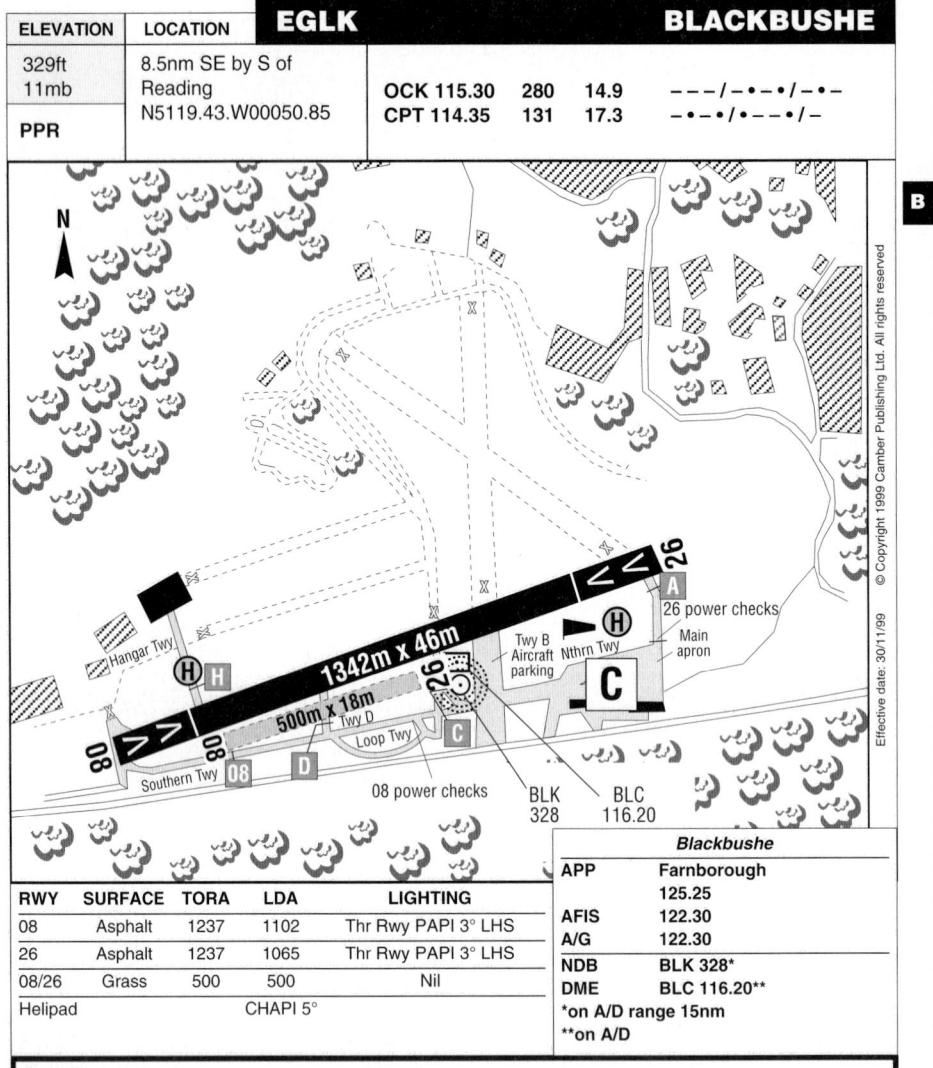

EGLK — BLACKBUSHE

ELEVATION	LOCATION
329ft 11mb **PPR**	8.5nm SE by S of Reading N5119.43, W00050.85

OCK 115.30	280	14.9	———/—•—•/—•—
CPT 114.35	131	17.3	—•——•/•———•/—

BLK 328
BLC 116.20

RWY	SURFACE	TORA	LDA	LIGHTING
08	Asphalt	1237	1102	Thr Rwy PAPI 3° LHS
26	Asphalt	1237	1065	Thr Rwy PAPI 3° LHS
08/26	Grass	500	500	Nil
Helipad				CHAPI 5°

	Blackbushe
APP	Farnborough 125.25
AFIS	122.30
A/G	122.30
NDB	BLK 328*
DME	BLC 116.20**

*on A/D range 15nm
**on A/D

Remarks
PPR by telephone or radio. Visual Aids to location: Abn White flashing. On PHs the AD is not available for ACFT required to use a licensed AD. APProaching Blackbushe remain North of the Woking-Basingstoke railway line to avoid ACFT using Farnborough. For noise abatement remain well clear of Yately to the North East and Hartley Witney West of the AD. Pilots are responsible for their passengers whilst on the airside of this airport. Due to planning restrictions the following ACFT may not land at this AD: Cessna Skymaster (C336/337/L); Dornier 28D Sky Servant (D08D/L); Gates Learjet 23,24,25,28,29 (LR23,24,25,28/L,29/M); Piaggio P166 (P166/L).

Warnings
The AD is frequently used outside the published Hrs of operation by fixed and rotary wing ACFT. Pilots operating at any time in the vicinity of the AD should therefore call Blackbushe AFIS/A/G to check if the AD is active. Pilots are further cautioned that no reply does not necessarily imply no traffic in the ATZ, and a very careful lookout should be maintained. Avoidance of the ATZ if at all possible is preferable. Because of increased helicopter activity, helicopter specific lighting aids have been installed on the northern Twy at the western end of the AD. These consist of Helipad, illuminated Tee and CHAPI 5.0° (Air Hanson's Helipad and APP. lights, plus lead-in strobes). Fixed-wing pilots should ignore indications from this lighting. An additional AD beacon situated on the roof of a hangar (287°, 0.3nm from the ARP) may be illuminated, but only outside notified AD Hrs. A section of disused Rwy01/19, to the south of Rwy 08/26, is marked as a Twy and the most southerly portion as an ACFT parking area. The grassed surface south of Rwy 08/26 between Twys C and D is unsuitable for use by certain types of helicopter due to its poor grading. Pilots are cautioned to positively ascertain that the grading of this area is suitable for their operational requirements. Visual glideslope guidance signals for both Rwy08 and 26 are visible to the south of the extended Rwy centrelines where normal obstacle clearance is not guaranteed. They should not be used until aligned with the Rwy. A public footpath crosses the centre of the AD from south east to north west. Fuel not normally available on Public Holidays. Caution large concentrations of birds on and in the vicinity of AD.

Paper 9 Appendix B Navigation

Effective date: 30/11/99   © Copyright 1999 Camber Publishing Ltd. All rights reserved

Operating Hrs 0700-1700 (Summer) 0800-1700 (Winter) and by arrangement

Circuits All circuits to the South of the AD
Single engined ACFT 800ft QFE
Twin engined and executive ACFT 1200 ft QFE
At night circuit height for all ACFT is 1000 ft QFE

Landing fee Single from £17.00 inc.VAT
Discount available for fuel uplift and club ACFT or PFA/AOPA members with card Single £9.00 inc VAT

Maintenance
Air Hanson Ltd **Tel:** 01252 890089
Fuel AVGAS 100LL AVTUR JET A1

Operator Blackbushe Airport Ltd
Blackbushe Airport
Camberley, Surrey
Tel: 01252 879449 (Management and Admin)
Tel: 01252 873338 (Tower) **Fax** 01252 874444

Restaurants Club facilities

Taxis
A2B Taxis **Tel:** 01276 64488/64499
Car Hire
Avis **Tel:** 01344 417417
Europcar **Tel:** 01276 451570

Weather Info AirSE BNMC

Blackbushe Circuit Diagram

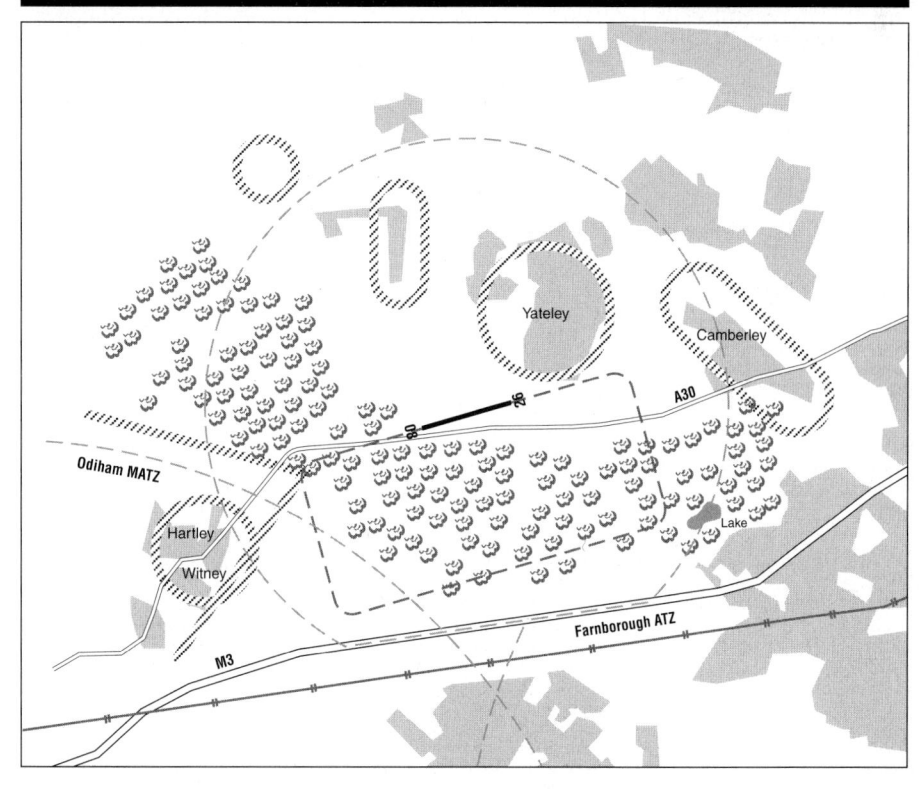

Paper 10 Navigation

It is planned to carry out a VFR cross-country flight from Newcastle (N5502.25 W00141.50) to Barrow (Walney Island) (N5407.87 W0315.81) via a turning point at Carlisle airfield (N5456.25 W0248.55).

Complete the attached flight log before answering questions 1 – 20.

1   What is the true track from Newcastle to Carlisle?
A   260°
B   261°
C   264°

2   What drift is being experienced on the first leg?
A   5°S
B   6°P
C   9°S

3   What is the magnetic heading on the first leg?
A   268°
B   261°
C   256°

4   What is the groundspeed on the first leg?
A   74kts
B   79sm/hr
C   69km/h

5   What is the airborne enroute time of the entire journey?
A   1hr 12mins
B   1hr 10mins
C   1hr 14mins

6   Given:
5kg of fuel for start, taxy and take-off;
plus an average fuel consumption of 13.7kg per hour at a specific gravity of 0.72 for 1hour 10 minutes,
plus a 30 minute holding reserve
plus 4kg for approach and landing
plus a reserve overhead the alternate of 10kg
what is the minimum fuel required in imperial gallons?
A   12.8imp. gals
B   42imp. gals
C   24.2imp. gals

7   What is the appropriate Flight Level for the first leg, in accordance with the quadrantal rule, given a QNH of 990mb?
A   FL65
B   FL60
C   FL55

8   On what frequency would you contact Newcastle approach?
A   126.35
B   114.25
C   124.375

Paper 10   Navigation

9 The dashed line originating at the NEW VOR and aligned south west / north east, annotated W911D, is:
A A class A airspace airway centreline
B An advisory route, class F airspace
C An advisory route, base FL150

10 Approaching Carlisle at 2500ft amsl the most appropriate course of action is to:
A Reduce altitude in order to pass through the Carlisle ATZ
B Not contact Carlisle because you are outside the ATZ
C Contact Carlisle at a range of around 10nm

11 What is the magnetic track from Carlisle to Barrow?
A 208°
B 204°
C 202°

12 What is the true heading on the second leg?
A 209°
B 198°
C 202°

13 What is the distance in KM from Carlisle to Barrow?
A 85km
B 51km
C 94km

14 What is the estimated airborne enroute time on the second leg?
A 38mins
B 42mins
C 40mins

15 An aircraft has a maximum total weight authorised of 726kg/1600lbs. It has a maximum useable fuel capacity of 85 litres. Ignoring balance and performance considerations, can the aircraft as loaded below carry full fuel and remain below the maximum total weight authorised?
Basic Aircraft 525kg
Pilot & Passenger 140kg
Baggage 10kg
Assume a specific gravity of 0.72
A Yes
B No
C Yes, but only if 10 litres of fuel are used before take-off

16 On the second leg, given a QNH of 990mb, what is the lowest useable Flight Level in accordance with the minimum safe altitude and the quadrantal rule?
A FL40
B FL60
C FL50

17 Approaching Barrow, the Warton RASA extends between _____ and the contact frequency is _____
A FL55 to above FL245, 129.525
B FL55 to FL155, 133.05
C SFC to FL55, 129.525

117

Paper 10 Navigation

18 What is the height (agl) of the mast at position (54°32'N) (03°36'W)?
A   450ft
B   272ft
C   722ft

19 You are located 20nm from Barrow, and you wish to descend from 6000ft to 2000ft to be level 5nm before reaching Barrow. If your groundspeed in the descent will be 100kts, what is the minimum rate of descent required?
A   520ft per minute
B   450ft per minute
C   490ft per minute

20 The reported surface wind at Barrow is 180/10-15 knots, the landing runway is 24. What is the maximum wind strength you can accept from this direction if the aircraft's maximum demonstrated crosswind component is 12 knots?
A   15 knots
B   10 knots
C   13 knots

Paper 10 Appendix A   Navigation

Latitude and longitude are given as an aid to identification but where locations and facilities are marked on the chart, their charted positions should be used.

From	To	FL/Alt	Safety Alt ft amsl	Tas kt	W/V	Trk T	Drift	Hdg T	Var	Hdg M	GS kt	Dist nm	Time hr/min
Newcastle N5502.25 W00141.50	Carlisle N5456.25 W0248.55	FL60		92	240/25				6W				
Carlisle N5456.25 W0248.55	Barrow (Walney Island) N5407.87 W0315.81	FL60		91	245/21				6W				
											Total		

Note: Safety Altitude is derived from the higher of:

1. the highest ground plus 1299ft;

   or

2. the highest structure plus 1000ft; rounded up to the next 100ft, within 5nm of track.

PRIVATE PILOT'S LICENCE

Aircraft General (Aeroplanes)

Time allowed: 1 hour 15 minutes

Instructions

1 The paper consists of 50 multiple choice questions, each carries 2 marks (total 100 marks). The pass mark is 70% (i.e. 35 questions or more must be answered correctly); marks are not deducted for incorrect answers.

2 Be sure to carefully read each question and ensure that you understand it before considering the answer choices. Only one of the answers is complete and correct; the others are either incomplete or based on a misconception.

3 Leave questions that seem difficult at first and return to these when the others have been completed.

4 Indicate the correct answer to each question by placing a tick in the appropriate box of the answer sheet. If you decide to change an answer, completely obliterate the original selection.

5 The back of the answer sheet can be used for working calculations.
DO NOT MARK THE QUESTION PAPER.

Paper 1   Aircraft General

1. The major component gasses of the earth's atmosphere are:
A. Helium, Nitrogen, Oxygen
B. Carbon Dioxide, Hydrogen, Oxygen
C. Nitrogen, Water vapour, Oxygen

2. The International Standard Atmosphere consists of:
A. Sea level pressure 1013.2mb, temperature +15°C, Lapse rate 1.98°C per 1,000', Density 1226 g/m^3
B. Sea level pressure 1013.2mb, temperature +15°F, Lapse rate 1.98°C per 1,000', Density 1226 g/m^3
C. Sea level pressure 1013.2mb, Temperature + 15°C Lapse rate and density do not apply

3. If the temperature of a parcel of air is increased, but pressure remains constant, the density will:
A. Remain constant
B. Increase
C. Decrease

4. You have calculated the take-off distance required based on sea level, ISA conditions. The actual conditions are a pressure altitude of 5,000ft and a temperature of +20°C. Which of the following statements is correct?
A. Density is less and take off distance will be reduced
B. Density altitude is higher and take off distance will be greater
C. Density altitude is lower and take off distance will be greater

5. When an aircraft is in equilibrium in straight and level, unaccelerated flight:
A. Lift, weight, thrust and drag are all equal
B. Weight equals drag
C. Lift is greater than thrust

6. Trailing edge flaps, used during take-off but at a greater setting than the recommended take-off configuration, will have the following effect on take-off performance:
A. Take-off distance is increased
B. Take-off distance is reduced, lift-off speed is slower
C. Take-off run is unchanged; rate of climb is increased

7. At the stalling angle of attack, the co-efficient of lift:
A. Is at its maximum
B. Is at its minimum
C. Is less than when flying at the best range airspeed

8. The use of ailerons initially causes the aircraft to:
A. Roll around the lateral axis
B. Roll around the longitudinal axis
C. Yaw around the lateral axis

9. When compared to the stalling speed in wings-level, unaccelerated flight; the stalling speed in a steep turn is:
A. Decreased
B. Increased
C. Same as for wings-level flight

Paper 1   Aircraft General

10 In most 'conventional' light aircraft, an increase in power in level flight will result in:
A No movement in pitch or trim
B The aircraft pitching nose-down
C The aircraft pitching nose-up

11 The angle between the chord line of an aerofoil and the relative airflow is:
A The angle of incidence
B The angle of attack
C The angle of co-efficient

12 If an aircraft is flying "nose heavy", and the pilot operates a conventional elevator trimmer to compensate:
A The elevator trim tab will not move, but the leading edge of the elevator will move up
B The trailing edge of the elevator trim tab will move down
C The trailing edge of the elevator trim tab will move up

13 Washout on an aeroplane wing means that there is a:
A Reduction of angle of incidence from the wing root towards the wing tip
B Reduction of angle of incidence from the wing tip towards the wing root
C Tendency for the wing tips to stall first to increase stability in the stall and during slow flight

14 The fin on an aeroplane:
A Helps to turn the aeroplane
B Balances the weight of the engine
C Assists directional stability

15 Carburettor icing is most likely in conditions of:
A Temperature 0°C, relative humidity 10%, climb power
B Temperature -5°C, relative humidity 30%, cruise power
C Temperature +12°C, relative humidity 65%, descent power

16 To achieve best power setting at altitude, the mixture control of an engine fitted with a fixed-pitch propeller is 'leaned' to achieve:
A A drop of 50 RPM from the 'full rich' RPM
B The peak RPM
C The lowest RPM without the engine stopping

17 The airspeed for maximum range will be achieved when:
A The aircraft is at or close to the angle of attack for minimum drag
B The aircraft is at or close to the angle of attack for maximum co-efficient of lift
C The aircraft is at the minimum speed for maintaining level flight

18 When gliding into a headwind, when compared with gliding in still air:
A Rate of descent is greater, glide range is reduced
B Rate of descent is greater, glide range is unchanged if airspeed is reduced
C Rate of descent is unchanged, glide range is reduced

19 During a prolonged climb, the engine temperatures of an air-cooled engine increase to their maximum limit. An appropriate response by the pilot would be to:
A Lean the mixture
B Increase airspeed
C Close the cowl flaps (if fitted)

Paper 1   Aircraft General

20   To be absolutely certain that the magnetos are not 'live':
A   The battery master must be off
B   It is impossible to be certain they are off, exercise caution at all times
C   The ignition keys must be out of the switch

21   Once a circuit breaker has popped:
A   2 minutes must elapse before resetting it
B   It can be reset immediately
C   Do not reset it at all

22   A fully charged 30 amp hour battery of an average light aircraft is (in theory) capable of supplying:
A   15 amps for 2 hours
B   30 amps for 30 hours
C   30 amps for 30 minutes

23   If a fuse blows during flight:
A   It should not be replaced until the aircraft has landed
B   It should be replaced with one of a higher rating to ensure it will not blow again
C   It should be replaced in the air with one of the same rating, but only once

24   If the alternator or generator fails during flight:
A   The battery will supply all the electrical loads for as long as required, so the flight can continue as planned
B   The master switch should be turned off, and the flight continued as planned
C   Electrical loads should be reduced to the bare minimum and a landing made as soon as practical

25   An aircraft has CG limits of 83 – 93 inches aft of the datum. The aircraft is loaded so that the actual CG is 83.5 inches aft of the datum. Compared with a CG position of 92.5 inches aft of the datum the effect on stalling speed and the flare for landing is:
A   The stall speed is increased and elevator forces will be lighter in the landing flare
B   The stall speed is decreased and elevator forces will be lighter in the landing flare
C   The stall speed is increased and elevator forces will be higher in the landing flare

26   The suction (vacuum) system operates the following instruments:
A   Altimeter, HI, Turn Co-ordinator
B   HI, Attitude Indicator (Artificial Horizon)
C   Turn Co-ordinator, HI, Attitude Indicator (Artificial Horizon)

27   The ball in the turn co-ordinator shows the:
A   Slip and skid of the aircraft
B   Rate of turn of the aircraft
C   The aircraft bank angle

28   Which of the following instrument is connected to the pitot pressure source?
A   The vertical speed indicator (VSI)
B   The altimeter
C   The airspeed indicator (ASI)

29   In a balanced turn, total lift acts:
A   Vertically
B   Perpendicular to the wings, in the direction of the turn
C   In direct opposition to weight

Paper 1   Aircraft General

30 The properly operating gyroscope of an Attitude Indicator has 'rigidity' meaning that:
A It tends to maintain its position in space
B It will not rotate unless considerable force is used
C It stays fixed relative to the aircraft

31 You wish to operate a UK-registered aircraft on MOGAS: where will you find authoritative information concerning such operation?
A In the aircraft's flight manual
B In an AIC
C In a CAA Airworthiness Directive

32 A suction (vacuum) pump operates the suction (vacuum)-driven instruments by:
A Drawing air through the instruments to the gyro rotors
B Blowing air through the instruments to the gyro rotors
C Sucking against diaphragms in the associated instruments

33 A 'normal' vacuum (suction) gauge reading is:
A 3.5 to 4.5 psi
B 4.5 to 5.5 inches of mercury
C 5.5 to 6.5 psi

34 The following instruments are connected to a static pressure source:
A Turn Co-ordinator, Attitude Indicator (Artificial Horizon), Airspeed indicator (ASI)
B Altimeter, Vertical speed indicator (VSI), Airspeed indicator (ASI)
C Heading Indicator (HI), Vertical speed indicator (VSI), Airspeed indicator (ASI)

35 The oil pressure relief valve is operated by:
A The oil pressure
B An electrical oil temperature sensor
C A pilot-selected control

36 The blade angle of a propeller is progressively reduced from hub to tip in order to:
A Maintain an efficient angle of attack along the whole blade
B Reduce centrifugal force
C Increase torque

37 An aircraft with 'direct' nosewheel steering usually has:
A Rods linking the rudder pedals and the nosewheel steering mechanism
B No need for differential braking
C A 'free-castoring' nosewheel

38 Certain instruments run on electrical power, in a typical light aircraft these will include:
A Fuel quantity gauges, oil pressure and Heading Indicator
B Oil temperature, turn co-ordinator and Vertical Speed Indicator
C Fuel quantity gauges and turn co-ordinator

39 Static pressure drawn from an alternate static source in the cockpit of an average light aircraft will be:
A Exactly the same as the outside 'ambient' pressure
B Less than the outside 'ambient' pressure
C The same as pitot pressure

Paper 1   Aircraft General

40   Using the graph below, the total weight/moment combination which is within limits in the utility category is:

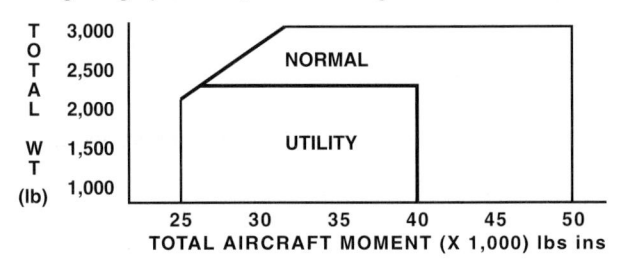

A   2,500lbs and moment 50,000lb ins
B   1,700lbs and moment 36,000lb ins
C   1,500lbs and moment 42,000lb ins

41   If an aircraft is fully loaded with adult passengers and maximum permitted baggage load:
A   The full fuel load may be carried, there is no need for a weight and balance check
B   The fuel required is worked out separately, and is loaded regardless of other items carried
C   The fuel load may have to be restricted

42   The ideal fuel/air mixture for efficient aero engine operation is:
A   15 parts air to 15 parts fuel (15:15)
B   15 parts fuel to 1 part air (15:1)
C   1 part fuel to 15 parts air (1:15)

43   After engine start the oil pressure should register within the green arc within a certain time, or the engine must be shut down immediately. The time allowed is normally:
A   10 seconds
B   30 seconds
C   2 minutes

44   If Carbon Monoxide gas enters the cabin, it:
A   Can be identified by its black colour
B   May be identified by its strong smell
C   Is not easy to identify because it is colourless and odourless

45   The use of an excessively weak (over lean) mixture at a high power setting can lead to:
A   Spark plug fouling (the build up of oil or lead deposits on the spark plugs)
B   Detonation (an 'explosive' combustion of the fuel air mixture in the cylinder)
C   Carburettor Icing (the formation of ice within the carburettor)

46   Under the Light Aircraft Maintenance Schedule, (LAMS) a Certificate of Airworthiness in the private category is valid for:
A   1 year
B   2 years
C   The period stated on the Certificate of Airworthiness

47   When testing the fuel system for water using a fuel tester, water may appear as:
A   Coloured bubbles in the fuel tester
B   Clear bubbles at the top of the fuel sample
C   Clear bubbles at the bottom of the fuel sample

Paper 1   Aircraft General

48 Carbon dioxide gas is:
A   Used in the inflation systems of lifejackets
B   Very poisonous and highly toxic
C   Commonly used to inflate light aircraft tyres

49 An aircraft with a Maximum Total Weight Authorised (MTWA) of less than 2730kg and a private category Certificate of Airworthiness (C of A) must be maintained in accordance with the approved maintenance schedule quoted on the C of A:
A   Except if otherwise authorised by the registered owner or operator
B   At all times
C   Except if otherwise authorised by a licensed engineer

50 Whilst in flight, a drop in RPM occurs and you suspect carb. icing. However, on applying carb. hot air, the engine initially runs more roughly. You should:
A   Return the carb. heat to cold immediately and not use it again
B   Return the carb. heat to cold immediately and apply more power as the spark plugs are fouled
C   Leave the carb. heat at hot until the rough-running clears

Paper 2   Aircraft General

1   The Sea Level pressure in the International Standard Atmosphere is:
A   1031mb
B   1013.2hPa
C   1003.2mb

2   The temperature lapse rate in the International Standard Atmosphere is:
A   1.98°C per 1,000ft up to 36,090ft
B   3°C per 1,000ft, up to 36,0900ft
C   1.98°C per 1,000ft without a defined upper limit

3   If temperature and pressure remain constant, an increase in humidity will cause:
A   A decrease in density
B   An increase in density
C   The density will be unchanged

4   In the dry atmosphere there is:
A   Approximately twice as much oxygen as other gases
B   Approximately three times as much nitrogen as oxygen
C   Approximately equal proportions of nitrogen and oxygen

5   The lift produced by an aerofoil can be attributed to:
A   An increase in the speed of airflow over the upper surface, resulting in a decrease in pressure, and a decrease in the speed of airflow past the under-surface, resulting in a decrease in pressure
B   A decrease in the speed of airflow over the upper surface, resulting in an increase in pressure and an increase in the speed of airflow past the under-surface resulting in an increase in pressure
C   An increase in the speed of airflow over the upper surface, resulting in a decrease in pressure

6   Which of the following statements concerning air density is correct?
A   Air density is inversely proportional to pressure and temperature
B   Air density is inversely proportional to pressure and proportional to temperature
C   Air density is proportional to pressure and inversely proportional to temperature

7   In straight and level flight, the resultant force of the tailplane and elevators acts in an upward direction if the position of the centre of pressure in relation to the centre of gravity is:
A   In front of
B   Behind
C   Located at the same point

8   Outside the boundary layer, the speed of the airflow over the top surface of an aerofoil, compared with the general airflow, is:
A   Greater than
B   Less than
C   Equal to

9   If the angle of attack of an aerofoil is increased, the coefficient of lift will:
A   Increase until the stalling angle of attack is reached
B   Decrease until the stalling angle of attack is reached
C   Remain constant

10 VNE is:
A The maximum indicated airspeed at which manoeuvres may be carried out
B The maximum indicated airspeed at which the aircraft may be flown in any circumstance
C The maximum indicated airspeed at which the aircraft may be flown in level flight, and may be exceeded during certain manoeuvres

11 In general, as airspeed is increased:
A All types of drag increase
B Parasite drag decreases, induced drag increases
C Parasite drag increases, induced drag decreases

12 Overall, the use of trailing edge flaps will:
A Increase lift and decrease drag during take-off
B Increase drag without increasing lift appreciably
C Increase lift and drag

13 High wing loading will:
A Increase the stalling speed, landing run and landing speed
B Increase lift, stalling speed and drag
C Decrease stalling speed, the landing run and landing speed

14 The chord line of an aerofoil is:
A A straight line through the centres of curvature at the leading and trailing edges of the aerofoil section
B A curved line each point of which is equidistant from the upper and lower boundaries of the aerofoil section
C A line which shadows the curvature of the top surface of the aerofoil section

15 The best angle of climb airspeed will result in:
A The best height gain over a specific distance
B The best height gain over a specific time
C The maximum excess power

16 Stalling speed:
A Increases by the square root of load factor
B Is inversely proportional to weight
C Is greatest at a rearward centre of gravity

17 Induced drag is:
A Caused by the difference in pressure between the upper and lower surfaces of an aerofoil
B At a minimum at the best range airspeed
C Greatest at small angles of attack

18 In order to increase flying control loads, a designer might:
A Restrict the control column movement
B Fit the control surface with a horn balance
C Fit the control surface with an anti-balance or anti-servo tab

19 The stalling angle of attack may be reduced when:
A Load factor is increased
B Leading edge slats are extended
C Trailing edge flaps are extended

Paper 2 Aircraft General

20 When airspeed is reduced:
A Parasite and induced drag will reduce
B Parasite drag will increase and induced drag will reduce
C Parasite drag will reduce and induced drag will increase

21 In a piston engine aircraft, maximum endurance will be achieved at:
A The best lift/drag ratio airspeed
B An airspeed which is approximately 75% of the best range airspeed
C The heading which gives the maximum tailwind component

22 After engine starting the starter warning light remains lit, this means:
A There is a risk of imminent serious electrical system damage
B The light is faulty and should be reported after the flight
C The starter system is faulty, it should be checked before the next start

23 To prevent flutter the control surfaces can be fitted with:
A Inset hinges
B Mass balance
C Spring tabs

24 A control surface can be fitted with a horn balance to:
A Allow the pilot to trim out control forces
B Assist the pilot in moving the control
C Assist the pilot in ground manoeuvring the aircraft the

25 Stability in pitch is also known as:
A Normal stability
B Lateral stability
C Longitudinal stability

26 The secondary effect of yaw is:
A Roll in the opposite direction to yaw
B Roll in the same direction as yaw
C Pitch

27 If the vent pipe to an aircraft fuel tank became blocked, it would:
A Create a higher pressure on the fuel in the tank, thus disrupting supply to the engine
B Create a lower pressure on the fuel in the tank, thus disrupting supply to the engine
C Make no difference to the fuel supply

28 High oil temperature and low oil pressure should be taken as indicating:
A Faulty gauges
B An electrical problem
C A serious engine problem with the danger of imminent mechanical failure

29 In a 60° angle of bank turn an aircraft stalls at 60 knots. In level flight what would you expect the stalling speed to be?
A 60 knots
B 45 knots
C 65 knots

Paper 2   Aircraft General

30 Cylinder head temperature can be reduced by:
A Enriching the mixture
B Weakening the mixture
C Decreasing the airspeed

31 If an aircraft with a fixed-pitch propeller is accelerated to a faster airspeed:
A RPM will increase even if the throttle setting is not changed
B RPM will be totally dependent of throttle setting
C The throttle setting will automatically reduce to maintain a constant RPM

32 An aircraft gliding at the recommended best range of glide airspeed, can cover 5nm from an altitude of 5,000ft in still air. Its lift/drag ratio is approximately:
A 10:1
B 6:1
C 1:10

33 Given a normally aspirated engine fitted with a fixed pitch propeller, carburettor icing is accompanied by:
A A fall in RPM
B A rise in RPM
C A rise in RPM together with a fall in oil temperature

34 If airspeed is reduced, one option to maintain constant lift is:
A Increase angle of attack
B Reduce weight
C Reduce drag

35 If the magnetos become disconnected from the cockpit magneto switch:
A They can be stopped by turning off the Master Switch
B They will stop working
C They will remain live, even if the magneto switch is selected 'off'

36 The mixture control can be used:
A Only above 5,000ft agl
B To stop the engine when Idle Cut Off (ICO) is selected
C To increase the amount of air entering the engine

37 A circuit breaker that has tripped due to over-load:
A Can be reset once but must not be held in
B Can be reset once and may be held in
C Cannot be reset at all

38 Magnetic deviation of the compass can be allowed for if the pilot refers to:
A Isogonals on an aeronautical chart
B The compass deviation card
C The POH/FM

39 The most reliable instrument indication to determine the direction of a spin is:
A The turn needle / aircraft symbol of a turn co-ordinator solely
B The turn needle / aircraft symbol of a turn co-ordinator if it agrees with the slip ball
C The Heading Indicator (HI)

Paper 2   Aircraft General

40   If in flight you use the rudder solely to turn the aircraft the effect will be:
A   Roll, followed by yaw
B   Yaw, against the direction in which the rudder pedal is applied
C   Excessive yaw, followed by roll in the same direction

41   Water in the pipe work of the pitot/static system:
A   Is a problem, as it may freeze and block the system
B   Is not a problem, as the system will filter water
C   Does not occur and so is not a problem

42   The high tension voltage of a magneto is produced by:
A   Boosting the supply from the generator
B   The aircraft battery
C   Inducing a current between the primary and secondary windings of a coil

43   Compression ratio is:
A   The rate at which air ignites in a diesel engine
B   The ratio of cylinder volume with the piston at Bottom Dead Centre, to the cylinder volume with the piston at Top Dead Centre
C   The ratio of the volume of one cylinder to the volume of all that engine's cylinders

44   An aircraft must be loaded so that the total fuel moment does not exceed 129.6kg/m. The fuel lever arm is 1.2m. Assuming a specific gravity of 0.72, how many litres of fuel can be loaded?
A   108 litres
B   150 litres
C   77 litres

45   If a BCF extinguisher is used within the cockpit:
A   It must not be used on an electrical fire
B   The cockpit should be ventilated once the fire is out
C   A BCF extinguisher must never be used in the cockpit

46   Running a piston engine at idling RPM for an excessive period can lead to:
A   Plug fouling
B   Excessive cooling of the cylinders
C   The engine burning too much oil

47   For flight over water and beyond gliding distance of land, lifejackets:
A   Should be kept in a compartment not accessible to passengers
B   Should be worn and inflated
C   Should be worn but not inflated

48   If the specific gravity of a fuel is 0.72 the weight of 100 imperial gallons of that fuel would be:
A   72lbs
B   720lbs
C   7,200lbs

49   Unless the POH/FM specifies otherwise, the correct action in the event of an engine fire in the air would be to:
A   Open the cockpit heater controls fully and operate the fire extinguisher into the vents
B   Shut down the engine immediately and close the cockpit heater controls
C   Keep running the engine at full throttle to draw the fire into the cylinders

Paper 2 Aircraft General

50 Maintenance carried out by an owner/pilot in accordance with the Air Navigation Order (General) regulations for an aircraft with a private category C of A:

A Must be recorded in the appropriate aircraft log book and signed by the pilot
B Must be recorded in the aircraft log book and certified by a licensed engineer
C Must be recorded on a separate record and produced to the CAA for inspection

Paper 3 Aircraft General

1 The force that acts in opposition to thrust is:
A Lift
B Drag
C Weight

2 In level flight the lift force is _____ drag force.
A Greater than
B Smaller than
C Equal to

3 An aircraft weighs 2500lbs and has a wing area of 155sq ft, what is its wing loading?
A 16lbs/sq ft
B 0.062lbs/sq ft
C 32lbs/sq ft

4 The airflow over the top surface of an aerofoil produces:
A A greater proportion of the total lift than the airflow past the lower surface
B An equal proportion of the total to that produced by the airflow past the lower surface
C A smaller proportion of the total lift than the airflow past the lower surface

5 The induced drag of an aircraft is:
A The drag due to the surface roughness
B The drag due to the frontal area
C The drag due to the lift being produced

6 For an aircraft to maintain level flight, if the wing centre of pressure is AFT of the centre of gravity and there is no thrust/drag couple, the tailplane load must be:
A Upward
B Downward
C Zero

7 During a sustained and steady climb, weight is:
A equal to thrust
B Less than lift
C Greater than lift

8 A frise aileron is designed to:
A To reduce to yawing moment opposing the turn
B To give an increased rate of roll
C To reduce drag on the inner wing in a turn

9 If a trim tab is operated in flight:
A It will provide aerodynamic forces which can cause the control surface to move
B It will provide aerodynamic force but the control surface cannot move
C The tab will only move when the control surface has moved

10 Controls are mass balanced in order to:
A Aerodynamically assist the pilot in moving the controls
B Prevent control flutter
C Provide equal control forces on all the controls

135

Paper 3 Aircraft General

11 The angle of attack is:
A The angle between the chord and the longitudinal axis
B The angle between the wing and lateral axis
C The angle between the chord and the relative airflow

12 Washout is used to ensure that the wing stalls first at the root, and is:
A An increase of angle of incidence from wing root to tip
B A decrease of chord from wing root to tip
C A decrease of angle of incidence from wing root to tip

13 Longitudinal control is obtained by:
A Ailerons
B Elevators
C Rudder

14 Yawing is a rotation about the:
A Normal axis
B Lateral axis
C Longitudinal axis

15 The force that acts perpendicular to the wings in a balanced turn is:
A The centrifugal force
B The total lift force
C The centripetal force

16 During a 'normal' wings-level stall without power, at the moment of the stall and without further input from the pilot the aircraft is expected to:
A Pitch nose-up and climb slightly
B Pitch nose-down and descend
C Pitch nose-up and maintain level flight

17 Within a four stroke engine the opening and closing of valves is controlled by a camshaft turning at half the speed of the engine, and during a complete 'Otto' cycle:
A The inlet valve opens once, the exhaust valve opens twice
B The inlet valve opens once, the exhaust valve opens once
C The inlet valve opens twice, the exhaust valve opens once

18 Within a four stroke engine, during a complete 'Otto' cycle, each piston:
A Moves up and down the cylinder twice
B Moves up and down the cylinder once
C Makes contact with the cylinder head once

19 A fuel load of 270 litres, with a specific gravity of 0.75, gives a total moment of 194.4kg/m. The lever arm for this load is:
A 0.96
B 1.96
C 9.60

Paper 3   Aircraft General

20 The part of a piston engine that converts the reciprocating movement of the pistons into the rotary movement needed to turn the propeller is the:
A   Conrod
B   Crankshaft
C   Camshaft

21 When the aircraft is operated at the minimum power required airspeed, it will achieve:
A   The maximum endurance
B   The maximum range
C   The minimum drag

22 An aircraft will always stall at:
A   The stalling airspeed quoted in the POH/FM
B   The stalling angle of attack
C   Minimum lift airspeed

23 A slot or slat in the leading edge of a wing will:
A   Re-energise the airflow over the wing's upper surface, delaying airflow separation
B   Move the centre of gravity rearwards, thus reducing stall airspeed
C   Reduce drag at the cruise airspeed

24 Aerodynamic balances designed to assist a pilot in deflecting a flight control surface may be:
A   A trim tab that moves in the same direction as the main control surface
B   A balance tab that moves in the opposite direction to the main control surface
C   A mass placed forward of the hinge line

25 If the elevator is moved in the pre-flight external inspection, the balance tab should:
A   Move in the same direction
B   Move in the opposite direction
C   Not move

26 When making an over-water flight:
A   Life jackets should be worn, inflated
B   Life jackets should be worn and inflated once over the sea
C   Life jackets should be worn, uninflated

27 When air is flowing through the narrowest point of a venturi:
A   Airflow speed will increase, static pressure will increase
B   Airflow speed will increase, static pressure will decrease
C   Airflow speed will decrease, static pressure will decrease

28 An explosive and uncontrolled combustion within a cylinder is called:
A   Pre-ignition, caused by the early burning of the fuel/air mixture
B   Detonation, caused by a fuel/air mixture too lean for the power setting selected
C   Plug foiling, caused buy the build-up of lead or oil deposits on the spark plugs

29 At a constant altitude, maximum power available:
A   Increases with increasing RPM, and is unaffected by airspeed changes
B   Increases with increasing RPM, but decreases with increasing airspeed
C   Increases with increasing RPM and airspeed

Paper 3   Aircraft General

30   In a glide with a tailwind, compared to gliding in still air at the same airspeed:
A   Glide range is unchanged, rate of descent is reduced
B   Glide range is increased, rate of descent is reduced
C   Glide range is increased, rate of descent is unchanged

31   In a climb at a steady speed, lift is:
A   Greater than weight
B   Less than weight
C   Equal to drag

32   Given the same ambient conditions, in which scenario is carburettor icing most likely?
A   High airspeed and high power setting
B   Cruise airspeed and cruise power setting
C   High airspeed, descent power setting

33   In a co-ordinated, 60 degree angle of bank turn maintaining level flight, what is the approximate increase in stalling airspeed compared with wings-level flight?
A   100%
B   40%
C   60%

34   An aircraft is constructed with dihedral to provide:
A   Lateral stability about the longitudinal axis
B   Longitudinal stability about the lateral axis
C   Lateral stability about the normal axis

35   On an aviation refuelling installation, what colour labels would you expect to indicate AVGAS 100LL and AVTUR Jet A-1 respectively?
A   Blue; Black
B   Red; Blue
C   Red; Black

36   When checking a fuel sample from a bayonet-type fuel strainer in particular:
A   The valve cannot remain open, it is not necessary to check that it has properly closed
B   The valve may remain stuck open, leading ultimately to considerable loss of fuel
C   The valve may remain stuck open, leading ultimately to an over-rich mixture

37   If an aircraft battery is completely discharged (flat), but the engine is started by some other means:
A   The battery should charge as normal once the alternator half of the Master Switch is selected
B   The battery is unlikely charge once the alternator half of the Master Switch is selected
C   The alternator does not require the battery in order to operate

38   Any water in the fuel system is most likely to cause:
A   Fuel contamination, leading to power loss
B   An over-rich mixture
C   An increase in Cylinder Head Temperature (CHT)

Paper 3   Aircraft General

39 You have been practising glide approaches to runway 27 when the surface wind was calm. The next day you practice glide approaches to the same runway, the surface wind is 260/18 knots. On that next day you should start the glide approach nearer to the runway and:

A   The rate of descent will be greater
B   The rate of descent will be less but the approach angle will be steeper
C   The rate of descent will be unchanged

40 Painted squares on the tyre wall and adjacent wheel hub are:

A   Tyre wear marks, the tyre is serviceable as long as they are visible
B   Creep marks, and should be aligned
C   Tyre pressure indicators, which should not line-up

41 With respect to a down-sloping runway, as opposed to a level runway:

A   Take-off distance is reduced, landing distance is increased
B   Take-off distance is increased, landing distance is increased
C   Take-off distance is reduced, landing distance is reduced

42 The colour of 100LL AVGAS fuel is:

A   Blue
B   Clear
C   Red

43 An aircraft has a take-off weight of 1009kg and a total moment of 1106 M.KG. If 250 litres of fuel, with a specific gravity of 0.72, is used and the fuel has a lever arm of 1.10, what is the calculated weight and moment at landing?

A   759kg; 911 M.KG
B   811kg; 908 M.KG
C   811kg; 1109 M.KG

44 An electrical fire is best tackled with a:

A   Water or foam extinguisher
B   Carbon dioxide, dry powder or BCF extinguisher
C   Dry powder extinguisher only

45 The period of validity of a Certificate of Airworthiness can be established from:

A   The POH/FM
B   The Certificate of Maintenance Review
C   The Certificate of Airworthiness

46 You have two batteries, each of 12 volts and 30 ampere-hour capacity. You want to connect these batteries to provide a capacity of 30 ampere hours, the batteries should be connected:

A   In series
B   In parallel
C   In the twilight zone

47 The time remaining to the next major inspection can be determined by:

A   The certificate of airworthiness
B   The certificate of maintenance review
C   The flight manual

Paper3   Aircraft General

48 You are calculating the take-off performance from Le Puy airfield (elevation of 2730 feet), where the air temperature is +14°C and the QNH is 1013mb. You already know the calculated take-off performance from Shoreham airfield (elevation 7ft) in ISA conditions. Which of the following statements is true:

A Density at Le Puy is less than at Shoreham, temperature deviation from ISA is -1°C, take-off distance will be longer

B Density at Le Puy is the same as at Shoreham, temperature deviation from ISA is 0°C take-off distance will be longer

C Density at Le Puy is less than at Shoreham, temperature deviation from ISA is +5°C, take-off distance will be longer

49 During a flight you begin to suffer from a headache, dizziness and drowsiness after turning on the cabin heater, you should suspect:

A Overheating

B Carbon Monoxide poisoning

C Electric shock

50 An aircraft is fitted with a 'centre-zero' reading ammeter (illustrated). The ammeter is presently indicating:

A A discharge, the battery is supplying all electrical power

B A discharge, the alternator is supplying all electrical power

C A positive charge, the battery is being charged by the alternator at about 5 ampere/hours

Paper 4 Aircraft General

1 If the air temperature at 5000ft amsl is +10°C, this deviation from ISA can be described as:
A ISA +5°C
B ISA -5°C
C ISA compliant

2 The amount of water vapour in the air compared to the maximum that the air could absorb at that temperature is the:
A Water vapour ratio, which is 100% when the air is saturated
B Relative humidity, increased relative humidity reduces density
C Water vapour ratio, which is 1:1 when the air is saturated

3 As altitude increases in the International Standard Atmosphere:
A The percentage of oxygen in the atmosphere reduces
B The percentage of oxygen in the atmosphere remains unchanged
C Density increases with reducing pressure

4 What is the function of the fin?
A To provide lateral stability
B To provide longitudinal stability
C To provide directional stability

5 At its MTWA of 5570kg, as aircraft has a best gliding range airspeed of 97kts. What might its best gliding range airspeed be at a weight of 4015kg?
A 109kts
B 91kts
C 103kts

6 Take-off run may be shortened by:
A The use of flaps
B Taking-off with a tail-wind
C An up-sloping runway

7 In relation to stalling angle of attack:
A Use of flaps increases the stalling angle of attack
B Use of slots and slats increases the stalling angle of attack
C Use of flaps or slots and slats does not alter stalling angle of attack

8 About which axis does an aircraft yaw?
A Normal
B Longitudinal
C Lateral

9 What is the purpose of wing 'slats'?
A To slow the aircraft down
B To increase the take off speed
C To delay the stall

10 In what conditions is carburettor ice most likely to form?
A OAT+5°C to -25°C, cruise power
B OAT -5°C to +25°C, descent power
C OAT -5°C to -25°C, descent power

Paper 4 Aircraft General

11 A 'bendable' trim tab, such as might be used on a rudder or aileron, is:
A Set by the authority when the initial C of A is issued, and not to be adjusted
B Designed to be ground adjustable
C Set by the manufacturer, and not to be adjusted by any other person or organisation

12 An aircraft is fitted with a fixed pitch propeller. If the aircraft accelerates in a dive, with a constant throttle setting, what will the effect be on engine RPM?
A It will increase
B It will decrease
C It will remain the same

13 Why is a propeller blade twisted along its length?
A To reduce centrifugal stress
B To reduce propeller torque
C To maintain a constant angle of attack along the blade

14 Adverse yaw can be minimised by:
A A butterfly tail
B Differential ailerons
C An aileron trim tab

15 Before engine starting, fuel can be delivered directly to the induction manifold by:
A The starter switch
B The primer
C The fuel selector

16 If trailing edge flaps are raised:
A The stalling angle of attack will be unchanged
B The stalling angle of attack will decrease
C The stalling angle of attack will increase

17 Best lift/drag ratio occurs:
A Just below stalling angle of attack
B Just below 0° angle of attack
C Neither of the above

18 What gas is the main constituent of the earth's atmosphere?
A Nitrogen
B Oxygen
C Carbon dioxide

19 The primary purpose of an anti-balance (anti-servo) tab is to:
A Aid movement of the flying control by reducing loads
B Increase flying control forces
C Prevent flutter

20 To theoretically supply 30 amps for 1 hour a battery would have to have a capacity of:
A 60 ampere hours
B 1 ampere hours
C 30 ampere hours

Paper 4   Aircraft General

21   What colour labelling indicates an AVTUR Jet A-1 installation?
A   Red
B   Black
C   Yellow

22   If the alternator fails in flight:
A   All electrical power from the magnetos to the spark plugs will be lost
B   The battery will supply electrical power from the magnetos to the spark plugs
C   The magnetos will continue to operate independently of the battery or alternator

23   Detonation in a piston engine can be caused by:
A   An over-lean mixture
B   An over-rich mixture
C   A cold engine

24   The altimeter senses:
A   Static pressure
B   Pitot pressure
C   Dynamic pressure

25   During a descent, the pitot tube becomes blocked, the ASI will subsequently:
A   Over – read
B   Under – read
C   Read correctly

26   During a descent, the static vent becomes blocked, subsequently the VSI will indicate:
A   A descent
B   Zero
C   A climb

27   A distribution point for electrical power to various services is known as:
A   A bus bar
B   A circuit breaker
C   A distributor

28   A POH/FM includes a CAA supplement. The POH/FM details one method of spin recovery, the supplement another. In a UK-registered aircraft should you:
A   Abide by the manual?
B   Abide by the CAA supplement?
C   Compromise between the two?

29   An aircraft propeller has a reducing blade angle from hub to tip in order to:
A   Maintain a constant angle of attack along the blade
B   Minimise weight
C   Increase angle of attack from hub to tip

30   Which of the following instruments would normally NOT be electrically powered in a light aircraft?
A   Fuel quantity gauges
B   Heading Indicator (HI)
C   Turn Co-ordinator

Paper 4 — Aircraft General

31 During a climb in an unpressurised aircraft, the altimeter may under-read if:
A   The static source become blocked
B   The pitot source becomes blocked
C   The alternate static source is used

32 A control lock is used:
A   To lock the trimmers in a fixed position
B   To lock the controls in steady straight and level flight
C   To lock the controls when the aircraft is parked

33 Three imperial gallons of oil, with a specific gravity of 0.84, are located at a point which has a lever arm of 14 inches. What is the total moment of this load?
A   11.76
B   353
C   42

34 The best airspeed to use for obstacle clearance after take-off is:
A   The best angle of climb airspeed
B   The best rate of climb airspeed
C   The VFE airspeed

35 Increasing the load carried by an aircraft:
A   Increases the angle of attack at which the stall occurs
B   Decreases the angle of attack at which the stall occurs
C   Does not affect the angle of attack at which the stall occurs

36 Increasing the load carried by an aircraft:
A   Increases stall speed at the same rate
B   Decreases stall speed by the square root of the load factor
C   Increases stall speed by the square root of the load factor

37 The pitot tube senses:
A   Static pressure
B   Dynamic pressure
C   Static and Dynamic pressure

38 An aircraft must always be loaded to remain within the specified centre of gravity limits. If flight is attempted with a C of G that exceeds the aft limit:
A   Stall speed is increased and the aircraft will feel tail heavy
B   The aircraft is designed not to get airborne
C   Control difficulties and possible loss of control of the aircraft may occur

39 An aircraft has a right-hand propeller (a propeller that rotates clockwise when viewed from behind). With an increase in power, how will propeller torque effect the aircraft?
A   It will roll the aircraft to the left
B   It will roll the aircraft to the right
C   Neither of the above are true

40 Which type of fire extinguisher must NOT be used on a petrol or electrical fire?
A   Gas
B   Dry powder
C   Water

Paper 4 Aircraft General

41 In a steady climb:
A Thrust = Lift
B Weight = Drag
C Lift is greater than Thrust

42 An aircraft as loaded has a weight of 702kg, a total moment of 77220 and a CG position of 110cm aft of datum. If 95 litres of fuel, with a specific gravity of 0.72, are loaded at a point that has a lever arm of 97cm, what is the new weight and CG position?
A 797kg; 121cm aft of datum
B 771kg; 108cm aft of datum
C 771kg; 112cm aft of datum

43 If 80 litres of a liquid weigh 68kg, what is its Specific Gravity?
A 0.58
B 0.85
C 0.545

44 An aircraft will achieve the maximum height increase in the minimum time when:
A Operating at the maximum angle of climb airspeed
B Operating at the maximum excess of thrust over drag
C Operating at the maximum excess of power available over power required

45 A pilot has calculated take off and landing performance based on a dry tarmac runway. It transpires that the runway is grass and wet, how will performance be effected?
A Take off and landing distances will be longer
B Take off distance will be longer, landing distance will be shorter
C Take off distance will be longer, landing distance will be the same

46 A duplicate inspection on a control system may be carried out by:
A The aircraft's owner and another PPL holder
B The aircraft's owner and a licensed engineer
C Two licensed engineers

47 If you take off from a concrete runway as opposed to your normal grass runway, your take off distance will be expected to:
A Increase
B Decrease
C Remained the same

48 An aircraft is fitted with a 'left-zero' reading ammeter (illustrated). The ammeter is currently indicating:

A The ammeter is supplying zero output
B The battery is fully charged
C The battery is below normal operating temperature

Paper 4   Aircraft General

49 If a licensed engineer has carried out work on a control system, the second part of the duplicate inspection may be carried out by:

A Any pilot
B Any pilot qualified on that type of aircraft
C Any commercial pilot

50 If an aircraft with a Maximum Total Weight Authorised (MTWA) of less than 2730kg and a private category Certificate of Airworthiness (C of A) has not been maintained in accordance with the approved maintenance schedule quoted on the C of A:

A The C of A is valid provided the work is signed-off by a licensed engineer
B The C of A is now invalid
C The C of A is valid provided the approved maintenance schedule is observed at the next inspection

PRIVATE PILOT'S LICENCE

Human Performance and Limitations

Time allowed: 30 minutes

Instructions

1 The paper consists of 20 multiple choice questions, each carries 5 marks (total 100 marks). The pass mark is 70% (i.e. 14 questions or more must be answered correctly); marks are not deducted for incorrect answers.

2 Be sure to carefully read each question and ensure that you understand it before considering the answer choices. Only one of the answers is complete and correct; the others are either incomplete or based on a misconception.

3 Leave questions that seem difficult at first and return to these when the others have been completed.

4 Indicate the correct answer to each question by placing a tick in the appropriate box of the answer sheet. If you decide to change an answer, completely obliterate the original selection.

5 The back of the answer sheet can be used for working calculations.
DO NOT MARK THE QUESTION PAPER.

Paper 1   Human Performance and Limitations

    Which of the following gases does the body maintains a greater store of?
- A   Oxygen
- B   Carbon Dioxide
- C   Carbon Monoxide

2   At altitudes above 10,000ft amsl aircrew require additional oxygen. This is due to the fall in the:
- A   Proportion of oxygen
- B   Temperature of oxygen
- C   Pressure of oxygen

3   During a flight above 10,000ft amsl a crewmember develops blue tinged lips and fingers and appears to be breathing rapidly. What is he is most likely to be suffering from?
- A   Hyperventilation
- B   Hypoxia
- C   Hypothermia

4   The mechanism that allows the middle ear to match the ambient pressure is known as:
- A   The sinuses
- B   The vestibular apparatus
- C   The Eustachian tubes

5   What is the average time of useful consciousness at 30,000ft?
- A   2-3 minutes
- B   45-75 seconds
- C   20-30 seconds

6   After diving with scuba equipment if a depth of 30ft has not been exceeded, the recommended time interval before flying is:
- A   12hrs
- B   24hrs
- C   48hrs

7   The parts of the eye that respond best to low light situations are the?
- A   Fovea
- B   Cones
- C   Rods

8   Smoking _____ the risk of the onset of hypoxia in a crew member at altitude.
- A   Has no effect on
- B   Reduces
- C   Increases

9   If Carbon Monoxide enters the cockpit, it can be detected by:
- A   Its taste
- B   Its odour
- C   A carbon monoxide detector

10   When are you fit to fly when suffering from a heavy cold?
- A   Never
- B   If remaining below 5,000ft
- C   If you have taken non-prescription medicine

11 A seat position which is lower than the Design Eye Position will:
A Reduce forward and downward visibility on the approach
B Improve forward and downward visibility on the approach
C Have no effect on visibility during a visual approach

12 An aircraft on a collision course with your own is most likely to:
A Remain stationary on the aircraft's windscreen
B Move across the aircraft's windscreen
C Not appear on the aircraft's windscreen

13 During a flight in a helicopter in bright overhead sunlight, a passenger complains of a feeling of mental unease and discomfort:
A The passenger is suffering motion sickness, advise him/her to move his/her head around
B The passenger may be effected by hypothermia, use supplemental oxygen
C The passenger may be effected by 'flicker effect', advise him/her to wear sunglasses or to close and cover his/her eyes

14 When not specifically focused on an object, the eyes tend to focus:
A 1-2 metres ahead
B 1-2 kilometres ahead
C At infinity

15 The most effective lookout technique is to:
A Stare straight ahead
B Move the head from side to side
C Use a regular, practised, scanning pattern

16 In relation to motion sickness:
A It is more likely to occur in children than adults
B It can be caused by conflicting information from the eyes, vestibular apparatus of the ears and other sensory organs
C It cannot occur to a pilot whilst flying an aircraft

17 If carrying out flying duties in the early hours of the morning, a pilot should expect his or her performance:
A To be unaffected
B To improve on normal
C To be worse than normal

18 During flight in hazy conditions:
A Turbulence is more likely
B Visibility is usually better into sun
C Large objects may appear more distant than they actually are

19 If a pilot is suffering from gastroenteritis:
A It can be treated and he/she may fly as normal
B He/she should not fly
C He/she can fly providing they do not inform their doctor or the authority

20 In relation to 'G' forces:
A Most people find negative 'G' more unpleasant than positive 'G'
B Most pilots can tolerate more negative 'G' than positive 'G' before G-LOC occurs
C Positive 'G' is normally reduced by pulling back on the control column

Paper 2

Human Performance and Limitations

1 The gas which forms the greater part of the atmosphere is:
A O_2
B CO_2
C N

2 When a person is deprived of the oxygen they need, they are suffering from:
A Hyperventilation
B Hypoxia
C Hysteresis

3 Susceptibility to hypoxia is increased by:
A Cold
B Heat
C Inactivity

4 One of the earliest symptoms of hypoxia is likely to be:
A Loss of vision
B Impaired judgement
C Loss of consciousness

5 The time of useful consciousness at 18,000ft will be:
A The same as at 36,000ft
B Less than at 36,000ft
C Greater than at 36,000ft

6 Spatial disorientation is:
A Never a problem for instrument qualified pilots
B A general term for a false perception of the aircraft's attitude
C Only a problem if one or more flight instruments have failed

7 If you suspect after a flight that exhaust gases are leaking into the cockpit:
A You should fly again immediately, with a safety pilot, to confirm if a problem exists
B You will probably be unfit to fly for a number of days
C You should be fit to fly within a hour

8 An aircraft on a collision course with yours can be difficult to spot because:
A It is most likely to remain stationary on the windscreen
B It is likely to move quickly across the windscreen
C It will appear to grow in size at a constant rate

9 Oxygen is transported around the body:
A By white blood cells
B By carbon dioxide molecules (carbolic acid)
C By haemoglobin

10 If 30ft is exceeded when diving using compressed air, you must not fly within:
A 12 hours
B 24 hours
C 48 hours

Paper 2 — Human Performance and Limitations

11 A light aircraft flying at 90knots has a head on course with a military jet flying at 420knots. Approximately how quickly are they closing in terms of seconds per mile?
A 7 seconds per mile
B 12 seconds per mile
C 29 seconds per mile

12 In the example above, if one pilot sights the other aircraft at a range of 2 miles, how much time is available to take avoiding action?
A 40 seconds
B 20 seconds
C 14 seconds

13 In relation to a practised lookout scan:
A It will be necessary to adjust the scan to compensate for 'blind spots' caused by the aircraft design and structure
B The aircraft will be designed not to have any 'blind spots'
C An aircraft hidden in a 'blind spot' cannot be on a collision course with you

14 As workload is increased from zero, pilot performance levels:
A Continuously increase
B Continuously decrease
C Gradually increase then decrease

15 Gastroenteritis is most often caused by:
A Food poisoning
B The common cold
C Hypoxia

16 After donating blood, you are advised not to fly:
A Within 24 hours
B Within 12 hours
C There is no recommended time interval, provided you have given less than 1 pint

17 If you are suffering from a heavy cold:
A You should not fly, even in a pressurised aircraft
B Flight in a pressurised aircraft is safe
C You can fly, provided you have taken appropriate medication

18 A group decision is often:
A Less risky than that which an individual member would have taken
B More risky than that which an individual member would have taken
C Of a poorer quality than that which an individual member would have taken

19 When approaching an upsloping runway, even when on the proper glideslope pilots may believe they are:
A Too high
B Too low
C Too fast

20 If you receive a local anaesthetic during dental treatment, you are advised not to fly for at least:
A 24 hours
B 2 hours
C 12 hours

Paper 3

Human Performance and Limitations

1 As altitude increases, the proportion of oxygen in the atmosphere:
A Remains approximately constant
B Increases due to the reducing temperature
C Increases due to the reducing pressure

2 The atmosphere contains approximately:
A 78% oxygen
B 21% oxygen
C 78% CO

3 The 'alveoli' are:
A Small air sacs in the lungs
B Small air sacs in the liver
C Small blood cells in the brain

4 The main function of haemoglobin is to:
A Transport carbon dioxide around the body
B Expell unwanted carbolic acid
C Transport oxygen around the body

5 A rise in carbon dioxide in the blood causes:
A A reduction in the respiration rate
B An increase in the respiration rate
C No change in the respiration rate

6 The partial pressure of oxygen:
A Remains the same with increasing altitude
B Reduces with increasing altitude
C Is mostly dependant on temperature

7 Moderate exercise:
A Increases oxygen demand and so can increase the degree of hypoxia
B Increases blood flow and so protects against hypoxia
C Does not effect the susceptibility to hypoxia

8 How can hypoxia best be described?
A As an excess of CO_2 in the body
B As an excess of nitrogen in the body
C As insufficient oxygen in the body

9 The three-pointer analogue altimeter display can be said to be:
A Accurate and easy to interpret, but unreliable
B Inaccurate, but reliable and easy to interpret
C Accurate and reliable, but easy to misinterpret

10 If searching for an object at night, the chances of seeing it are best when:
A Looking slightly to one side of the object
B Looking directly at the object
C Closing one eye then looking directly at the object

Paper 3

Human Performance and Limitations

11 To maintain situational awareness a pilot should:
A Consider only expected information
B Discard conflicting information
C Consider all possible information

12 Body Mass Index (BMI) is calculated by the formulae:
A Weight in kg divided by height in metres squared
B Height in metres divided by weight in kg
C Weight in kg divided by height in feet

13 The BMI figure over which a man can be considered to be overweight is:
A 20
B 25
C 15

14 Approximately how many units of alcohol should be eliminated from the blood in three hours?
A 3 units
B 6 units
C 4 units

15 You receive a general anaesthetic for a minor cosmetic operation. You are advised not to fly for at least the following:
A 24 hours
B 12 hours
C 48 hours

16 The onset of hyperventilation is:
A Less likely above 10,000ft
B Not directly connected with altitude
C Characterised by a red skin colour

17 The hazardous attitude "macho" can best be characterised by the phrase:
A "It won't happen to me"
B "I'll show them how good I am"
C "Don't tell me"

18 The effects of alcohol:
A Increase with increasing altitude
B Decrease with increasing altitude
C Are unaffected by decreasing altitude

19 An approaching aircraft that is on a constant bearing tends to:
A Increase in apparent size at a constant rate
B Increase in apparent size quickly at first, then more slowly
C Increase in apparent size slowly at first, then more quickly

20 The most important consideration in flight instrument display layout is:
A Cost
B Colour
C Standardisation

Paper 4   Human Performance and Limitations

1   Hyperventilation means breathing:
A   More deeply and less frequently than is necessary
B   More deeply and more frequently than is necessary
C   More deeply but less frequently than necessary

2   Stress, apprehension or motion sickness could cause:
A   Hyperventilation
B   Hypoxia
C   Introventilation

3   Cockpit controls that operate different systems should:
A   Look and feel different
B   Look and feel identical, but be labelled
C   Be colour coded

4   The vision requirement for pilots requires the ability to read a car number plate at about:
A   20 metres
B   30 metres
C   40 metres

5   The amount of oxygen in the atmosphere:
A   Is 78% of the total of all gases present
B   Is highest at ground level
C   Is constant at all altitudes

6   Donating bone marrow:
A   Is permitted subject to at least 48 hours elapsing prior to next flight
B   Is not recommended for aircrew who are actively flying
C   Imposes no restrictions on subsequent flying

7   Which particular item of pilot equipment is believed to significantly increase accident survivability in the case of flight in aerobatic/open cockpit aircraft:
A   A protective helmet
B   A flying suit
C   A silk scarf

8   To enable the pilot to attain the Design Eye Postion, the pilot's seat:
A   Should be adjustable for height
B   Should be fixed in position
C   Should be adjustable by an engineer only

9   With regard to the circadian rhythm of body temperature, at what time is the body temperature at its lowest?
A   11:00
B   19:00
C   05:00

10 'Situational awareness' – the accurate perception of conditions effecting you and your aircraft – is:
A   Undesirable, as it 'over-loads' the pilot
B   Desirable in a pilot, it means knowing what is happening around you
C   Best achieved by concentrating on one aspect to exclusion of all others

Paper 4 Human Performance and Limitations

11 A light aircraft flying at 120 knots directly towards an oncoming jet with a TAS of 300 knots. If one of the pilots spots the other aircraft at a range of 4nm, how long does he have to avoid a collision?
A   15 seconds
B   35 seconds
C   25 seconds

12 Which of the following is not a symptom of hypoxia?
A   Dusty red colour of finger nails and extremities
B   Over-deep, over-rapid breathing
C   Dizziness

13 Which of the following graphs best represents the "Arousal/Performance" graph?

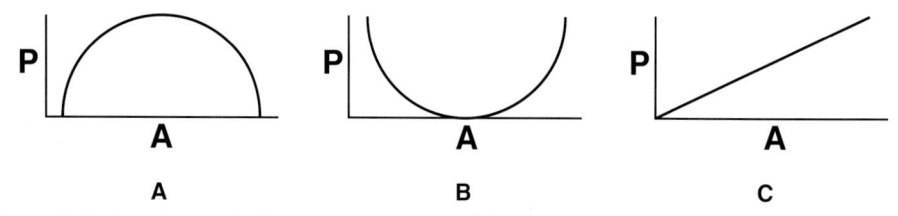

A
B
C

14 Pilot performance is adversely affected by:
A   Excessive arousal only
B   Too high and too low arousal
C   Unaltered arousal

15 If a pilot's seat is too low the effect could be to:
A   Lower the Design Eye Position
B   Increase the pilots view ahead of and below the aircraft's nose
C   Place the pilot's eyes below the Design Eye Position

16 Conflicting information being received from eyes, vestibular apparatus of the ears and other sensory organs can cause:
A   Motion Sickness
B   Gastroenteritis
C   DCS

17 The eustachain tubes:
A   Allow the pressure in the inner ear to equalise with the pressure in the outer ear
B   Allow the pressure in the middle ear to equalise with the ambient pressure
C   Allow the lungs to vent to the trachea

18 Generally, a unit of alcohol is taken as being equivalent to:
A   ½ pint of beer OR a standard glass of wine OR a single measure of spirit
B   1 pint of beer OR 2 standard glasses of wine OR a double measure of spirit
C   2 pints of beer OR 4 standard glasses of wine OR a treble measure of spirit

19 Decompression Sickness (DCS) can occur:
A   Only during scuba diving
B   When flying within 24 hours of scuba diving
C   Only after hypoxia has occured

Paper 4   Human Performance and Limitations

20   Which of the following altimeter presentations is the least ambiguous?

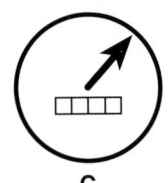

Paper 5

Human Performance and Limitations

1 When flying at 25,000ft in a pressurised aircraft you begin to suffer headaches and nausea, you should suspect:
A Hyperventilation
B Hypoxia
C Hypothermia

2 What time, approximately, is required to eliminate two units of alcohol from the blood?
A 1/2 hour
B 1 hour
C 2 hours

3 Does low temperature increase susceptibility to hypoxia?
A Yes, because it is necessary to generate more energy which increases the demand for oxygen
B No, because the body's metabolism slows, reducing the need for oxygen consumption
C No, because the body's metabolism increases

4 In flight in IMC a pilot experiences an unexpected accelerating and climbing sensation, he should:
A Move the control column forward
B Reduce power
C Trust, and act upon, the information from the flight instruments

5 The three-pointer altimeter display is:
A Completely unambiguous at all levels
B More difficult to interpret below 10,000ft
C More difficult to interpret above 10,000ft

6 Night vision may be:
A Improved by bright lighting conditions in the cockpit
B Improved by higher CO levels
C Significantly worse for a smoker than a non-smoker

7 'Flicker effect', which can cause an epileptic-type fit in a susceptible person, can be caused by:
A Bright navigation lights
B Sunlight through helicopter rotor blades, or a windmilling propeller
C A red rotating beacon

8 In the case of an impending impact, the upper body can best protected by:
A Use of upper torso restraint
B Releasing upper torso restraint and bracing with arms straight
C Leaning back prior to impact

9 If two aircraft are approaching each other at a closing speed of 540 knots, how much time is available to take avoiding action when they are five miles apart?
A 24 seconds
B 34 seconds
C 14 seconds

10 A good treatment for a passenger suffering from motion sickness is for the passenger to:
A Move his/her eyes around the cockpit
B Moving his/her head whilst keeping the eyes focused ahead
C Avoid moving his/her head

Paper 5 Human Performance and Limitations

11 Which of the following statements concerning 'flicker effect', which can cause an epileptic-type fit in a susceptible person, is the most accurate:
A   It can occur in a helicopter or fixed-wing aircraft
B   It can only occur in a helicopter
C   It cannot occur in an aviation environment

12 A pilot may experience the illusory perception of pitching up when actually in level flight, when the aircraft is:
A   Decelerating
B   Accelerating
C   Rolling

13 The eye datum of Design Eye Position is established:
A   To enable the pilot to see all the flight instruments with minimum scan movement of the head
B   To determine the eventual size of the Flight deck and where window frames will be positioned so as not to interfere with the pilot's field of view
C   So that the pilot can maintain an adequate view of all the important displays inside and of the world outside with minimal head movement

14 A microlight aircraft flying at 60 knots is on a collision course with a military jet flying at 480 knots. If they see each other at range of three miles, how long do they have before a collision will occur?
A   35 seconds
B   30 seconds
C   20 seconds

15 In a proper lookout scan the eyes are most likely to:
A   Focus at one spot directly ahead
B   Move smoothly over the area to be scanned
C   Move in a series of jerks over the area to be scanned

16 Where two pilots of differing experience are flying together:
A   The less experienced pilot must not contradict the more experienced
B   The more experienced pilot should not expect his judgement to be questioned
C   Either pilot should always openly express any doubts or concerns

17 A more experienced pilot-in-command should encourage a less experienced co-pilot to:
A   Keep quiet, do as told and learn something
B   Discuss any problems after the flight is over
C   Always express any doubts or queries

18 At night a pilot may best search for an object by looking slightly to one side of it because:
A   The rods concentrate around the fovea, where the light from the object is now falling
B   The cones are less around the fovea, and the cones work better in low light
C   There are more rods away from the fovea

19 To enhance lookout into an empty visual field, a pilot should:
A   Make an effort to 'defocus' the eyes
B   Make an effort to focus on a distant object, such as the horizon
C   Close one eye

20 During a visual night approach to a brightly lit runway in dark surroundings:
A   There is an increased risk of undershooting
B   There is an increased risk of overshooting
C   There is an increased risk of flying too slowly

Paper 6 Human Performance and Limitations

1 Compared to a non-smoker, a tobacco smoker will experience the onset of hypoxia:
A At a higher altitude
B At a lower temperature
C At a lower altitude

2 The first body organ to be adversely affected by a lack of oxygen is :
A The heart
B The brain
C The eyes

3 Assuming that 1 unit of alcohol equals ½ pint of beer, a man would reach the approximate "damage threshold" at:
A 8 pints per day/30 pints per week
B 6 pints per day/25 pints per week
C 3 pints per day/15 pints per week

4 Whilst re-fuelling an aircraft you spill a significant quantity of aviation fuel onto your skin and adjacent clothing. What should you do?
A Immediately discard the effected clothing and wash the effected skin with cold water
B Nothing, unless you are a smoker
C Nothing, aviation fuel has no known adverse effects in these circumstances

5 Smoking 20 cigarettes a day can adversely affect:
A Night vision
B Mental reasoning
C Hearing

6 The effect of altitude on the gastro-intestinal tract may cause stretching of the small bowel, if gas is present in this part of the system. This can be known as:
A Gastroenteritis
B Barotruma
C Boyles disease

7 A pilot suffering from decompression sickness should:
A Land as soon as possible and seek medical assistance
B Decrease the cabin pressure to relieve the symptoms
C Continue the flight at a lower altitude and carry out exercises to relieve any pains in the affected areas

8 At night you are making a visual approach to an isolated airfield, where the runway is well lit but there are few other lights visible:
A There is no danger of optical illusion if you concentrate solely on the runway
B There is an optical illusion that may cause you to approach too fast
C There is an optical illusion that may cause you to approach too low

9 The rate of breathing is most sensitive to changes in:
A Oxygen
B Nitrogen
C Carbon Dioxide

10 The most common cause of in flight incapacitation is:
A Heart attack
B Severe disorientation
C Acute gastroenteritis

11 During flight at 5,000ft, somebody experiencing breathing problems and dizziness is most likely to be suffering from:
A Hypoxia
B Hyperventilation
C Hypothermia

12 In VMC a pilot suffers spatial disorientation, he should:
A React based on visual information
B Trust 'seat of the pants' information
C Make control inputs based on vestibular senses

13 A light twin with an airspeed of 160 knots is closing head on with a military jet whose airspeed is 450 knots. If the pilots see each other at a range of 4km, how much time is available to react?
A 12 seconds
B 20 seconds
C 30 seconds

14 When flying with another pilot, you should express any serious concerns:
A Only if the other pilot has less experience or qualifications than you
B Always
C After the flight has been completed

15 The tendency of an individual to acquiesce to a group decision is known as:
A Competency
B Conventionality
C Conformity

16 The approximate threshold for alcohol intake above which physical damage may be sustained is:
A The same for men and women
B Higher for women than for men
C Higher for men than for women

17 During a night flight, you are advised of conflicting traffic in your 12 o'clock. For the best chance of spotting the traffic you should look:
A About 10 degrees either side of dead-ahead
B Dead-ahead
C It depends on the aircraft's heading

18 To increase the value of a displayed variable, an associated knob should ideally turn:
A Anticlockwise
B In either direction
C Clockwise

19 When the eyes are at rest, they tend to focus:
A At infinity
B At 1-2 metres ahead
C It depends on age

20 You are approaching a runway that is larger than you are used to. You may perceive that:
A You are closer to it than you actually are
B You are further from it than you actually are
C You are approaching faster than you actually are

Paper 7 — Human Performance and Limitations

1 Which of the following are symptoms of hypoxia?
A Impaired judgement, hyperventilation, nausea
B Dizziness, loss of co-ordination, tunnel vision
C All of the above

2 If disorientated in IMC the pilot should believe:
A Vision and inner ear input
B Cochlea input
C The flight instruments

3 When oxygen is being used in a light aircraft:
A Smoking is permissible if the commander chooses to allow it
B There must be no smoking
C Smoking is permissible for passengers only

4 The sinuses are:
A Air filled cavities in the skull
B Air sacs in the lungs
C Tubes joining the middle ear to the throat

5 Which of the following does the body have a greater store of?
A Oxygen
B Carbon Monoxide
C Carbon Dioxide

6 The capacity of the eye to resolve details is termed:
A Visual Acuity
B Fovea Accommodation
C Retinal focusing

7 Excessive consumption of alcohol can damage the health. For men, an approximate 'safe' limit of alcohol consumption is:
A 4 units daily
B 40 units weekly
C 8 units daily

8 After scuba diving using compressed air to a depth of 25 metres:
A You should not fly within 12 hours
B You should not fly within 24 hours
C You should not fly within 48 hours

9 Smoking, or alcohol in the blood:
A Has no effect on night vision
B Reduces night vision at increased altitude
C Increases night vision at increased altitude

10 If a pilot is seated below the design eye position (DEP) during an approach, at about 200ft agl he/she is most likely to:
A Lose sight of a portion of the overshoot
B See more runway than if seated at the DEP
C Lose sight of a portion of the undershoot

11 You should be trained as a pilot to consider all input, to constantly up-date your circumstances and to plan ahead. This desirable action is known as:
A   Situational awareness
B   Conformality
C   Convergence

12 The 'balance' mechanism of the ear is:
A   Known as the spatial apparatus and found in the inner ear
B   Known as the vestibular apparatus and found in the middle ear
C   Known as the vestibular apparatus and found in the inner ear

13 Time of useful consciousness at altitude is:
A   Increased by sitting quietly
B   Increased by moderate activity
C   Not effected by activity

14 Confirmation bias:
A   Is the action of seeking the quickest solution to a problem to avoid consulting others
B   Is the act of group problem solving
C   Tends to make the pilot accept information that confirms his/her diagnosis of a problem and reject information that does not fit into his/her theory

15 Referring to the diagram below, where does optimal arousal occur?

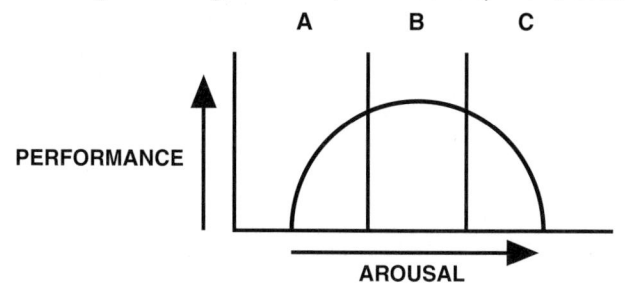

16 Particularly in an inexperienced passenger, a difference between the messages the brain receives from the eyes and from the ears can lead to:
A   Motion sickness
B   Gastroenteritis
C   Titenitus

17 Hyperventilation is:
A   The number one cause of in-flight incapacitation
B   A condition brought on by lack of oxygen
C   A condition in which there is too little carbon dioxide in the body

18 If a pilot experiences "spatial disorientation" whilst flying on instruments, the best solution is to:
A   Trust the balance senses alone
B   Request ATC assistance
C   Refer to, and believe in, the flight instruments

19 In the cockpit of a 'complex' single engine piston aircraft:
A   The undercarriage and flap controls should look and feel the same
B   The undercarriage and flap controls should look and feel different
C   The undercarriage and flap controls should be next to each other

20 A circular instrument with fixed scale moving pointers is:
A   An analogue display instrument, and can be misinterpreted
B   An analogue display instrument and poor for displaying bearing information
C   A digital display instrument and ideal for displaying range information

Paper 8

Human Performance and Limitations

1. A pilot displaying symptoms of dizziness, tingling at the fingertips and hot or cold flushes may be suffering from:
   - A Hypoxia
   - B Hypoglycaemia
   - C Hyperventilation

2. When approaching a runway wider than the pilot is used to, due to visual illusion the pilot may believe that the aircraft is:
   - A At too fast an airspeed
   - B Low on the approach
   - C Not on the centre-line

3. For effective lookout scanning it is necessary to:
   - A Focus on a nearby object
   - B Focus on a distant object
   - C Allow the eyes to rest

4. It is recommended that breathing apparatus is used when flying:
   - A above 5000 feet agl
   - B above 10,000 feet agl
   - C above 10,000 feet amsl

5. Pushing forward abruptly on the control column from a flight condition of 1G is most likely to lead to:
   - A Positive G
   - B Negative G
   - C Decreased airspeed

6. Hyperventilation is best overcome by:
   - A Increasing stress levels, and/or moderate activity
   - B Stopping the use of supplemental oxygen
   - C Restoring normal breathing rate

7. Carbon Monoxide is:
   - A Found at higher levels in a smoker's body than a non-smokers
   - B Necessary to regulate the breathing rate
   - C Generally beneficial to night vision

8. The symptoms of headaches, breathlessness, impaired judgement and eventual loss of consciousness can relate to excessive concentrations of which gas?
   - A O_2
   - B CO_2
   - C CO

9. Full dark adaptation of the eye takes approximately:
   - A 30 minutes
   - B 7 minutes
   - C 5 minutes

10. If an emergency occurs in flight, the best course of action is to:
    - A Request ATC assistance immediately
    - B Act immediately, using the emergency checklist
    - C Assess the situation, consider the options and then choose the appropriate course of action

11 Flying with a "hangover", but more than 12 hours after last drinking alcohol:
A   Is considered safe at low altitudes
B   Is permitted for 2 crew operations
C   Increases the chance of committing piloting errors

12 One characteristic of excessive stress is that:
A   It can always be alleviated in the long-term by cognitive coping
B   It is not a problem for a properly trained pilot
C   What is considered a 'stressful' situation varies between individuals

13 Drinking excessive amounts of tea and coffee before, or during, flight can lead to:
A   A distracting desire to empty bladder, with consequent loss of concentration
B   Insomnia, fatigue and anxiety
C   All of the above

14 The approximate 'safe' daily intake of caffeine is approximately:
A   100mg per day
B   900mg per day
C   400mg per day

15 The hazardous attitude that is best summed up in the phrase "it won't happen to me" is:
A   Anti-authority
B   Resignation
C   Complacency

16 Whilst flying in hazy conditions, a distant object is likely to appear to be:
A   Bigger than it actually is
B   Closer than it actually is
C   Further away than it actually is

17 Approximately how many units of alcohol should be eliminated from the blood in 1 hour?
A   2 units
B   1 unit
C   4 units

18 When using supplemental oxygen in-flight:
A   Smoking is permitted
B   Smoking is not permitted
C   Smoking by passengers only is permitted

19 A pilot is most likely to experience the illusory perception of "pitching up" during:
A   The landing roll
B   The beginning of descent from cruise
C   A go-around

20 An in-cockpit warning system should ideally:
A   Alert, report and guide
B   Not disturb the pilot whilst he/she is concentrating
C   Be capable of being disarmed for the duration of the flight by the pilot

Paper 9 — Human Performance and Limitations

1 At 30,000ft the percentage of oxygen present in the atmosphere is:
A 78%
B Dependent on ambient pressure
C 21%

2 High light levels at high altitude can be particularly dangerous because they:
A Contain more UV light
B Cause the iris to close, blinding the pilot
C Cause the pupil to dilate

3 When on collision course with another aircraft, that aircraft will appear to:
A Grow bigger at a constant rate
B Grow bigger slowly at first, and then grow bigger rapidly at close range
C Remain at a constant image size

4 When a pilot is being subjected to prolonged positive "G" loading, an early symptom of impending unconsciousness is:
A Red-out
B Greying out – partial loss of vision
C Loss of hearing

5 A major function of the inner ear is to:
A Detect angular and linear accelerations of the head
B Prevent direct sound damaging the otoliths
C Connect the ear to the nasal passage

6 The most obvious early symptom of a person suffering from Carbon Monoxide poisoning is:
A They may have blue lips and finger tips
B They may have hearing loss
C They may have cherry red lips and flushed cheeks

7 If you suspect that you have suffered from prolonged exposure to exhaust gases in flight, you should consider yourself:
A Fit to fly after 1-2 hours
B Unfit to fly for at least several days
C Unfit to fly except with another pilot

8 The symptoms of hypoglycaemia can best be avoided by:
A Eating regularly, and supplementing with glucose containing sweets or sweet drinks
B Reducing alcohol intake
C Maintaining a comfortable cabin temperature

9 Decompression sickness (DCS) is caused by:
A Nitrogen coming out of solution in the blood to form bubbles in body tissues:
B A rapid increase of pressurisation in the cabin
C Pains in the shoulder and elbow

10 When a collision course with an aircraft on a reciprocal track, the size of the approaching aircraft:
A Increases gradually and is therefore difficult to detect
B Increases rapidly, just prior to impact
C Is easier to detect if the pilot keeps his/her eyes moving constantly

Paper 9 — Human Performance and Limitations

11 The most common cause of sudden in-flight incapacitation is:
A   A heart attack
B   A blood clot
C   Acute gastroenteritis

12 The decision of an individual group member is generally considered to be:
A   Usually better than the average group decision
B   Usually the same as the average group decision
C   No better than the average group decision

13 At what time of the day is the body temperature usually highest?
A   1800
B   0800
C   1200

14 If 1 unit of alcohol equals 1 glass of wine, a woman would reach the approximate 'damage threshold' at:
A   3 glasses per day/14 glasses per week
B   6 glasses per day/25 glasses per week
C   8 glasses per day/30 glasses per week

15 When looking at an object during a night flight, it is best to look:
A   Slightly to one side of the object
B   Away from the object by about 45 degrees, to catch it in peripheral vision
C   Directly at the object

16 In a disorientation situation (e.g. an aerobatic manoeuvre which has gone wrong) which of the following will give the pilot the most reliable guidance:
A   The eyes
B   The balance sense
C   Smell

17 Individuals are more likely to comply with a decision made by someone of:
A   Greater age
B   Greater experience
C   Greater wealth

18 In terms of 'life stresses, the correct descending order such events, starting with the most stressful, is:
A   Death of spouse, divorce, marriage
B   Marriage, divorce of spouse, family death
C   Divorce, family death, marriage

19 The four flying instruments arranged in the standard 'T' consist of:
A   ASI, AI, ALT, HI
B   ASI, ALT, VSI, HI
C   ASI, AI, ALT, VSI

20 The potentially dangerous condition of hypoglycaemia can be caused by:
A   Over-consumption of alcohol
B   Sudden reduction in cabin pressure
C   Lack of food for many hours, followed by sudden physical exercise or mental anxiety

Paper 10 — Human Performance and Limitations

1 Following a forced landing in hostile terrain, the survival priorities, in order, are:
A Food, water, location, protection
B Water, location, protection, food
C Protection, location, water, food

2 In NW Europe, winter sea temperatures may be as low as 2°C. A person NOT equipped with an immersion suit or dingy has a life expectancy in such waters of around:
A 30 minutes
B 5 hours
C 24 hours

3 Hyperventilation, or over-breathing, can be:
A Cured by hypoxia
B Confused with hypoxia
C Treated by increasing altitude

4 Apparent personality change, impaired judgement, muscular, memory and consciousness impairment, are all symptoms of:
A Hyperventilation
B Anoxia
C Hypoxia

5 Carbon Monoxide, produced by smoking, binds to haemoglobin which has _____ affinity for it than oxygen.
A An equal
B A lesser
C A greater

6 Time of useful consciousness can be increased by:
A A lower temperature
B Smoking
C Reducing stress and workload

7 Cockpit controls that operate different systems should:
A Be placed close together and feel identical
B Look and feel different to each other
C As similar as possible, but labelled

Answer the following 2 questions on the diagram below.

8 Label 1 refers to the...
A Iris
B Pupil
C Lens

9 Label 2 refers to the...
A Retina
B Optic Nerve
C Fovea

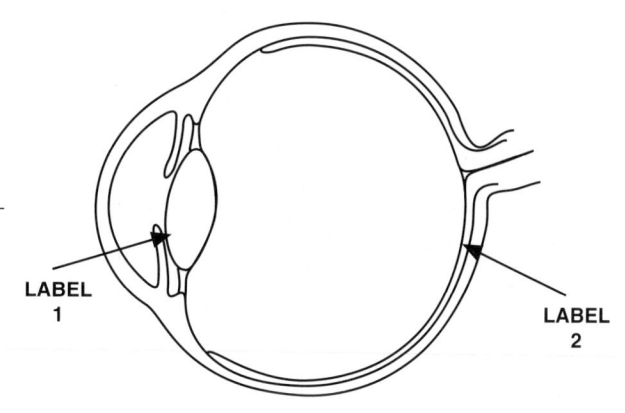

10 The most toxic of the exhaust gases is?
A Carbon Dioxide
B Carbon Monoxide
C Carbohydrate

11 A less experienced co-pilot, believing that a more experienced pilot-in-command has chosen a potentially dangerous course of action should:
A Express openly any doubts
B Try to subtly discuss the subject later
C Say nothing, but adopt the "brace for impact" position

12 A possible antidote for an impulsive attitude is to:
A Take time and think before acting
B Use supplemental oxygen
C Only consider the first option thought of

13 The 'pitch-up' illusion can result from:
A An aircraft deceleration
B An aircraft acceleration
C An aircraft yawing movement

14 To reduce stress and increase performance before a cross-country flight, it is best to:
A Allow plenty of time for proper pre-flight planning
B Ignore any adverse factors that might effect the flight
C Eat as little as possible prior to flight

15 The amount of stress on an individual is mainly due to:
A Actual demand and actual ability
B Perceived demand and actual ability
C Perceived demand and perceived ability

16 The most comfortable temperature for an 'average' person in normal clothing is approximately:
A +10°C
B +30°C
C +20°C

17 Three pints of beer, or six glasses of wine, or six standard spirit measure, equate to:
A 6 units of alcohol
B 3 units of alcohol
C 9 units of alcohol

18 The common symptoms of gastroenteritis include:
A Vomiting, diarrhoea
B Abdominal cramp pains, fever
C All the above

19 Group problem solving will _____ the problem solving ability of the ablest member of the group:
A Rarely improve upon
B Always improve upon
C Usually be dramatically better than

Paper 10   Human Performance and Limitations

20 The standard instrument 'T' panel is shown below, select the answer which correctly describes the instrument layout:

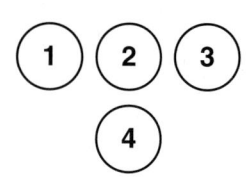

	1	2	3	4
A	ASI	AI	HI	ALT
B	ALT	AI	ASI	HI
C	ASI	AI	ALT	HI

PRIVATE PILOT'S LICENCE

Radiotelephony (RTF)

Time allowed: 30 minutes

Instructions

1 The paper consists of 18 multiple choice questions, each carries 5 marks; marks are not deducted for incorrect answers. Question 19 carries 10 marks: 5 marks are deducted for each item omitted a further 3 marks are deducted for placing the items in the incorrect order. The minimum mark for the question is zero. The pass mark is 70%

2 Be sure to carefully read each question and ensure that you understand it before considering the answer choices. Only one of the answers is complete and correct; the others are either incomplete or based on a misconception.

3 Leave questions that seem difficult at first and return to these when the others have been completed.

4 Indicate the correct answer to each question by placing a tick in the appropriate box of the answer sheet. If you decide to change an answer, completely obliterate the original selection.

5 The back of the answer sheet can be used for working calculations.
DO NOT MARK THE QUESTION PAPER.

Paper 1 Radiotelephony

1 The primary reference for an aeronautical radio communications frequency is:
A An airways flight guide
B The AIC's
C The AIP

2 A controller passes you a VDF bearing which is accurate to within 2°, this is classified as class…
A 1
B A
C 5

3 As aircraft height is increased, the range of VHF communications from that aircraft:
A Decreases
B Stays the same
C Increases

4 The phrase that means 'confirm that you have received and understood this message' is:
A Acknowledge
B Affirm
C Confirm

5 The word 'climb' means:
A Begin a climb and await further instructions
B Climb, and level-out at any level below that specified
C Climb to and maintain the specified level

6 You begin an RT transmission, and then realise that the radio is set to the wrong frequency. To indicate that the ATSU should ignore the message you should use the word:
A Disregard
B Ignore
C Correction

7 An ATSU wants you to set the code 7000 on your transponder and select mode C. The correct RT instruction would be:
A Set 7000, mode Charlie
B Squawk 7000 Charlie
C Send down 7000 with Charlie

8 How should a time of ten to ten in the morning be transmitted?
A Ten to Ten Alpha Mike
B Niner Fifty
C Fife Zero or Zero Niner Fife Zero

9 An altimeter setting of 1030 mb/hPa would normally be transmitted as:
A Wun Zero Tree Zero millibars
B Zero Tree Zero hectopascals
C Wun Zero Tree Zero

10 Which of the following items IS required to be read back?
A An instruction to maintain an altitude
B An instruction backtrack a non-active runway
C Surface wind when passed to a landing aircraft

Paper 1   Radiotelephony

11   An aircraft may abbreviate its call sign:
A   When satisfactory two-way RTF communications have been established
B   At the pilot's discretion, if no conflicting call sign is in use
C   Only after the ATSU has first abbreviated the aircraft's call sign

12   A 'distress' or 'urgency' call:
A   Should initially be made on the frequency in use
B   Should only be made on 121.5 MHz
C   Should be made to the nearest airfield

13   A pilot planning to cross an active MATZ is advised to establish two-way RTF contact the MATZ ATSU:
A   Only when within the MATZ
B   5 minutes or 15 miles from the MATZ boundary, whichever is greater
C   5 minutes or 15 miles from the airfield, whichever is greater

14   Which of the following items are NOT required to be read back?
A   Any item if an ATSU requests it
B   Speed instructions
C   Conflicting traffic information

15   How should a frequency of 119.725 be transmitted?
A   9.725MHz
B   19.725MHz
C   119.72

16   A surface wind of 240/15 should be transmitted as:
A   Too Fower Zero degrees Fifteen knots
B   Too Fower Zero degrees Wun Fife knots
C   Too Hundred and Forty Degrees Fifteen knots

17   A 'departure' clearance is:
A   A clearance to take-off
B   A clearance to taxy onto the active runway to hold
C   Routing for an aircraft to follow after take-off

18   When can you change frequency without informing the ATSU you are presently in communication with?
A   At the pilot's discretion, if the ATSU was only giving an FIS or alerting service
B   Once beyond 25nm from a TOWER or APPROACH ATSU
C   Never

19   You are a solo student pilot flying a Grumman AA-5 G-DINA 2 miles to the north of Nottingham airfield at 2500 feet on the QNH heading 090° when you experience a complete engine failure. You have Nottingham in sight and you plan to land on runway 27. Detail your radio call (you are already in contact with the air/ground station at Nottingham):

Paper 2   Radiotelephony

1   The ATC instruction used to instruct the pilot to check and confirm the current level against the transponder Mode C read-out is:
A   Verify your level
B   Cross-check Mode C and Confirm
C   Confirm and verify Mode C read-out

2   How would you classify a radio transmission that is readable but with difficulty?
A   Readability 3
B   Readability 2
C   Readability 4

3   The correct RTF word or phrase that mean 'I intend to call [unit] on [frequency]' is:
A   Changing to…
B   Freecall…
C   QSY…

4   Where an ATSU permits a call sign to be abbreviated, the correct abbreviation of Thurston G-ASMY would be:
A   Thurston MY
B   Thurston G-MY
C   Thurston G-ASMY

5   The RT word 'descend' means:
A   Descend to and maintain the specified level
B   Descend to any level above that specified
C   Descend, and an instruction to level out will follow when you reach the cleared level

6   An ATSU instruction to set the transponder to the 'standby' position should be transmitted as:
A   Select standby
B   Squawk mode 0
C   Squawk standby

7   A radio frequency of 119.65MHz would be transmitted as:
A   Wun Nineteen dayseemal Sixty-five
B   Wun Nineteen dayseemal Six Fife
C   Wun Wun Niner dayseemal Six Fife

8   At an airfield with ATC in operation, when a pilot has completed the pre take-off checks and is ready to take-off, the pilot should report:
A   'Ready for departure'
B   'Ready for take-off'
C   'Ready in turn'

9   An ATSU passes the airfield METAR to an arriving aircraft. The pilot should read back the following information:
A   The complete METAR
B   The altimeter pressure settings
C   The surface wind and altimeter pressure settings

10 You are instructed by an ATSU to 'standby'. The correct response is:
A 'Standing By [call sign]'
B 'Roger standby [then pass message]'
C No response is expected

11 The correct point to report 'downwind' in the visual circuit is:
A When abeam the upwind end of the runway in use
B When abeam the runway mid point
C When beginning the turn onto the downwind leg

12 What is the correct wording to initiate an urgency message?
A Urgency, Urgency, Urgency
B Difficulty message
C Pan Pan, Pan Pan, Pan Pan

13 What is the transponder code to indicate an emergency situation?
A 7700
B 7600
C 7777

14 The following message from an ATC unit; 'G-CD, after the landing Cherokee, line-up and wait', is what type of message?
A A limited clearance
B A provisional clearance
C A conditional clearance

15 A recorded broadcast of an airfield's weather and arrival/departure information is known as:
A AFIC – Aerodrome Flight Information Conditions
B ATIS – Automatic Terminal Information Service
C AFIB – Automatic Flight Information Bulletin

16 A flight unable to comply with IFR, but which is cleared to enter a control zone in conditions that do not meet VMC criteria, may operate under a:
A Specified VFR (SVFR) Clearance
B Special VFR (SVFR) Clearance
C Single VFR (SVFR) Clearance

17 Which of the following does NOT need to be included in a 'Mayday' call by ICAO requirements?
A Aircraft call sign
B Aircraft position
C Pilot's qualifications

18 If the pilot has a very urgent message concerning the safety of the aircraft or some person in it, or some person or vehicle in sight, he/she should use the spoken words:
A Mayday Mayday Mayday
B Pan Pan
C Priority Message

19 You are a student pilot flying solo on a cross country flight from Luton to Shobdon, and you have become completely lost. Your last known position was overhead Banbury at time 15. Your aircraft is G – BNHK, a Cessna 152. Your altitude is 3000 feet on the Cotswold QNH of 1020, heading is 260° and you estimate that you have 1 hour of fuel remaining, the aircraft has a transponder. You are unable to contact the ATSUs on your plan. On what frequency are you going to call for a position fix, and detail the radio message?

Paper 3 Radiotelephony

1 A controller passes you a VDF bearing which is accurate to within 5°, this is classified as class…
A B
B A
C 5

2 The RT word that means 'permission for proposed action is granted' is:
A Acknowledged
B Affirm
C Approved

3 A correct abbreviated call sign for an aircraft with the registration G-DASH would be:
A G-SH
B SH
C G-DA

4 Turning onto final approach at a range of 6nm from the runway threshold, the pilot should report:
A Finals
B Extended Finals
C Long Final

5 An ATSU instruction to climb to and maintain Flight Level 75 should be transmitted as:
A Climb to and maintain Flight Level Seven Fife
B Climb and maintain Flight Level Seven Fife
C Climb Flight Level Seven Fife

6 A compulsory position report should contain the following information (in order):
A position, heading, level, speed
B callsign, position, level
C callsign, position, time, level, next position and ETA

7 Which of the following DOES NOT require a read back by the pilot?
A A wind shear warning
B Type of radar service being provided
C A VDF bearing

8 A pilot has completed the pre take-off checks and checked the traffic situation. Which of the following is the correct request by the pilot for clearance to take-off?
A 'G-RD ready for take-off'
B 'G-BARD ready for departure'
C 'G-RD request take-off'

9 In the visual circuit, the phrase 'Late Downwind' means:
A The aircraft is further along the downwind leg than where a 'downwind' call is normally made
B The aircraft is behind its landing ETA
C The aircraft has landing traffic ahead

10 An ATSU instructs you to 'contact [ATSU] on [frequency]'. You should:
A Change to that frequency immediately without making further transmissions on that frequency
B Transmit your call sign, then change frequency
C Make a full read back of the instruction

Paper 3   Radiotelephony

11 An aircraft that is in serious and/or imminent danger and requires immediate assistance is in a _____ situation:
A Urgency
B Distress
C Difficulty

12 An aircraft callsign of Channel 2239 should be transmitted as:
A Channel Twenty-two Thirty-nine
B Too Too Tree Niner
C Channel Too Too Tree Niner

13 When providing a Radar Information Service (RIS):
A The controller will provide traffic information, the pilot decides on what avoiding action to take
B The controller will provide traffic information on any known conflicting traffic and advise on avoiding action
C The controller will provide traffic information of all other aircraft on his radar screen

14 To establish a Flight Information Service (FIS), once instructed to 'pass your message' which of the following items, in order, should you transmit?
A Aircraft type, position, heading, altitude/level, intentions,
B Aircraft type, point of departure, altitude/level, next turning point with ETA, intentions
C Aircraft type, heading, altitude/level, destination point with ETA,

15 The spoken abbreviation 'SSR' means:
A Service Stopped – Radar
B Secondary Surveillance Radar
C Special Service Requested

16 The FIS service provided by an FIR controller (e.g. callsign London Information):
A Can provide separation from all traffic in the open FIR
B Automatically provides a RIS or RAS
C Can only provide flight details of 'known' traffic

17 If a pilot reports 'final' the aircraft is:
A More than 8 miles from the runway threshold
B Between 4 and 8 miles from the runway threshold
C Less than 4 miles from the runway threshold

18 An aircraft which uses the callsign suffix 'heavy' on initial contact with an ATSU is:
A Operating at more than 1000kg MAUW
B In the ICAO Heavy wake turbulence category
C Operating at or near it's MAUW

19 You are flying a Slingsby G – BNSP, solo, 5 miles west of Finningley disused airfield at FL 55 heading 110° and talking to Sheffield Approach on 128.525, when the engine begins to run rough – you suspect an engine failure is possible and you decide to divert to Finningley disused airfield. You are a PPL. Detail your emergency message:

Paper 4 Radiotelephony

1 The RT word(s) that means 'this is a separation between messages' is:
A Correction
B Break
C New message

2 An ATSU wishes you to climb to and maintain an altitude of 3500ft. This instruction would be transmitted as:
A Climb to and maintain Tree Tousand Fife Hundred feet
B Climb Tree Fife Zero Zero feet
C Climb to Tree Tousand Fife Hundred feet

3 Where a read back IS NOT required, the phrase to indicate you have understood the message and will co-operate with it is:
A Roger
B Affirm
C Wilco

4 The correct abbreviation of Neatax G-LEAR would be:
A Neatax AR
B Neatax GAR
C No abbreviation is permitted

5 An aircraft gives an ETA of 'Wun Fife'. This time will be:
A 15:00 UTC
B 15 minutes from the time of transmission
C 15 minutes past the hour

6 'Distress' and 'Urgency' messages are:
A Only to be made on 121.5MHz
B Two of three classifications of emergency message, the other is 'uncertainty'
C The two classifications of emergency message

7 A radio frequency of 128.50 would be transmitted as:
A Too Ait point Fife Zero
B Too Ait Dayseemal Fife Zero
C Wun Too Ait Dayseemal Fife Zero

8 During an approach to land, you decide to make a 'missed approach', once established in this manoeuvre you should report:
A [callsign] missed approach
B [callsign] going around
C [callsign] climbing away

9 A controller gives you a VDF bearing which is accurate to within 10°, this is classified as class…
A B
B D
C C

10 A pilot requests departure information, and is given the runway in use, the surface wind, the number of aircraft in the circuit and the QNH. The pilot should read back:
A Runway in use, surface wind, number of aircraft in the circuit, QNH
B Runway in use, QNH
C No read back is required

181

Paper 4   Radiotelephony

11 A 'departure' clearance is:
A The route to be followed after take-off
B Clearance to take-off
C Clearance to enter the departure runway

12 An aircraft is inbound to an airfield within controlled airspace. The pilot makes an initial call to the approach frequency and is instructed to 'standby'. The pilot should:
A Orbit at the present position
B Continue into controlled airspace via the flight plan route and await further instructions
C Await a further call from the ATSU, but not assume that any clearance has been given

13 You make initial contact with an ATSU, request a Radar Advisory Service, and are given a transponder code to 'squawk'. That in itself:
A Means you are receiving a RAS
B Means you are receiving some type of radar-based service
C Does not imply that you are receiving any form of radar service

14 During a cross country flight you become lost and cannot contact any of your planned ATSUs. You decide to call 'Scottish Centre' for assistance, on what frequency will you make that call?
A 121.5MHz
B The ATIS frequency for the nearest major airfield
C The relevant FIS frequency for that part of the FIR

15 When can a distress (Mayday) message be simulated between an aircraft and an ATSU?
A Never
B Only on 121.5MHz
C Only if the aircraft uses the words 'Practice Mayday'

16 A pilot requesting a MATZ penetration should pass which of the following details (in order) when invited to 'pass your message'?
A Aircraft type, position, heading, MATZ ETA
B Aircraft type, altitude/level, destination ETA
C Aircraft type, position, heading, altitude/level, intentions

17 A SVFR clearance:
A Is offered at the discretion of ATC, and accepted at the pilot's discretion
B Must be offered by ATC if conditions in the control zone are less than VMC
C Absolves the pilot from all provisions of the low flying rules in relation to built-up areas

18 A pilot MUST read back:
A Altimeter settings, runway in use, traffic information
B SSR operating instructions, surface winds, airways clearances
C Speed and heading instructions, VDF information, Frequency changes

19 You are downwind in the circuit at Biggin Hill in a Robin DR400 G – BPZP when you suffer a bird strike that shatters the canopy and effects the handling of the aircraft. You decide to make an immediate landing on runway 03. You are at 1000 feet on the QFE, heading 200° and have one passenger – you are a PPL. You are in communication with Biggin Tower and decide to make a distress call. Detail that call:

Paper 5 Radiotelephony

1   When making an 'overhead join' from 1000ft above the circuit height, at what point would you commence the descent to circuit height?
A   Once within the ATZ, but not within 500ft of circuit height until on the 'deadside'
B   Once on the deadside of the runway, which is always the right-hand side
C   Once on the deadside of the runway, turning in the circuit direction

2   A correct abbreviated call sign for an aircraft with the registration G-BCSL would be:
A   G-SL
B   SL
C   G-BC

3   To request a MATZ crossing, it is recommended that you should contact the relevant ATSU:
A   15nm or 5 minutes from the MATZ boundary (whichever is greater)
B   15nm or 5 minutes from the MATZ boundary (whichever is less)
C   At any time before reaching the MATZ boundary

4   The RTF phrase that may be used to indicate an inexperienced pilot is:
A   Low Hours
B   Tyro
C   In xp

5   An ATSU wants you to set your transponder to standby and reselect the assigned mode and code. The correct RTF phraseology is:
A   Re-select [code] [mode]
B   Re-try [code] [mode]
C   Re-cycle [code] [mode]

6   Which of the following most accurately represents items that MUST be read-back by a pilot?
A   Speed instructions, clearance to backtrack an active runway, a frequency change, runway in use
B   Heading instructions, a VDF bearing, type of radar service being offered, range and bearing of conflicting traffic, route clearance
C   Altimeter settings, level instructions, a METAR, clearance to cross an active runway, an SSR code

7   When an aircraft's transponder is set to 'Standby' or 'SBY':
A   On the controller's radar screen the abbreviation 'SBY' appears next to the aircraft's primary return
B   On the controller's radar screen the code selected is 'frozen' until the next code is selected
C   No secondary return is seen on the controller's screen

8   The Morse code • • • – – – • • • (SOS) indicates:
A   An urgency (Pan) situation
B   A difficulty situation
C   A distress (Mayday) situation

9   Upon hearing a Mayday call, all other aircraft on the frequency:
A   Must maintain radio silence under all circumstances
B   Can break radio silence if they can offer assistance to the aircraft in distress
C   Can only break radio silence if they wish to change frequency

10   How would you classify a radio transmission that is unreadable ?
A   Readability 1
B   Readability 0
C   Readability 4

Paper 5   Radiotelephony

11   The RTF phrase for 'I have received all of your last transmission' is:
A   'Roger', which also implies that any instructions will be complied with
B   'Roger', which does not mean that any instructions will be complied with
C   'Roger', which means that a response is required

12   The spoken abbreviation 'DF' means:
A   Dedicated Frequency
B   Direction Finding
C   Delay Flight

13   Which of the following is true of a Radar Advisory Service (RAS)?
A   The controller will pass details of conflicting traffic, the pilot decides what avoiding action is required
B   The controller will pass details of known conflicting traffic, and advise on avoiding action
C   The controller will pass details of avoiding action, without passing information on conflicting traffic

14   During a cross country flight you become lost and cannot contact any of your planned ATSUs. You decide to call for position fixing assistance. Assuming there are no immediate safety, fuel, weather or daylight concerns what type of call should you make?
A   An alerting service call
B   A practice position fix call
C   An urgency (Pan Pan) call

15   During a visual go-around, and unless there are specific instructions otherwise, you would normally climb:
A   To the 'dead' side of the runway
B   To the 'live' side of the runway
C   Straight ahead directly over the runway

16   What is the correct wording to initiate a distress message?
A   Distress, Distress, Distress
B   Emergency call
C   Mayday, Mayday, Mayday

17   An aircraft is instructed by ATC to 'expedite' a descent. This means the pilot should:
A   Increase the aircraft's airspeed
B   Increase the aircraft's rate of descent
C   Reduce the current rate of descent

18   A 'Volmet' broadcast transmits:
A   The current TAFs (forecasts) for selected airfields
B   The current METARS (actuals) for selected airfields
C   The current METAR and arrival/departure information for a single airfield

19   You are a PPL flying with one passenger in a Piper Malibu aircraft with a call sign of Autoair 03. You suffer a complete engine failure when 1 mile north of Lymington, altitude 1500 feet. Your heading is 340° and you are talking to Southampton Approach. You intend to make a forced landing at Beaulieu disused airfield. Write out the correct distress call.

Paper 6 Radiotelephony

1 When may the frequency 121.5MHz be used for practising an emergency procedure?
A Never
B Only if the call is prefixed with 'practice'
C Only for a simulated urgency message

2 A radio transmission classified as Readability 2 can be said to be:
A Readable
B Readable now and then
C Unreadable

3 If an ATSU wishes to instruct you to call another ATSU that already has your details, they will use the word/phrase:
A Contact
B Change to
C Freecall

4 The correct abbreviation of the callsign Speedbird 5536 is:
A Speedbird 36
B Speedbird 5536
C 5536

5 If instructed to 'go around' the pilot should:
A Acknowledge the instruction first, then carry-out a missed approach
B Act upon the instruction immediately
C Acknowledge the instruction first, but continue the approach if you cannot see any danger

6 A heading of 140° would be transmitted as:
A Fower Zero
B Wun Hundred and Forty
C Wun Fower Zero

7 When an ATC unit has acknowledged correct read back of a departure clearance:
A The aircraft still requires a separate take-off clearance
B The aircraft can take-off within two minutes
C The aircraft can take-off when ready

8 An ATSU passes the following arrival information to an inbound aircraft:
'Runway in use 24, surface wind 300 degrees 5 knots, visibility 15 kilometres, weather nil. Cloud scattered at 2500. Temperature +15, dewpoint +8. QNH 1025, QFE for 24 1015.'
Given a call sign of Raven 09, how would this information be read back?
A 'Roger the weather Raven 09'
B 'Copy the weather Raven 09'
C 'Runway 24, QNH 1025, QFE 1015 Raven 09'

9 During a flight over inhospitable terrain you spot an aircraft that has made a successful forced landing, with survivors requiring assistance. You should:
A Make a Mayday call on the frequency in use
B Make a Pan Pan call on the frequency in use
C Change to 121.5 and make a Pan call

Paper 6 Radiotelephony

10 Which of the following items are NOT required in a compulsory position report?
A Time
B ETA at next position point
C Heading

11 A transponder without 'altitude read-out' capability is described as:
A Mode A
B Four figure only
C Cheap

12 The standard format of a conditional clearance is:
A [Aircraft callsign]/[condition]/[clearance]
B [Aircraft callsign]/[clearance]/[condition]
C [condition]/[clearance]/[Aircraft callsign]

13 During an initial contact to request MATZ penetration the pilot should pass:
A [station addressed] [callsign] [position]
B [station addressed] [callsign] [position] [heading] [request]
C [station addressed] [callsign] 'request MATZ penetration'

14 The abbreviation FIS means:
A Final Instruction Sent
B First Initiate Standby
C Flight Information Service

15 When receiving a Radar Advisory Service (RAS):
A The controller will pass information on any known conflicting traffic and advise on avoiding action
B The controller will pass information on any known conflicting traffic, the pilot decides what avoiding action is necessary
C The controller will pass information on conflicting traffic that the pilot spots

16 You are in the visual circuit at an airfield whose callsign has the suffix 'Radio'. After reporting 'final' you receive the message "Roger, surface wind 180/10'. The correct response is:
A You should make no response
B 'Roger'
C 'Request landing clearance'

17 An aircraft broadcasts a 'Mayday' call on the frequency you are using, but the ATSU does not reply. You should:
A Maintain radio silence
B Tell the 'Mayday' aircraft to 'say again'
C Relay the 'Mayday' call to the ATSU

18 You fly regularly to an airfield, which usually has a callsign '[ATSU name] information'. One day the callsign is '[ATSU name] radio'. This means that:
A The airfield is now unlicensed
B A trainee radio operator is using the radio under supervision
C Only an air/ground radio service is available at this time

19 You are in a Piper Arrow G-BNZG flying across the English Channel to the Channel Islands when you spot a small boat in difficulties 10 miles south of the Isle of Wight. You are at altitude 3000 feet and begin a right-hand orbit to keep the boat in sight while you fix the exact position. You are talking to London Information, and you want to request Coastguard assistance. You are a PPL with an IMC rating. Detail your emergency message:

Paper 7 Radiotelephony

1 How would you classify a radio transmission that is perfectly readable?
A Readability 1
B Readability 5
C Readability A

2 An ATSU makes an error in a transmission. To indicate an error has occurred, and preface the proper version, they will use the phrase:
A Correction
B Say again
C Disregard

3 You did not receive properly an ATSU transmission to you. You should:
A Request them to 'say again'
B Request them to 'restate'
C Request them to 'repeat'

4 Which of the following services would you NOT expect a FIR FIS controller to provide?
A Filing of a flight plan
B Alerting service
C Radar service

5 An altimeter setting of 995 millibars would be transmitted as:
A Niner Niner Fife
B Niner Ninety-five
C Niner Niner Fife millibars

6 Which of the following most accurately represents items that must be read back by a pilot?
A A departure clearance, clearance to continuing holding short of an active runway, an instruction to 'recycle' a transponder code, any message when a read back is requested by ATC
B An altimeter setting, clearance to land, a frequency change, runway in use, a descent instruction, a met report of an active Cumulonimbus
C Any level instruction, an airways clearance (when it is the same as flight plan), a QFE, a QDM, a visibility report if it is below 1000 metres

7 The pilot of an aircraft with the call sign of G-ER has requested departure information, and in reply is given 'Runway in use 15, surface wind 170/10, QNH 1015'. What would be the correct read back?
A 'Runway in use 15, surface wind 170/10, QNH 1015 G-ER'
B 'Runway 15, QNH 1015 G-ER'
C 'Roger the information, G-ER'

8 A radio frequency of 128.175 would be transmitted as:
A Wun Too Ait dayseemal Wun Seven Fife
B Wun Too Ait Wun Seven Fife
C Wun Too Ait dayseemal Wun Seven

9 It is not your day. You are making a Pan call, when your conversation is interrupted by a Mayday call. You should:
A Continue your call over the Mayday call
B Resume your Pan conversation as soon as the Mayday transmission ends
C Maintain silence whilst the Mayday is in progress

Paper 7   Radiotelephony

10. You are at the holding point for the active runway, and in reply to your request for departure ATC reply 'cleared immediate take-off'. After acknowledging this message you may:
- A Taxy onto the runway immediately and commence take-off without stopping
- B Complete your pre take-off checks, provided you begin your take-off within 2 minutes
- C Either of the above, at the pilot's option

11. You have established two-way communication on a frequency of 119.65, when you experience an emergency that necessitates a 'Mayday' call. On what frequency should the call be made?
- A 121.5
- B 119.65MHz
- C The FIR FIS frequency

12. When receiving a Radar Advisory Service (RAS) or a Radar Information Service (RIS), which of the following is true:
- A The controller and the pilot are jointly responsible for terrain separation
- B The controller is solely responsible for terrain separation
- C The pilot is wholly responsible for terrain separation

13. At an airfield whose ATSU uses the suffix 'information' you receive the following message 'G-FE land at your discretion, surface wind 250/5'. You should reply:
- A '250/5 G-FE'
- B 'Wilco G-FE'
- C 'Cleared to land G-FE'

14. In response to the instruction 'contact Liverpool approach on 119.85', the correct acknowledgement would be:
- A 'Wilco [call sign]'
- B 'Roger, changing frequency'
- C 'Liverpool Approach 119.85 [call sign]'

15. In relation to a dedicated FIR FIS, which of the following is true?
- A It can be used to file a flight plan
- B It can provide an ATC service or Flight Information Service only
- C It can provide a RAS or RIS for aircraft within 30nm of the ATSU

16. The three types of ATSU are:
- A Control unit, Information unit, Alerting unit
- B ATC, AFIS, A/G
- C Approach, Tower, Ground

17. The abbreviation TMA means:
- A Terminal Control Area
- B TCAS Mandatory Airspace
- C Thunderstorm Manoeuvring Avoidance

18. Which of the following may not be practised on 121.5MHz?
- A An urgency situation (Pan Pan)
- B A distress situation (Mayday)
- C Both the above

19. You hear a Mayday call from G-BNCR, a Piper Warrior with an engine fire, 4 miles south of Thame at altitude 2000 feet heading 270°. The pilot, a CPL is flying solo and intends to make an immediate forced landing. If the ATSU (Wycombe tower) does not hear the call, how would you relay it (your call sign is G-BXPS)?

Paper 8 Radiotelephony

1 What exactly is the aviation VHF frequency spoken as 'WUN WUN AIT DAYSEEMAL SIX TOO'?
A 118.60
B 1186.25
C 118.625

2 A controller passes you a VDF bearing whose accuracy is worse than 10°, this is classified as class...
A Unclassified
B D
C C

3 To indicate that your message is ended, and you do expect a reply, you may use the word:
A Over
B Out
C Reply

4 To request a station to proceed in giving their flight details the correct phrase is:
A Go ahead
B Pass your message
C Pass your flight details

5 Your callsign is G-AB, you awaiting take-off clearance, there is a C172 on final for runway 24. If the ATSU were to give you a conditional clearance to line-up after that aircraft had landed, which message would you expect?
A Line-up and wait after the landing C172, G-AB
B G-AB, line-up and wait after the landing C172
C G-AB, after the landing C172, line-up and wait

6 After reporting established on final, you are instructed by an ATSU to 'Continue approach'. This means:
A You are cleared to land
B Continue the approach, you are not yet cleared to land
C You are cleared to go-around

7 The established visual circuit is left-hand on runway 26. You make a visual go-around after approaching 26, during the climb you should:
A Route directly over runway 26
B Turn left to fly to the left of runway 26
C Turn right to fly to the right of runway 26

8 To correctly make an overhead join from 2000ft you should:
A Route to the airfield overhead, then descend to circuit height on the deadside
B Descend to circuit height and join the circuit on the downwind leg
C Descend to circuit height, cross the downwind leg to the deadsise and join crosswind from there

9 In an emergency message the pilot may use the word 'tyro':
A Only if communicating with a military unit
B To indicate an inexperienced pilot
C To indicate that you are flying solo

Paper 8
Radiotelephony

10 An aircraft ahead of you in the visual circuit announces the intention to make a 'touch and go'. You can expect it will:
A Land and stop on the runway
B Land, stop on the runway, wait for not more than 2 minutes then take-off again
C Land and then take-off straight away without stopping

11 You are orbiting, waiting to make an approach to an airfield. If your fuel situation becomes critical you should:
A Make a 'fuel critical' message to receive priority over other traffic
B Request 'fuel emergency' status to receive priority over other traffic
C Make a Distress or Urgency message as appropriate

12 You are flying VFR outside controlled airspace, and have not been allocated a transponder code by an ATSU:
A You may squawk 7000
B You may not use a squawk without ATC instructions
C You may squawk 4321

13 An aircraft is cleared backtrack the runway in use. This instruction must be:
A Ignored, it has no practical use
B Acted upon, but does not need to be acknowledged
C Read back

14 The RT phrase 'Squawk standby' means:
A Set the transponder to the standby position
B Standby for a new squawk code, continue squawking the existing code
C Squawk the conspicuity code

15 A controller reports to you 'not receiving mode Charlie'. This means:
A Your altimeter subscale is incorrectly set
B The controller cannot see the aircraft's 'secondary' return
C The controller cannot see any height read-out from the aircraft's transponder

16 A controller giving you a radar service describes a conflicting aircraft as 'unknown traffic'. This means:
A The ATSU does not know the traffic's flight details
B The traffic is not in contact with any ATSU
C The traffic is a UFO

17 A squawk of 7600 indicates to a controller that:
A The aircraft has experienced a communications radio failure
B The aircraft has suffered a radionavigation aid radio failure
C The aircraft is subject to unlawful interference

18 An aircraft may abbreviate its callsign:
A At any time if there is no similar callsign in use already
B Only if the ATSU has already done so
C Only after requesting specific permission from the ATSU to do so

19 You are flying 1 mile west of Clevedon at FL50 heading 160°, in a Rockwell Commander, G-DASH when the engine begins to run rough. You decide to divert to Bristol airfield, whose approach service you are already talking to. You are a PPL with 2 passengers. Write out the correct urgency call:

Paper 9 Radiotelephony

1 An ATSU instruction to climb to and maintain Flight Level 45 could be transmitted as:
A Climb to Flight Level Forty-five
B Climb Flight Level Fower point Fife
C Climb Flight Level Fower Fife

2 How would you classify a radio transmission that is readable?
A Readability 3
B Readability 2
C Readability 4

3 To indicate 'no; OR that is not correct; OR permission is not granted' the correct RT word is:
A Negatory
B Negative
C Nullify

4 The correct abbreviation of Britannia G-ABCD would be:
A Britannia G-CD
B Britannia G-ABCD
C Britannia CD

5 Having contacted a LARS unit and been asked to 'pass your message', which of the following describes the items to be given, in the correct order?
A Aircraft type, position, heading, intentions
B Position, altitude/level, intentions, request for RAS/RIS
C Aircraft type, position, heading, altitude/level, intentions, request for RAS/RIS

6 What is the meaning of the phrase 'Freecall'?
A Suggest you contact [ATSU], they do not have your details
B Suggest you contact [ATSU], they do have your details
C Suggest you maintain a listening watch only on that frequency

7 A cloud base of 2800 feet would be transmitted as:
A Twenty Ait Zero Zero feet
B Too dayseemal Ait Tousand feet
C Too Tousand Ait Hundred feet

8 When should a pilot use the phrase 'take-off'?
A Never
B To request clearance to take-off
C Only after the ATSU has given take-off clearance

9 Which of the following is NOT one of the three classes of ATSU?
A AG
B AFIS
C ATIS

10 What is the transponder code to indicate that the aircraft has suffered a communications radio failure?
A 7700
B 7600
C 6000

Paper 9   Radiotelephony

11 The two classes of emergency message are:
A Urgency and Distress
B Difficulty and Distress
C Distress and Security

12 The Air Traffic Radar Service, in which the controller provides traffic information only, is a:
A Radar Information Service
B Radar Advisory Service
C Radar Indicator Service

13 At an airfield with an ATC unit, you accept a 'land after' clearance (there is one aircraft already on the runway, taxying to the end to vacate). Who is responsible for maintaining separation between the aircraft?
A The controller
B You, as the pilot of the following aircraft
C The pilot of the aircraft already on the runway

14 After reporting 'downwind' you are receive the instruction 'cleared to final number 1'. This means:
A You are number one in the landing sequence
B No other aircraft will take-off or land before you
C You are the only aircraft in the circuit

15 Flying on a Sunday, you receive no reply after three consecutive calls on a MATZ frequency. You can assume:
A You have suffered a radio failure
B The ATSU is closed, you may fly through the airfield's ATZ
C The ATSU is closed, you may not fly through the airfield's ATZ

16 What would be the correct read back of the following arrival information, by the pilot of an aircraft with the call sign G-VU:
'Runway 16, surface wind 130/15, QNH 1014 QFE 1009, four in the circuit'
A 'Runway 16, surface wind 130/15, QNH 1014 QFE 1009, four in the circuit G-VU'
B 'Runway 16, QNH 1014, QFE 1009 G-VU'
C 'Runway 16, QNH 1014, QFE 1009, traffic copied'

17 You are receiving an FIS service from a FIR controller on a very busy frequency. When you wish to change frequency:
A You can do so without calling the controller
B You can do so without calling the ATSU provided you contact them by telephone after landing
C You must inform the controller

18 You hear a 'Mayday' being broadcast. Your initial action should be:
A Write down details of the Mayday, maintain radio silence and be ready to offer assistance if you can
B After the ATSU has acknowledged the Mayday, do so also
C Instruct the 'Mayday' aircraft to change frequency to 121.5MHz

19 List, in the correct order, the items to be transmitted in an Urgency radio message:

Paper 10 Radiotelephony

1 Pilots are recommended to make contact with the appropriate ATSU 15 miles or 5 minutes before reaching:
A A LARS area
B An ATZ
C A MATZ boundary

2 An ATSU instruction to maintain altitude 2200 feet would be transmitted as:
A Maintain Flight Level 2.2
B Maintain Too Tousand Too Hundred feet
C Maintain Twenty-two Hundred feet

3 After landing, a 'runway vacated' call can be made by the pilot:
A When the aircraft reaches the end of the runway
B As the aircraft turns to backtrack the runway
C Once the aircraft clears (passes the holding point of) the runway

4 A Radar Advisory Service (RAS):
A Is only available to aircraft operating under IFR
B Is only available within controlled airspace
C Is only available to flights already operating under a RIS

5 A cloud base of 1400 feet would be transmitted as:
A Fourteen Hundred feet
B Wun Tousand Fower Hundred feet
C Wun Fower Zero Zero feet

6 When can a pilot tell an ATSU to 'standby'?
A Never
B Only in an urgency or distress situation
C At any time

7 Arriving at an airfield with the callsign INFORMATION, when you advise 'downwind' the response is 'Report final, on aircraft ahead'. Your correct response is:
A 'Wilco [callsign]'
B 'Cleared final number 2 [Call sign]'
C 'Roger [Call sign]'

8 The transponder code 7700:
A Can only be selected on ATC instructions
B Can be used to simulate an emergency, as long as you have broadcast this intention to the ATSU
C Should only be used in a genuine emergency

9 In an emergency situation, who can impose radio silence on all other aircraft?
A The ATSU
B The aircraft in difficulties
C Both A & B

10 An aircraft has a very urgent message concerning the safety of an aircraft or some person in it, or some person or vehicle in sight of the aircraft. This is a _____ situation:
A Urgency
B Difficulty
C Distress

Paper 10 Radiotelephony

11 The suffix to be used for simulating an urgency situation is:
A Non-emergency
B Practice
C Tyro

12 What type of ATSU uses the callsign 'information'
A An ATSU providing a service in the 'open FIR'
B An AFIS unit
C An AFIS or air/ground unit

13 Which of the following most accurately represents items that must be read back by the pilot?
A Speed instructions, VDF information, runway in use, a regional altimeter setting
B Runway in use, level instructions, landing RVR, type of radar service
C Heading instructions, a route clearance, an ILS frequency, clearance to backtrack an active runway

14 Which of the following is true of a Radar Information Service (RIS)?
A The controller and the pilot are jointly responsible for traffic separation
B The controller is solely responsible for traffic separation
C The pilot is wholly responsible for separation from other aircraft, whether or not the controller has given traffic information

15 The phrase 'unable comply' means:
A I do not understand your instruction
B I cannot carry out your instruction
C I did not hear your instruction

16 When will a 'land after' clearance NOT be given to a pilot?
A When the following aircraft is bigger than the leading aircraft
B When the following aircraft has a faster approach speed than the leading aircraft
C At night

17 You receive the clearance 'G-UD cleared to land 19, surface wind 190/15'. The correct read back is:
A 'Cleared to land 19 G-UD'
B 'Wilco G-UD'
C 'Roger G-UD'

18 An aircraft with the call sign Monarch 874B may abbreviate that callsign to:
A Mike 874 Bravo
B 874 Bravo
C Monarch 874 Bravo

19 List, in the correct order, the items to be transmitted in a Distress radio message:

Answers and Reference

Air Law

Paper 1

1	C	PPL2 Air Law; Flight Crew Licencing; The Private Pilot's Licence
2	C	PPL2 Air Law; Flight Crew Licencing
3	A	PPL2 Air Law; Rules of the Air and Air Traffic Control; Marshalling Signals
4	B	PPL2 Air Law; Rules of the Air and Air Traffic Control; Aerobatics
5	C	PPL2 Air Law; Aircraft Operation; Pre-flight actions
6	C	PPL2 Air Law; Aviation law Documents; Basis of Aviation Law
7	C	PPL2 Air Law; VFR/IFR; Special VFR
8	B	PPL2 Air Law; Flight Crew Licencing; Use of the Radio
9	C	PPL2 Air Law; Rules of the Air and Air Traffic Control; Light Signals
10	B	PPL2 Air Law; Rules of the Air and Air Traffic Control; Distress, Difficulty & Urgency Signals
11	A	PPL2 Air Law; Aircraft Operation; Carriage of Dangerous Goods
12	A	PPL2 Air Law; Rules of the Air and Air Traffic Control; Ground-to-Air Visual Signals
13	C	PPL2 Air Law; Aircraft Documentation; Documents & Records
14	A	PPL2 Air Law; Rules of the Air and Air Traffic Control; The Rules of the Air
15	A	PPL2 Air Law; Rules of the Air and Air Traffic Control; Aerobatics
16	C	PPL2 Air Law; VFR/IFR; IFR Flight
17	A	PPL2 Air Law; Flight Crew Licencing; Student Pilot Privileges
18	C	PPL2 Air Law; Rules of the Air and Air Traffic Control; Distress, Difficulty & Urgency Signals
19	C	PPL2 Air Law; Rules of the Air and Air Traffic Control; The Low Flying Rules
20	A	PPL2 Air Law; Rules of the Air and Air Traffic Control; Rules for Avoiding Collisions
21	C	PPL2 Air Law; Aeronautical Information Service; Flight Plans
22	B	PPL2 Air Law; Rules of the Air and Air Traffic Control; Distress, Difficulty & Urgency Signals
23	B	PPL2 Air Law; Aircraft Operation; Pre-flight actions
24	A	PPL2 Air Law; Aeronautical Information Service; Aeronautical Information Circulars
25	A	PPL2 Air Law; Flight Crew Licencing; Weather Requirements

Answers and Reference Air Law

Paper 2

1	C	PPL2 Air Law; Aircraft Documentation; Aircraft, Engine and Propeller Logbooks
2	A	PPL2 Air Law; Aeronautical Information Service; Search and Rescue
3	C	PPL2 Air Law; VFR/IFR; IFR Flight
4	C	PPL2 Air Law; Rules of the Air and Air Traffic Control; Lights to be Displayed by Aircraft
5	B	PPL2 Air Law; Flight Crew Licencing; Personal Flying Logbook
6	C	PPL2 Air Law; Rules of the Air and Air Traffic Control; Distress, Difficulty & Urgency Signals
7	B	PPL2 Air Law; Rules of the Air and Air Traffic Control; Landing and Take-off
8	C	PPL2 Air Law; Rules of the Air and Air Traffic Control; Rights of Way in Flight
9	C	PPL2 Air Law; Altimeter Setting Procedures; Altimeter Pressure Settings
10	B	PPL2 Air Law; Altimeter Setting Procedures; Transition Level
11	B	PPL2 Air Law; Rules of the Air and Air Traffic Control; Ground-to-Air Visual Signals
12	B	PPL2 Air Law; Rules of the Air and Air Traffic Control; The Low Flying Rules
13	B	PPL2 Air Law; Rules of the Air and Air Traffic Control; Aerodrome Lighting
14	A	PPL2 Air Law; Flight Crew Licencing; Weather Requirements
15	B	PPL2 Air Law; Aeronautical Information Service; Aeronautical Information Circulars
16	C	PPL2 Air Law; Rules of the Air and Air Traffic Control; Taxiway Signals and Markings
17	A	PPL2 Air Law; Flight Crew Licencing; Nature of Flight
18	C	PPL2 Air Law; Aircraft Operation; Passenger Briefing
19	A	PPL2 Air Law; Rules of the Air and Air Traffic Control; Distress, Difficulty & Urgency Signals
20	B	PPL2 Air Law; VFR/IFR; IFR Flight
21	C	PPL2 Air Law; Aircraft Operation; Pre-flight actions
22	C	PPL2 Air Law; Rules of the Air and Air Traffic Control; Rules for Avoiding Aerial Collisions & Rights of Way in Flight
23	C	PPL2 Air Law; Aircraft Documentation; Documents & Records
24	A	PPL2 Air Law; Flight Crew Licencing; Nature of Flight
25	B	PPL2 Air Law; Rules of the Air and Air Traffic Control; Lights to be Displayed by Aircraft

Answers and Reference   Air Law

Paper 3

#	Ans	Reference
1	A	PPL2 Air Law; Aircraft Documentation; Pilot Maintenance
2	B	PPL2 Air Law; Rules of the Air and Air Traffic Control; Visual Signals Visible to an Aircraft on the Ground
3	A	PPL2 Air Law; Rules of the Air and Air Traffic Control; Lights to be Displayed by Aircraft
4	C	PPL2 Air Law; Rules of the Air and Air Traffic Control; Rights of Way in Flight
5	C	PPL2 Air Law; Flight Crew Licencing; Medical Requirements
6	B	PPL2 Air Law; Flight Crew Licencing; Medical Requirements
7	A	PPL2 Air Law; Rules of the Air and Air Traffic Control; Lights to be Displayed by Aircraft
8	B	PPL2 Air Law; Airspace Restrictions, Prohibited, Restricted and Danger Areas
9	A	PPL2 Air Law; En-Route Procedures, Use of Transponder
10	C	PPL2 Air Law; Rules of the Air and Air Traffic Control; Rights of Way on the Ground
11	B	PPL2 Air Law; Aeronautical Information Service; Aeronautical Information Circulars
12	B	PPL2 Air Law; Rules of the Air and Air Traffic Control; Distress, Difficulty & Urgency Signals
13	A	PPL2 Air Law; Rules of the Air and Air Traffic Control; Aerodrome Lighting
14	A	PPL2 Air Law; Rules of the Air and Air Traffic Control; Rights of Way on the Ground
15	A	PPL2 Air Law; Rules of the Air and Air Traffic Control; Lights to be Displayed by Aircraft
16	A	PPL 2 Air Law; Rules of the Air and Air Traffic Control; Lights to be Displayed by Aircraft
17	A	PPL2 Air Law; Rules of the Air and Air Traffic Control; Landing and Take-off
18	C	PPL2 Air Law; Rules of the Air and Air Traffic Control; Order of Landing
19	B	PPL2 Air Law; Flight Crew Licencing; Weather Requirements
20	C	PPL2 Air Law; Flight Crew Licencing; Personal Flying Logbook
21	B	PPL2 Air Law; Rules of the Air and Air Traffic Control; Rights of Way on the Ground
22	C	PPL2 Air Law; VFR/IFR; VMC Minima
23	C	PPL2 Air Law; Flight Crew Licencing; Weather Requirements
24	B	PPL2 Air Law; Rules of the Air and Air Traffic Control; Runway and Taxiway Markings
25	B	PPL2 Air Law; VFR/IFR; Special VFR

Answers and Reference

Air Law

Paper 4

1	B	PPL2 Air Law; Aeronautical Information Service; Flight Plans
2	B	PPL2 Air Law; Flight Crew Licencing; Nature of Flight
3	C	PPL2 Air Law; Aeronautical Information Service; Flight Plans
4	B	PPL2 Air Law; Rules of the Air and Air Traffic Control; Taxiway Signals and Markings
5	C	PPL2 Air Law; Arrival/Traffic Pattern Procedures; Landing Clearance
6	C	PPL2 Air Law; Rules of the Air and Air Traffic Control; Ground-to-Air Visual Signals
7	B	PPL2 Air Law; Flight Crew Licencing; Weather Requirements
		PPL2 Air Law; VFR/IFR; VMC Minima
8	C	PPL2 Air Law; Rules of the Air and Air Traffic Control; Light Signals
9	B	PPL2 Air Law; Aeronautical Information Service; Search and Rescue
10	A	PPL2 Air Law; Aeronautical Information Service; Search and Rescue
11	B	PPL2 Air Law; Aircraft Documentation; Technical Log
12	A	PPL2 Air Law; Flight Crew Licencing; Medical Requirements
13	A	PPL2 Air Law; Flight Crew Licencing; Personal Flying Logbook
14	C	PPL2 Air Law; Aircraft Operation; Drunkeness in Aircraft
15	C	PPL2 Air Law; Flight Crew Licencing; Daylight Requirement
16	B	PPL2 Air Law; Rules of the Air and Air Traffic Control; The Low Flying Rules
17	A	PPL2 Air Law; Rules of the Air and Air Traffic Control; The Low Flying Rules
18	C	PPL2 Air Law; Rules of the Air and Air Traffic Control; Ground-to-Air Visual Signals
19	B	PPL2 Air Law; Rules of the Air and Air Traffic Control; Ground-to-Air Visual Signals
20	A	PPL2 Air Law; Rules of the Air and Air Traffic Control; Light Signals
21	A	PPL2 Air Law; Flight Crew Licencing; Use of the Radio
22	B	PPL 2 Air Law; Rules of the Air and Air Traffic Control; Lights to be Displayed by Aircraft
		PPL 2 Air Law; Rules of the Air and Air Traffic Control; Rules for Avoiding Collisions
		PPL 2 Air Law; Rules of the Air and Air Traffic Control; Rights of Way in Flight
23	B	PPL 2 Air Law; Rules of the Air and Air Traffic Control; Rules for Avoiding Collisions
24	C	PPL2 Air Law; VFR/IFR; IFR Flight
25	A	PPL2 Air Law; Aircraft Documentation; Weight Schedule

Meteorology

Paper 1

1	A	PPL 3 Meteorology; The Motion of the Atmosphere; Depressions and Anticyclones
2	C	PPL 3 Meteorology; The International Standard Atmosphere; The Parameters of the ISA
3	B	PPL 3 Meteorology; Icing; Piston Engine Icing
4	C	PPL 3 Meteorology; Visibility; Fog and Mist
5	A	PPL 3 Meteorology; Depressions
6	B	PPL 3 Meteorology; Depressions
7	A	PPL 3 Meteorology; Depressions
8	C	PPL 3 Meteorology; Weather Hazards; Thunderstorms
9	B	PPL 3 Meteorology; Depressions
10	C	PPL 3 Meteorology; Depressions
11	C	PPL 3 Meteorology; Aviation Weather Reports and Forecasts
12	B	PPL 3 Meteorology; Formation of Clouds: *also* Visibility; Fog and Mist
13	A	PPL 3 Meteorology; Motion of the Atmosphere; Local Winds
14	C	PPL 3 Meteorology; Icing
15	A	PPL 3 Meteorology; Icing; Piston Engine Icing
16	B	PPL 3 Meteorology; Properties of the Atmosphere; Composition and Structure
17	C	PPL 3 Meteorology; Aviation Weather Reports and Forecasts
18	A	PPL 3 Meteorology; Aviation Weather Reports and Forecasts
19	B	PPL 3 Meteorology; Aviation Weather Reports and Forecasts
20	B	PPL 3 Meteorology; Aviation Weather Reports and Forecasts

Paper 2

1	B	PPL 3 Meteorology; The Motion of the Atmosphere; Local Winds
2	A	PPL 3 Meteorology; Pressure and Altimetry
3	A	PPL 3 Meteorology; Properties of the Atmosphere; Composition and Structure
4	C	PPL 3 Meteorology; Air Masses; Formation of Air Masses
5	B	PPL 3 Meteorology; The Motion of the Atmosphere
6	C	PPL 3 Meteorology; Aviation Weather Reports and Forecasts
7	A	PPL 3 Meteorology; Humidity and Stability; Temperature Inversion
8	C	PPL 3 Meteorology; The Motion of the Atmosphere; Measurement of Pressure
9	B	PPL 3 Meteorology; Pressure and Altimetry; Altimetry
10	C	PPL 3 Meteorology; The International Standard Atmosphere
11	C	PPL 3 Meteorology; The Motion of the Atmosphere; Measurement of Wind
12	B	PPL 3 Meteorology; The Motion of the Atmosphere; Coriolis Force, Geostrophic Wind
13	B	PPL 3 Meteorology; The Motion of the Atmosphere; Variation of Wind Velocity with Altitude
14	B	PPL 3 Meteorology; Clouds and Precipitation; Formation of Clouds
15	A	PPL 3 Meteorology; Humidity and Stability; Humdity
16	C	PPL 3 Meteorology; The Motion of the Atmosphere; Turbulence and Windshear
17	C	PPL 3 Meteorology; Aviation Weather Reports and Forecasts
18	B	PPL 3 Meteorology; Aviation Weather Reports and Forecasts
19	C	PPL 3 Meteorology; Aviation Weather Reports and Forecasts
20	C	PPL 3 Meteorology; Aviation Weather Reports and Forecasts

Answers and Reference   Meteorology

Paper 3

#	Ans	Reference
1	B	PPL 3 Meteorology; The Motion of the Atmosphere; Pressure Gradient
2	C	PPL 3 Meteorology; The International Standard Atmosphere
3	A	PPL 3 Meteorology; Humidity and Stability; Temperature Lapse Rate
4	A	PPL 3 Meteorology; The Motion of the Atmosphere; Coriolis Force and Geostrophic Wind
5	C	PPL 3 Meteorology; The Motion of the Atmosphere; Pressure Gradient
6	B	PPL 3 Meteorology; Anticyclones and Ridges
7	A	PPL 3 Meteorology; Air Masses
8	B	PPL 3 Meteorology; Clouds and Precipitation; Precipitation
9	C	PPL 3 Meteorology; Clouds and Precipitation; Formation of Clouds
10	C	PPL 3 Meteorology; Weather Hazards, Thunderstorms
11	B	PPL 3 Meteorology; Aviation Weather Reports and Forecasts
12	A	PPL 3 Meteorology; Weather Hazards, Thunderstorms
13	C	PPL 3 Meteorology; The Motion of the Atmosphere; Depressions and Anticyclones
14	A	PPL 3 Meteorology; Depressions; Occluded Fronts
15	A	PPL 3 Meteorology; Clouds and Precipitation; Formation of Clouds
16	A	PPL 3 Meteorology; Aviation Weather Reports and Forecasts
17	C	PPL 3 Meteorology; Aviation Weather Reports and Forecasts
18	C	PPL 3 Meteorology; Aviation Weather Reports and Forecasts
19	C	PPL 3 Meteorology; Aviation Weather Reports and Forecasts
20	B	PPL 3 Meteorology; Aviation Weather Reports and Forecasts

Paper 4

#	Ans	Reference
1	C	PPL 3 Meteorology; Air Masses
2	A	PPL 3 Meteorology; The Motion of the Atmosphere; Local Winds
3	B	PPL 3 Meteorology; Depressions; The Warm Front
4	A	PPL 3 Meteorology; Depressions; The Cold Front
5	C	PPL 3 Meteorology; Humidity and Stability; Humidity
6	B	PPL 3 Meteorology; Aviation Weather Reports and Forecasts
7	B	PPL 3 Meteorology; Air Masses
8	A	PPL 3 Meteorology; Visibility; Haze
9	C	PPL 3 Meteorology; Aviation Weather Reports and Forecasts
10	A	PPL 3 Meteorology; Weather Hazards; Flight In Mountainous Areas
11	B	PPL 3 Meteorology; Icing; Piston Engine Icing
12	B	PPL 3 Meteorology; Depressions; The Warm Front
13	A	PPL 3 Meteorology; Humidity and Stability; Atmospheric Stability
14	B	PPL 3 Meteorology; Depressions; The Warm Front
15	C	PPL 3 Meteorology; Depressions; The Warm Front *also* The Cold Front
16	C	PPL 3 Meteorology; The Motion of the Atmosphere; Depressions and Anticyclones
17	A	PPL 3 Meteorology; Aviation Weather Reports and Forecasts
18	A	PPL 3 Meteorology; Depressions
19	B	PPL 3 Meteorology; Aviation Weather Reports and Forecasts
20	C	PPL 3 Meteorology; Aviation Weather Reports and Forecasts

Answers and Reference Meteorology

Paper 5

1	C	PPL 3 Meteorology; Weather Hazards, Flight in Mountainous Areas
2	B	PPL 3 Meteorology; Humidity and Stability; Atmospheric Stability
3	B	PPL 3 Meteorology; Humidity and Stability; Humidity
4	A	PPL 3 Meteorology; Motion of the Atmosphere *also* Pressure and Altimetry
5	C	PPL 3 Meteorology; Anticyclones and Ridges; Anticyclones
6	A	PPL 3 Meteorology; Motion of the Atmosphere; Depressions and Anticyclones
7	B	PPL 3 Meteorology; Motion of the Atmosphere; Variation of Wind Velocity with Altitude
8	C	PPL 3 Meteorology; Clouds and Precipitation; Classification of Clouds
9	A	PPL 3 Meteorology; Motion of the Atmosphere; Pressure Gradient
10	A	PPL 3 Meteorology; Humidity and Stability; Humidity
11	C	PPL 3 Meteorology; Humidity and Stability; Temperature Lapse Rate
12	A	PPL 3 Meteorology; Clouds and Precipitation
13	A	PPL 3 Meteorology; Visibility; Fog and Mist
14	B	PPL 3 Meteorology; Icing
15	C	PPL 3 Meteorology; Air Masses; Characteristics or Air Masses
16	B	PPL 3 Meteorology; Aviation Weather Reports and Forecasts
17	C	PPL 3 Meteorology; Aviation Weather Reports and Forecasts
18	B	PPL 3 Meteorology; Aviation Weather Reports and Forecasts
19	B	PPL 3 Meteorology; Aviation Weather Reports and Forecasts
20	C	PPL 3 Meteorology; Aviation Weather Reports and Forecasts *also* Weather Hazards; Thunderstorms

Paper 6

1	B	PPL 3 Meteorology; Depressions; The Cold Front
2	B	PPL 3 Meteorology; Properties of the Atmosphere; Pressure, Temperature and Density
3	A	PPL 3 Meteorology; Pressure and Altimetry
4	B	PPL 3 Meteorology; Humidity and Stability; Temperature Inversion
5	C	PPL 3 Meteorology; The International Standard Atmosphere
6	A	PPL 3 Meteorology; The Motion of the Atmosphere; Coriolis Force, Geostrophic Wind
7	C	PPL 3 Meteorology; The Motion of the Atmosphere; Depressions and Anticyclones *also* Anticyclones
8	B	PPL 3 Meteorology; Aviation Weather Reports and Forecasts
9	C	PPL 3 Meteorology; The Motion of the Atmosphere; Variation of Wind Velocity with Altitude
10	A	PPL 3 Meteorology; Humidity and Stability; Atmospheric Stability
11	A	PPL 3 Meteorology; Weather Hazards; Flight in Mountainous Areas
12	C	PPL 3 Meteorology; Weather Hazards; Thunderstorms
13	B	PPL 3 Meteorology; Properties of the Atmosphere; Composition and Structure
14	B	PPL 3 Meteorology; Visibility; Fog and Mist
15	C	PPL 3 Meteorology; Depressions; The Warm Front
16	C	PPL 3 Meteorology; Icing; Hoar Frost *also* Visibility; Fog and Mist
17	C	PPL 3 Meteorology; Aviation Weather Reports and Forecasts
18	A	PPL 3 Meteorology; Aviation Weather Reports and Forecasts
19	C	PPL 3 Meteorology; Aviation Weather Reports and Forecasts
20	A	PPL 3 Meteorology; Aviation Weather Reports and Forecasts

Answers and Reference — Meteorology

Paper 7

#	Ans	Reference
1	A	PPL 3 Meteorology; Visibility; Fog and Mist
2	B	PPL 3 Meteorology; Depressions; Occluded Fronts
3	A	PPL 3 Meteorology; Icing
4	C	PPL 3 Meteorology; Clouds and Precipitation; Formation of Clouds
5	B	PPL 3 Meteorology; Pressure and Altimetry
6	A	PPL 3 Meteorology; Humidity and Stability; Change of State
7	A	PPL 3 Meteorology; The Motion of the Atmosphere; Depressions and Anticyclones
8	C	PPL 3 Meteorology; The International Standard Atmosphere
9	B	PPL 3 Meteorology; The Motion of the Atmosphere; Measurement of Wind
10	B	PPL 3 Meteorology; The Motion of the Atmosphere; Depressions and Anticyclones
11	A	PPL 3 Meteorology; Properties of the Atmosphere; Composition and Structure
12	B	PPL 3 Meteorology; Weather Hazards; Flight in Mountainous Areas
13	A	PPL 3 Meteorology; Weather Hazards; Flight in Mountainous Areas
14	A	PPL 3 Meteorology; Weather Hazards; Flight in Mountainous Areas
15	C	PPL 3 Meteorology; Depressions; The Cold Front
16	B	PPL 3 Meteorology; Aviation Weather Reports and Forecasts
17	C	PPL 3 Meteorology; Aviation Weather Reports and Forecasts
18	C	PPL 3 Meteorology; Aviation Weather Reports and Forecasts
19	A	PPL 3 Meteorology; Aviation Weather Reports and Forecasts
20	B	PPL 3 Meteorology; Aviation Weather Reports and Forecasts

Paper 8

#	Ans	Reference
1	C	PPL 3 Meteorology; Properties of the Atmosphere; Composition and Structure
2	A	PPL 3 Meteorology; The International Standard Atmosphere
3	C	PPL 3 Meteorology; Clouds and Precipitation; Formation of Clouds
4	B	PPL 3 Meteorology; Properties of the Atmosphere; Composition and Structure *also* International Standard Atmosphere
5	A	PPL 3 Meteorology; The International Standard Atmosphere
6	B	PPL 3 Meteorology; Clouds and Precipitation; Formation of Clouds
7	C	PPL 3 Meteorology; Humidity and Stability; Temperature Lapse Rate
8	A	PPL 3 Meteorology; Humidity and Stability; Temperature Inversion
9	A	PPL 3 Meteorology; The Motion of the Atmosphere *also* Pressure and Altimetry
10	C	PPL 3 Meteorology; The Motion of the Atmosphere; Pressure Gradient
11	B	PPL 3 Meteorology; The Motion of the Atmosphere; Variation of Wind Velocity with Altitude
12	B	PPL 3 Meteorology; Weather Hazards; Flight in Mountainous Areas
13	A	PPL 3 Meteorology; Weather Hazards; Thunderstorms
14	B	PPL 3 Meteorology; Aviation Weather Reports and Forecasts
15	C	PPL 3 Meteorology; Clouds and Precipitation; Formation of Clouds
16	A	PPL 3 Meteorology; Weather Hazards; Thunderstorms
17	B	PPL 3 Meteorology; Air Masses
18	C	PPL 3 Meteorology; Weather Hazards; Thunderstorms
19	A	PPL 3 Meteorology; Depressions; The Warm Front
20	C	PPL 3 Meteorology; Depressions; The Occluded Front

Answers and Reference   Meteorology

Paper 9

1	B	PPL 3 Meteorology; Depressions; The Warm Front *also* The Cold Front
2	C	PPL 3 Meteorology; Clouds and Precipitation; Formation of Clouds
3	C	PPL 3 Meteorology; Clouds and Precipitation; Formation of Clouds *also* Weather Hazards; Flight in Mountainous Areas
4	B	PPL 3 Meteorology; The International Standard Atmosphere
5	A	PPL 3 Meteorology; Aviation Weather Reports and Forecasts
6	B	PPL 3 Meteorology; Weather Hazards; Thunderstorms
7	C	PPL 3 Meteorology; Visibility; Fog and Mist
8	B	PPL 3 Meteorology; Aviation Weather Reports and Forecasts
9	B	PPL 3 Meteorology; The Motion of the Atmosphere; Local Winds
10	A	PPL 3 Meteorology; The International Standard Atmosphere
11	A	PPL 3 Meteorology; Aviation Weather Reports and Forecasts
12	C	PPL 3 Meteorology; The Motion of the Atmosphere; Measurement of Wind
13	B	PPL 3 Meteorology; Depressions; The Cold Front
14	C	PPL 3 Meteorology; Icing; Hoar Frost
15	C	PPL 3 Meteorology; Aviation Weather Reports and Forecasts
16	A	PPL 3 Meteorology; Aviation Weather Reports and Forecasts
17	B	PPL 3 Meteorology; Depressions
18	B	PPL 3 Meteorology; Aviation Weather Reports and Forecasts
19	B	PPL 3 Meteorology; Aviation Weather Reports and Forecasts
20	B	PPL 3 Meteorology; Aviation Weather Reports and Forecasts

Paper 10

1	C	PPL 3 Meteorology; The International Standard Atmosphere *also* Conversion of Temperature
2	B	PPL 3 Meteorology; The Motion of the Atmosphere; Local Winds
3	C	PPL 3 Meteorology; Anticyclones
4	B	PPL 3 Meteorology; Depressions; The Occluded Front
5	A	PPL 3 Meteorology; The Motion of the Atmosphere; Local Winds
6	B	PPL 3 Meteorology; Icing; Piston Engine Icing
7	C	PPL 3 Meteorology; Visibility; Fog and Mist
8	C	PPL 3 Meteorology; Aviation Weather Reports and Forecasts
9	A	PPL 3 Meteorology; Aviation Weather Reports and Forecasts
10	C	PPL 3 Meteorology; Visibility; Fog and Mist
11	B	PPL 3 Meteorology; Humidity and Stability; Atmospheric Stability
12	A	PPL 3 Meteorology; Pressure and Altimetry
13	A	PPL 3 Meteorology; Visibility; Fog and Mist
14	A	PPL 3 Meteorology; The International Standard Atmosphere
15	C	PPL 3 Meteorology; Aviation Weather Reports and Forecasts
16	B	PPL 3 Meteorology; Aviation Weather Reports and Forecasts *also* Temperature Lapse Rate
17	A	PPL 3 Meteorology; Aviation Weather Reports and Forecasts
18	C	PPL 3 Meteorology; Aviation Weather Reports and Forecasts
19	A	PPL 3 Meteorology; Aviation Weather Reports and Forecasts
20	B	PPL 3 Meteorology; Aviation Weather Reports and Forecasts

Navigation

Paper 1

1	B	Flight plan, (PPL 3 Navigation; Aeronautical Maps; Measurement of Direction)
2	C	Flight plan, (PPL 3 Navigation; Aeronautical Maps; Scale and Distance)
3	C	Flight plan, (PPL 3 Navigation; Navigation Principles 2: Time, Speed and Distance)
4	C	Flight plan, (PPL 3 Navigation; Navigation Principles 2: Time, Speed and Distance)
5	A	Flight plan, (PPL 3 Navigation; Navigation Principles 2: Time, Speed and Distance)
6	C	Study of map
7	C	Study of map
8	A	PPL 3 Navigation; Fuel Planning; Fuel Planning
9	A	PPL 3 Navigation; Fuel Planning; Fuel Planning
10	A	Study of map and map key, (PPL2 Air Law; Airspace Restrictions; Prohibited, Restricted and Danger Areas)
11	B	Study of map and map key, (PPL2 Air Law; Airspace Restrictions; Prohibited, Restricted and Danger Areas)
12	A	Study of map and map key, (PPL 3 Navigation; Vertical Navigation; Minimum Safety Altitude)
13	B	Study of map key; (PPL2 Air Law; Division of Airspace and Air Traffic Services; Airspace Classifications)
14	A	Study of map and map key; (PPL 3 Navigation; Practical Navigation 1 Dead Reckoning and Map Reading; Map Reading Principles
15	C	Study of map and map key, (PPL 3 Navigation; Vertical Navigation; Obstructions)
16	C	Study of map and map key; (PPL 3 Navigation; Aeronautical Maps; Airfields
17	A	PPL 3 Navigation; Navigation Principles 2: Time, Speed and Distance
18	B	Study of map; (PPL2 Air Law; Airspace Restrictions; Other Hazards to Flight)
19	A	Study of map and map key, (PPL 3 Navigation; Vertical Navigation; Minimum Safety Altitude)
20	A	Study of map and map key, (PPL 3 Navigation; Vertical Navigation; Obstructions)

Answers and Reference

Navigation

Latitude and longitude are given as an aid to identification but where locations and facilities are marked on the chart, their charted positions should be used.

From	To	FL/Alt	Safety Alt ft amsl	Tas kt	W/V	Trk T	Drift	Hdg T	Var	Hdg M	GS kt	Dist nm	Time hr/min
Gloucestershire N5153.65 W00210.03	Peterborough (Sibson) N5233.35 W00023.18	2500	2400	90	240/10	060	0	060	4W	064	100	76	46
											Total		

Alternate

Peterborough (Sibson) N5233.35 W00023.18	Peterborough (Conington) N5228.08 W00015.07	2500	1800	90	240/10	134	6°P	140	4°W	144	92	7	4.5

Note: Safety Altitude is derived from the higher of:

1. the highest ground plus 1299ft;

   or

2. the highest structure plus 1000ft; rounded up to the next 100ft, within 5nm of track.

Answers and Reference — Navigation

Paper 2

1	C	Flight plan, (PPL 3 Navigation; Navigation Principles 2: Time, Speed and Distance)
2	B	Flight plan, (PPL 3 Navigation; Aeronautical Maps; Scale and Distance)
3	C	Flight plan, (PPL 3 Navigation; Aeronautical Maps; Measurement of Direction)
4	B	Flight plan, (PPL 3 Navigation; Navigation Principles 1: The Triangle of Velocities)
5	C	Flight plan, (PPL 3 Navigation; Navigation Principles 1: The Triangle of Velocities)
6	A	PPL 3 Navigation; Fuel Planning; Fuel Planning
7	B	Study of map; (PPL3 Navigation, Vertical Navigation, Altimeter Settings)
8	C	Study of map
9	A	Study of map; (PPL2 Air Law; Rules of the Air and ATC; The Low Flying Rules)
10	A	Study of map
11	B	Study of map
12	A	Study of map; (PPL2 Air Law; Rules of the Air and ATC; Aerodrome Traffic Zones)
13	A	Study of map key
14	C	PPL3 Navigation; Fuel Planning; Fuel Volume Conversions
15	C	Study of map
16	A	PPL3 Navigation; Vertical Navigation; Vertical Navigation Calculations
17	A	Study of map and map key
18	A	PPL3 Navigation; Fuel Planning; Fuel Volume Conversions
19	A	Study of map key; (PPL2 Air Law; Airspace Restrictions; Prohibited, Restricted and Danger Areas)
20	C	Study of map and map key; (PPL2 Air Law; Airspace Restrictions; Other Hazards to Flight)

Answers and Reference

Navigation

Latitude and longitude are given as an aid to identification but where locations and facilities are marked on the chart, their charted positions should be used.

From	To	FL/Alt	Safety Alt ft amsl	Tas kt	W/V	Trk T	Drift	Hdg T	Var	Hdg M	GS kt	Dist nm	Time hr/min
Audley End N5200.52 E00013.57	Croft Farm N5205.13 W00208.15	2400	2400	95	190/15	273	9°S	264	4W	268	94	87	55
											Total		

Alternate

From	To	FL/Alt	Safety Alt	Tas	W/V	Trk T	Drift	Hdg T	Var	Hdg M	GS	Dist	Time
Croft Farm N5205.13 W00208.15	Ledbury N5200.17 W00228.50	2500	2500	95	210/10	249	4°S	245	4W	249	87	13	9

Note: Safety Altitude is derived from the higher of:

1. the highest ground plus 1299ft;

   or

2. the highest structure plus 1000ft; rounded up to the next 100ft, within 5nm of track.

Answers and Reference Navigation

Paper 3

1	B	Flight plan; (PPL 3 Navigation; Aeronautical Maps; Measurement of Direction)
2	B	Flight plan; (PPL 3 Navigation; Aeronautical Maps; Scale and Distance)
3	B	Flight plan; (PPL 3 Navigation; Navigation Principles 2: Time, Speed and Distance)
4	A	Flight plan; (PPL 3 Navigation; Fuel Planning; Fuel Planning)
5	B	PPL 3 Navigation; Performance; Fuel Planning
6	A	PPL 3 Navigation; Performance; Crosswind Component
7	B	Map, (PPL 3 Navigation; Navigation Principles 2: Time, Speed and Distance)
8	A	Study of map, (PPL 3 Navigation; Vertical Navigation; Obstructions)
9	B	Study of map
10	B	PPL 3 Navigation; Aeronautical Maps; Measurement of Direction
11	A	PPL2 Radiotelephony; En-Route Procedures; MATZs
12	A	PPL 3 Navigation; Fuel Planning; Fuel Planning
13	C	Study of mao
14	C	PPL3Navigation; Off-Track Calculations and Track Markings; The One in Sixty Rule
15	B	Study of map and map key,
16	C	PPL 3 Navigation; Vertical Navigation; Altimeter Settings
17	A	PPL3 Navigation; Vertical Navigation; Vertical Navigation Calculations
18	A	Flight plan; (PPL 3 Navigation; Vertical Navigation; Minimum Safety Altitude)
19	B	Study of map key
20	A	Study of map and map key

Answers and Reference

Navigation

Latitude and longitude are given as an aid to identification but where locations and facilities are marked on the chart, their charted positions should be used.

From	To	FL/Alt	Safety Alt ft amsl	Tas kt	W/V	Trk T	Drift	Hdg T	Var	Hdg M	GS kt	Dist nm	Time hr/min
Goodwood N5051.55 W00045.55	Grove N5136.28 W00126.09	3000	2300	85	250/20	330	12°S	318	4.5W	332.5	80	51	38
Grove N5136.28 W00126.09	Shobdon N5214.48 W00252.88	3500	2800	85	270/15	306	6°S	300	5W	305	72	66	55
											Total	117	93

Note: Safety Altitude is derived from the higher of:

1. the highest ground plus 1299ft;

    or

2. the highest structure plus 1000ft, rounded up to the next 100ft, within 5nm of track.

Answers and Reference   Navigation

Paper 4

1	A	Flight plan, (PPL 3 Navigation; Aeronautical Maps; Measurement of Direction)
2	C	Flight plan, (PPL 3 Navigation; Aeronautical Maps; Scale and Distance)
3	C	Flight plan, (PPL 3 Navigation; Navigation Principles 2: Time, Speed and Distance)
4	A	Flight plan, (PPL 3 Navigation; Fuel Planning; Fuel Planning *and* Fuel Volume Conversions)
5	B	PPL 3 Navigation; Performance; Fuel Planning
6	A	PPL 3 Navigation; Performance; Crosswind Component
7	C	PPL 3 Navigation; Navigation Principles 2: Time, Speed and Distance
8	B	Study of map and map key, (PPL 3 Navigation; Vertical Navigation; Obstructions)
9	C	Study of map
10	B	Study of map and map key
11	C	Study of map and map key, (PPL2 Air Law; Airspace Restrictions; Prohibited, Restricted and Danger Areas)
12	A	PPL 3 Navigation; Fuel Planning; Fuel Planning
13	C	Study of map
14	C	Study of map and map key
15	B	PPL 3 Navigation; Performance; Crosswind Component
16	C	PPL 3 Navigation; Performance; Crosswind Component
17	C	Study of Appendix A
18	A	Flight plan, (PPL 3 Navigation; Vertical Navigation; Minimum Safety Altitude)
19	A	Study of Appendix A
20	B	Study of Appendix A

Answers and Reference

Navigation

Latitude and longitude are given as an aid to identification but where locations and facilities are marked on the chart, their charted positions should be used.

From	To	FL/Alt	Safety Alt ft amsl	Tas kt	W/V	Trk T	Drift	Hdg T	Var	Hdg M	GS kt	Dist nm	Time hr/min
Shoreham N5050.07 W00017.67	Canterbury N5116.73 E00104.73	2000	2100	85	175/15	061	9°P	070	4W	074	90	56	37
Canterbury N5116.73 E00104.73	Stapleford N5139.15 E00009.35	2000	1900	85	190/20	304	8°S	292	4W	296	91	38	25
											Total	94	62

Note: Safety Altitude is derived from the higher of:

1. the highest ground plus 1299ft;
   or
2. the highest structure plus 1000ft; rounded up to the next 100ft, within 5nm of track.

Answers and Reference   Navigation

Paper 5

1	A	Flight plan, (PPL 3 Navigation; Aeronautical Maps; Scale and Distance)
2	C	Flight plan, (PPL 3 Navigation; Navigation Principles 1: The Triangle of Velocities)
3	B	Flight plan, (PPL 3 Navigation; Fuel Planning; Fuel Planning *and* Fuel Volume Conversions)
4	B	Flight plan, (PPL 3 Navigation; Aeronautical Maps; Measurement of Direction)
5	C	Study of map
6	A	Flight plan; (PPL3 Navigation, Vertical Navigation, Altimeter Settings)
7	C	Study of map; (PPL2 Air Law; Division of Airspace and Air Traffic Services; Airspace Classifications)
8	A	Study of map and map key
9	C	Study of map and map key, (PPL2 Air Law; Airspace Restrictions; Prohibited, Restricted and Danger Areas)
10	B	Flight plan, (PPL 3 Navigation; Navigation Principles 2: Time, Speed and Distance)
11	A	Flight plan, (PPL 3 Navigation; Aeronautical Maps; Measurement of Direction)
12	C	Study of map
13	C	Study of map; (PPL2 Air Law; Division of Airspace and Air Traffic Services; Airspace Classifications)
14	B	Flight plan; (PPL 3 Navigation; Fuel Planning; Fuel Planning)
15	B	Study of map; (PPL2 Air Law; Division of Airspace and Air Traffic Services; Airspace Classifications)
16	A	PPL2 Air Law; Rules of the Air and ATC; The Low Flying Rules
17	B	Study of map
18	A	Study of map and map key
19	B	PPL 3 Navigation; Fuel Planning; Fuel Planning
20	B	Study of map key

Answers and Reference — Navigation

Latitude and longitude are given as an aid to identification but where locations and facilities are marked on the chart, their charted positions should be used.

From	To	FL/Alt	Safety Alt ft amsl	Tas kt	W/V	Trk T	Drift	Hdg T	Var	Hdg M	GS kt	Dist nm	Time hr/min
Hucknall N5300.85 W00113.10	Hawarden N5310.68 W00258.67	3000	3200	85	260/15	279	3°S	276	5W	281	71	64	54
Hawarden N5310.68 W00258.67	Manchester N5321.22 W00216.50	2000	1800	90	280/20	067	7°S	060	5W	065	106	27	15
											Total	91	69

Note: Safety Altitude is derived from the higher of:

1. the highest ground plus 1299ft;

   or

2. the highest structure plus 1000ft; rounded up to the next 100ft, within 5nm of track.

216

Answers and Reference   Navigation

Paper 6

#	Ans	Reference
1	A	Flight plan, PPL3 Navigation; Aeronautical Maps; Converting Units of Distance
2	C	Flight plan, (PPL 3 Navigation; Navigation Principles 1: The Triangle of Velocities)
3	A	Flight plan, (PPL 3 Navigation; Aeronautical Maps; Measurement of Direction)
4	B	Flight plan, (PPL 3 Navigation; Navigation Principles 1: The Triangle of Velocities)
5	B	Flight plan, PPL3 Navigation; Aeronautical Maps; Converting Units of Distance
6	A	Flight plan, (PPL3 Navigation, Vertical Navigation, Altimeter Settings)
7	A	PPL 3 Navigation; Fuel Planning; Fuel Planning
8	B	Flight plan, (PPL 3 Navigation; Aeronautical Maps; Scale and Distance)
9	A	Flight plan, (PPL 3 Navigation; Navigation Principles 1: The Triangle of Velocities)
10	A	Study of map and map key, (PPL Navigation; Aeronautical Maps; Airfields)
11	C	Study of map and map key, (PPL2 Air Law; Airspace Restrictions; Other Hazards to Flight)
12	C	Study of map,
13	A	PPL2 Air Law, Airspace Restrictions; Other Hazards to Flight
14	B	PPL 3 Navigation; Navigation Principles 2: Time, Speed and Distance
15	C	Study of map and map key, (PPL2 Air Law; Airspace Restrictions; Prohibited, Restricted and Danger Areas
16	A	Study of map
17	A	Study of map key, (PPL 3 Navigation; Vertical Navigation; Minimum Safety Altitude)
18	B	Study of map, (PPL2 Air Law, Rules of the Air and ATC, The Low Flying Rules)
19	B	PPL 3 Navigation; Performance; Fuel Planning
20	C	Study of map

Answers and Reference

Navigation

Latitude and longitude are given as an aid to identification but where locations and facilities are marked on the chart, their charted positions should be used.

From	To	FL/Alt	Safety Alt ft amsl	Tas kt	W/V	Trk T	Drift	Hdg T	Var	Hdg M	GS kt	Dist nm	Time hr/min
Skegness N5310.40 E00020.00	Hucknall N5300.85 W00113.10	2000	1900	85	010/20	260	13°P	273	5W	278	89	57	38.5
Hucknall N5300.85 W00113.10	Netherthorpe N5319.02 W00111.77	2000	2100	85	350/15	003	2°S	001	5W	006	69	18	15.5
										Total		75	54

Note: Safety Altitude is derived from the higher of:

1. the highest ground plus 1299ft;

   or

2. the highest structure plus 1000ft; rounded up to the next 100ft, within 5nm of track.

218

Answers and Reference Navigation

Paper 7

1	B	Flight plan, (PPL 3 Navigation; Aeronautical Maps; Measurement of Direction)
2	A	Flight plan, (PPL 3 Navigation; Navigation Principles 1: The Triangle of Velocities)
3	B	Flight plan, (PPL 3 Navigation; Navigation Principles 1: The Triangle of Velocities)
4	B	Flight plan, (PPL 3 Navigation; Fuel Planning; Fuel Planning *and* Fuel Volume Conversions)
5	A	PPL 3 Navigation; Performance; Fuel Planning *and* Weight and Balance
6	A	PPL 3 Navigation; Performance; Crosswind Component
7	A	PPL 3 Navigation; Navigation Principles 2: Time, Speed and Distance
8	A	PPL3 Navigation; Off-Track Calculations and Track Markings; The One in Sixty Rule
9	B	Study of map; (PPL2 Air Law; Rules of the Air and ATC; The Low Flying Rules)
10	A	Study of map and map key
11	C	Study of map; (PPL2 Air Law; Rules of the Air and ATC; Aerodrome Traffic Zones)
12	C	PPL3 Navigation; Off-Track Calculations and Track Markings; The One in Sixty Rule
13	A	Study of map; (PPL2 Air Law; Division of Airspace and Air Traffic Services; Airspace Classifications)
14	C	Study of map
15	B	Study of map key
16	A	PPL3 Navigation; Vertical Navigation; Vertical Navigation Calculations
17	B	PPL 3 Navigation; Performance; Crosswind Component
18	B	Study of map key; (PPL2 Air Law; Airspace Restrictions; Other Hazards to Flight)
19	B	Study of appendix A
20	A	Study of appendix A

Answers and Reference

Navigation

Latitude and longitude are given as an aid to identification but where locations and facilities are marked on the chart, their charted positions should be used.

From	To	FL/Alt	Safety Alt ft amsl	Tas kt	W/V	Trk T	Drift	Hdg T	Var	Hdg M	GS kt	Dist nm	Time hr/min
Bournemouth N5046.80 W00150.55	Dunkeswell N5051.60 W00314.08	2000	2600	90	220/20	275	10°S	265	5W	270	77	53	41.5
Dunkeswell N5051.60 W00314.08	Bristol N5122.96 W00243.15	1500	3000	95	260/25	031	13°S	018	5W	023	109	37	20.5
										Total		90	62

Note: Safety Altitude is derived from the higher of:

1. the highest ground plus 1299ft;

   or

2. the highest structure plus 1000ft, rounded up to the next 100ft, within 5nm of track.

220

Answers and Reference Navigation

Paper 8

1	B	Flight plan, (PPL 3 Navigation; Navigation Principles 1: The Triangle of Velocities)
2	A	Flight plan, (PPL 3 Navigation; Navigation Principles 1: The Triangle of Velocities)
3	C	Flight plan, (PPL 3 Navigation; Navigation Principles 1: The Triangle of Velocities)
4	C	Study of map; (PPL3 Navigation, Vertical Navigation, Altimeter Settings)
5	B	Flight plan, (PPL 3 Navigation; Navigation Principles 2: Time, Speed and Distance)
6	C	Study of map and map key
7	C	PPL3 Navigation; Vertical Navigation; Vertical Navigation Calculations
8	B	Study of map and map key, (PPL 3 Navigation; Vertical Navigation; Obstructions)
9	B	Flight plan, (PPL 3 Navigation; Fuel Planning; Fuel Planning *and* Fuel Volume Conversions)
10	B	PPL3 Navigation; Off-Track Calculations and Track Markings; The One in Sixty Rule
11	C	Flight plan, (PPL 3 Navigation; Aeronautical Maps; Measurement of Direction)
12	C	Flight plan, PPL3 Navigation; Aeronautical Maps; Converting Units of Distance
13	B	Study of map; (PPL2 Air Law; Rules of the Air and ATC; Aerodrome Traffic Zones)
14	B	Study of map and map key, (PPL2 Air Law; Rules of the Air and ATC; The Low Flying Rules)
15	C	Study of map
16	C	PPL 3 Navigation; Performance; Fuel Planning *and* Weight and Balance
17	A	Study of map and map key
18	C	Study of map and map key
19	C	Study of map key, (PPL 3 Navigation; Vertical Navigation; Minimum Safety Altitude)
20	A	PPL2 Air Law; Rules of the Air and ATC; Aerodrome Traffic Zones

Answers and Reference

Navigation

Latitude and longitude are given as an aid to identification but where locations and facilities are marked on the chart, their charted positions should be used.

From	To	FL/Alt	Safety Alt ft amsl	Tas kt	W/V	Trk T	Drift	Hdg T	Var	Hdg M	GS kt	Dist nm	Time hr/min
Gloucester Staverton N5153.65 W00210.03	Northampton Sywell N5218.29 W00047.48	3000	2200	92	190/22	064	12°P	076	5W	081	103	56	32.5
Northampton Sywell N5218.29 W00047.48	Cambridge N5212.30 E00010.50	2000	2000	90	180/18	099	11°P	110	5W	115	85	36	25.5
										Total		92	58

Note: Safety Altitude is derived from the higher of:

1   the highest ground plus 1299ft;

    or

2   the highest structure plus 1000ft; rounded up to the next 100ft, within 5nm of track.

222

Answers and Reference — Navigation

Paper 9

1	B	Flight plan, (PPL 3 Navigation; Aeronautical Maps; Measurement of Direction)
2	A	Flight plan, (PPL 3 Navigation; Navigation Principles 1: The Triangle of Velocities)
3	A	Flight plan, (PPL 3 Navigation; Navigation Principles 1: The Triangle of Velocities)
4	A	Flight plan, PPL3 Navigation; Aeronautical Maps; Converting Units of Distance
5	C	Flight plan, (PPL 3 Navigation; Navigation Principles 2: Time, Speed and Distance)
6	C	PPL 3 Navigation; Performance; Fuel Planning
7	A	Study of map
8	B	Study of map and map key, (PPL 3 Navigation; Vertical Navigation; Minimum Safety Altitude)
9	C	Study of map and map key
10	A	Study of map and map key
11	C	Flight plan, (PPL 3 Navigation; Aeronautical Maps; Measurement of Direction)
12	A	Flight plan, (PPL 3 Navigation; Navigation Principles 2: Time, Speed and Distance)
13	B	Study of map, (PPL2 Air Law; Division of Airspace and Air Traffic Services; Airspace Classifications)
14	A	PPL 3 Navigation; Navigation Principles 2: Time, Speed and Distance
15	C	PPL3 Navigation; Vertical Navigation; Vertical Navigation Calculations
16	A	PPL2 Radiotelephony; En-Route Procedures; MATZs
17	B	PPL 3 Navigation; Performance; Crosswind Component
18	C	Study of appendix A
19	A	Study of appendix A
20	A	Study of appendix A

Answers and Reference
Navigation

Latitude and longitude are given as an aid to identification but where locations and facilities are marked on the chart, their charted positions should be used.

From	To	FL/Alt	Safety Alt ft amsl	Tas kt	W/V	Trk T	Drift	Hdg T	Var	Hdg M	GS kt	Dist nm	Time hr/min
Bembridge IOW N5040.68 W00106.55	Thruxton N5112.62 W00135.90	3000ft	2100	85	270/18	330	12°S	318	5W	323	75	37	29.5
Thruxton N5112.62 W00135.90	Blackbushe N5119.43 W00050.85	2500ft	2300	82	290/22	076	8°S	068	5W	073	100	29	17.5
											Total	66	47

Note: Safety Altitude is derived from the higher of:

1 the highest ground plus 1299ft;

 or

2 the highest structure plus 1000ft; rounded up to the next 100ft, within 5nm of track.

Answers and Reference Navigation

Paper 10

1	B	Flight plan, (PPL 3 Navigation; Aeronautical Maps; Measurement of Direction)
2	A	Flight plan, (PPL 3 Navigation; Navigation Principles 1: The Triangle of Velocities)
3	B	Flight plan, (PPL 3 Navigation; Navigation Principles 1: The Triangle of Velocities)
4	B	Flight plan, PPL3 Navigation; Aeronautical Maps; Converting Units of Distance
5	C	Flight plan, (PPL 3 Navigation; Navigation Principles 2: Time, Speed and Distance)
6	A	PPL 3 Navigation; Fuel Planning; Fuel Planning *and* Fuel Volume Conversions
7	B	Flight plan, PPL3 Navigation; Vertical Navigation; Altimeter Settings
8	C	Study of map
9	B	Study of map and map key, (PPL2 Air Law; Division of Airspace and Air Traffic Services; Airspace Classifications)
10	C	PPL2 Radiotelephony, Pre-flight, Use of the AIP *also* Arrival/Traffic Pattern Procedures, Inbound to an Airfield
11	B	Flight plan, (PPL 3 Navigation; Aeronautical Maps; Measurement of Direction)
12	A	Flight plan, (PPL 3 Navigation; Navigation Principles 1: The Triangle of Velocities)
13	C	Flight plan, PPL3 Navigation; Aeronautical Maps; Converting Units of Distance
14	C	Flight plan, (PPL 3 Navigation; Navigation Principles 2: Time, Speed and Distance)
15	B	PPL 3 Navigation; Performance; Fuel Planning
16	B	Flight plan, PPL3 Navigation; Vertical Navigation; Altimeter Settings
17	A	Study of map
18	A	Study of map and map key, (PPL 3 Navigation; Vertical Navigation; Obstructions)
19	B	PPL3 Navigation; Vertical Navigation; Vertical Navigation Calculations
20	C	PPL 3 Navigation; Performance; Crosswind Component

Answers and Reference — Navigation

Latitude and longitude are given as an aid to identification but where locations and facilities are marked on the chart, their charted positions should be used.

From	To	FL/Alt	Safety Alt ft amsl	Tas kt	W/V	Trk T	Drift	Hdg T	Var	Hdg M	GS kt	Dist nm	Time hr/min
Newcastle N5502.25 W00141.50	Carlisle N5456.25 W0248.55	FL60	3500	92	240/25	261	5°S	256	6W	261	69	39	34
Carlisle N5456.25 W0248.55	Barrow (Walney Island) N5407.87 W0315.81	FL60	4600	91	245/21	199	10°P	209	6W	215	76	51	40
										Total		90	74

Note: Safety Altitude is derived from the higher of:

1. the highest ground plus 1299ft;

    or

2. the highest structure plus 1000ft; rounded up to the next 100ft, within 5nm of track.

226

Aircraft General (Aeroplanes)

Paper 1

#	Ans	Reference
1	C	PPL4 Technical; The Atmosphere and Properties of Air; The Atmosphere
2	A	PPL4 Technical; The Atmosphere and Properties of Air; The Atmosphere
3	C	PPL4 Technical; The Atmosphere and Properties of Air; The Atmosphere
4	B	PPL4 Technical; The Atmosphere and Properties of Air; The Atmosphere *also* Loading and Performance; Take-off Performance
5	C	PPL4 Technical; Principles of Flight – The Four Forces; The Four Forces Acting on an Aircraft in Flight
6	A	PPL4 Technical; Take-off and Initial Climb; Forces in the Take-off Run
7	A	PPL4 Technical; Principles of Flight – The Four Forces; Lift
8	B	PPL4 Technical; Stability and Control; The Three Planes of Movement *also* Control in Roll
9	B	PPL4 Technical; Stalling; Factors Effecting Stalling Airspeed
10	C	PPL4 Technical; Stability and Control; Control in Pitch
11	B	PPL4 Technical; Principles of Flight – The Four Forces; Lift
12	B	PPL4 Technical; The Flying Controls; The Elevator
13	A	PPL4 Technical; The Airframe; Wing Design
14	C	PPL4 Technical; Stability and Control; Stability in Yaw
15	C	PPL4 Technical; The Aero Engine and Propeller; Carburettor Icing *also* Engine Handling; Descent
16	B	PPL4 Technical; Engine Handling; In the Cruise
17	A	PPL4 Technical; Loading and Performance; Cruise Performance
18	C	PPL4 Technical; Descending; Gliding Performance
19	B	PPL4 Technical; Engine Handling; Climbing
20	B	PPL4 Technical; The Aero Engine and Propeller; The Ignition System
21	A	PPL4 Technical; The Electrical System; Electrical Systems
22	A	PPL4 Technical; The Electrical System; Aircraft Batteries
23	C	PPL4 Technical; The Electrical System; Electrical Systems
24	C	PPL4 Technical; The Electrical System; Electrical Failure
25	C	PPL4 Technical; Stability and Control; Stability in Pitch *also* Stalling; Factors Effecting Stalling Airspeed
26	B	PPL4 Technical; The Aircraft Instruments; The Suction System
27	A	PPL4 Technical; The Aircraft Instruments; The Turn Co-ordinator
28	C	PPL4 Technical; The Aircraft Instruments; The Pitot-Static System
29	B	PPL4 Technical; Turning; The Basics
30	A	PPL4 Technical; The Aircraft Instruments; The Attitude Indicator
31	C	PPL4 Technical; The Aero Engine and Propeller; Fuel Grades
32	A	PPL4 Technical; The Aircraft Instruments; The Suction System
33	B	PPL4 Technical; The Aircraft Instruments; The Suction System
34	B	PPL4 Technical; The Aircraft Instruments; The Pitot-Static System
35	A	PPL4 Technical; The Aero Engine and Propeller; The Oil System
36	A	PPL4 Technical; The Aero Engine and Propeller; Propellers
37	A	PPL4 Technical; The Undercarriage; Undercarriage Legs
38	C	PPL4 Technical; The Electrical System; The Master Switch
39	B	PPL4 Technical; The Aircraft Instruments; The Pitot-Static System
40	B	PPL4 Technical; Loading and Performance; Centre of Gravity

Answers and Reference Aircraft General (Aeroplanes)

41	C	PPL4 Technical; Loading and Performance; Weight Limits
42	C	PPL4 Technical; The Aero Engine and Propeller; The Induction System
43	B	PPL4 Technical; Engine Handling; Starting
44	C	PPL4 Technical; The Heating and Ventilation Systems; The Heating and Ventilation System
45	B	PPL4 Technical; Engine Handling; In The Cruise
46	C	PPL4 Technical; Airworthiness; Aircraft Documents
47	C	PPL4 Technical; The Aero Engine and Propeller; Fuel System Serviceability Checks and Handling
48	A	PPL4 Technical; Safety Equipment; Survival Equipment
49	B	PPL4 Technical; Airworthiness; Aircraft Documents
50	C	PPL4 Technical; The Aero Engine and Propeller; Carburettor Icing

Answers and Reference Aircraft General (Aeroplanes)

Paper 2

1	B	PPL4 Technical; The Atmosphere and Properties of Air; The Atmosphere
2	A	PPL4 Technical; The Atmosphere and Properties of Air; The Atmosphere
3	A	PPL4 Technical; The Atmosphere and Properties of Air; The Atmosphere
4	B	PPL4 Technical; The Atmosphere and Properties of Air; The Atmosphere
5	C	PPL4 Technical; Principles of Flight – The Four Forces; Lift
6	C	PPL4 Technical; The Atmosphere and Properties of Air; The Atmosphere
7	A	PPL4 Technical; Level Flight; Power + Attitude = Performance
8	A	PPL4 Technical; Principles of Flight – The Four Forces; Lift
9	A	PPL4 Technical; Principles of Flight – The Four Forces; Lift
10	B	PPL4 Technical; The Aircraft Instruments; The Airspeed Indicator (ASI)
11	C	PPL4 Technical; Principles of Flight – The Four Forces; Drag
12	C	PPL4 Technical; The Flying Controls; The Flaps
13	A	PPL4 Technical; Principles of Flight – The Four Forces; Weight
14	A	PPL4 Technical; Principles of Flight – The Four Forces; Lift
15	A	PPL4 Technical; Climbing; Climb Performance
16	A	PPL4 Technical; Stalling; Factors Effecting Stalling Airspeed *and* Stall Accident Scenarios
17	A	PPL4 Technical; Principles of Flight – The Four Forces; Drag
18	C	PPL4 Technical; The Flying Controls; The Elevator
19	B	PPL4 Technical; The Flying Controls; Slats, Slots and Airbrakes *and* Stalling; Factors Effecting Stalling Airspeed
20	C	PPL4 Technical; Principles of Flight – The Four Forces; Drag
21	B	PPL4 Technical; Loading and Performance; Cruise Performance
22	A	PPL4 Technical; Engine Handling; Starting
23	B	PPL4 Technical; The Flying Controls; The Elevator
24	B	PPL4 Technical; The Flying Controls; The Elevator
25	C	PPL4 Technical; Stability and Control; The Three Planes of Movement *also* Stability in Pitch
26	B	PPL4 Technical; Stability and Control; Stability in Yaw
27	B	PPL4 Technical; The Aero Engine and Propeller; The Fuel System
28	C	PPL4 Technical; The Aero Engine and Propeller; The Oil System
29	B	PPL4 Technical; Stalling; Factors Effecting Stalling Airspeed
30	A	PPL4 Technical; Engine Handling; In the Cruise
31	A	PPL4 Technical; The Aero Engine and Propeller; Propellers
32	B	PPL4 Technical; Descending; Gliding Performance
33	A	PPL4 Technical; Engine Handling; In the Cruise
34	A	PPL4 Technical; Principles of Flight – The Four Forces; Lift
35	C	PPL4 Technical; The Aero Engine and Propeller; The Ignition System
36	B	PPL4 Technical; Engine Handling; In the Cruise *and* After-landing and Shut Down
37	A	PPL4 Technical; The Electrical System; Electrical Systems
38	B	PPL4 Technical; The Aircraft Instruments; The Magnetic Compass
39	A	PPL4 Technical; Spinning; Spin Recovery
40	C	PPL4 Technical; Stability and Control; Stability in Yaw
41	A	PPL4 Technical; The Aircraft Instruments; The Pitot-Static System
42	C	PPL4 Technical; The Aero Engine and Propeller; The Ignition System
43	B	PPL4 Technical; The Aero Engine and Propeller; The Otto Cycle
44	B	PPL4 Technical; Loading and Performance; Centre of Gravity

Answers and Reference Aircraft General (Aeroplanes)

45	B	PPL4 Technical; Safety Equipment; Fire Extinguishers
46	A	PPL4 Technical; Engine Handling; Taxying, Power Checks, Take-off
47	C	PPL4 Technical; Safety Equipment; Survival Equipment
48	B	PPL4 Technical; Loading and Performance; Centre of Gravity
49	B	PPL4 Technical; Engine Handling; Engine Troubleshooting
50	A	PPL4 Technical; Airworthiness; Pilot Maintenance

Answers and Reference   Aircraft General (Aeroplanes)

Paper 3

1	B	PPL4 Technical; Principles of Flight – The Four Forces; The Four Forces Acting on an Aircraft in Flight
2	A	PPL4 Technical; Principles of Flight – The Four Forces; The Four Forces Acting on an Aircraft in Flight
3	A	PPL4 Technical; Principles of Flight – The Four Forces; Weight
4	A	PPL4 Technical; Principles of Flight – The Four Forces; Lift
5	C	PPL4 Technical; Principles of Flight – The Four Forces; Drag
6	B	PPL4 Technical; Level Flight; Power + Attitude = Performance
7	C	PPL4 Technical; Climbing; Climb Performance
8	A	PPL4 Technical; Stability and Control; Control in Roll
9	A	PPL4 Technical; Stability and Control; Control in Pitch
10	B	PPL4 Technical; The Flying Controls; The Elevator
11	C	PPL4 Technical; Principles of Flight – The Four Forces; Lift
12	C	PPL4 Technical; The Airframe; Wing Design
13	B	PPL4 Technical; Stability and Control; Stability in Pitch
14	A	PPL4 Technical; Stability and Control; The Three Planes of Movement
15	B	PPL4 Technical; Turning; The Basics
16	B	PPL4 Technical; Stalling; Symptoms of the Stall
17	B	PPL4 Technical; The Aero Engine and Propeller; The Otto Cycle
18	A	PPL4 Technical; The Aero Engine and Propeller; The Otto Cycle
19	A	PPL4 Technical; Loading and Performance; Centre of Gravity
20	B	PPL4 Technical; The Aero Engine and Propeller; Principles of Piston Engines
21	A	PPL4 Technical; Loading and Performance; Cruise Performance
22	B	PPL4 Technical; Stalling; The Basics
23	A	PPL4 Technical; The Flying Controls; Slats, Slots and Airbrakes
24	B	PPL4 Technical; The Flying Controls; The Elevator
25	B	PPL4 Technical; The Flying Controls; The Elevator
26	C	PPL4 Technical; Safety Equipment; Survival Equipment
27	B	PPL4 Technical; The Atmosphere and Properties of Air; Air in Motion
28	B	PPL4 Technical; Engine Handling; In the Cruise
29	C	PPL4 Technical; Level Flight; Power + Attitude = Performance
30	C	PPL4 Technical; Descending; Gliding Performance
31	B	PPL4 Technical; Climbing; Climb Performance
32	C	PPL4 Technical; The Aero Engine and Propeller; Carburettor Icing *also* Engine Handling; Descent
33	B	PPL4 Technical; Stalling; Stall Accident Scenarios
34	A	PPL4 Technical; Stability and Control; The Three Planes of Movement *also* Stability in Roll
35	C	PPL4 Technical; The Aero Engine and Propeller; Fuel System Serviceability, Checks and Handling
36	B	PPL4 Technical; The Aero Engine and Propeller; Fuel System Serviceability, Checks and Handling
37	B	PPL4 Technical; The Electrical System; The Master Switch
38	A	PPL4 Technical; The Aero Engine and Propeller; Fuel System Serviceability, Checks and Handling
39	C	PPL4 Technical; Descending; Gliding Performance
40	B	PPL4 Technical; The Undercarriage; Serviceability Checks
41	A	PPL4 Technical; Loading and Performance; Take-off Performance *and* Landing Performance
42	A	PPL4 Technical; The Aero Engine and Propeller; Fuel Grades
43	B	PPL4 Technical; Loading and Performance; Centre of Gravity

Answers and Reference Aircraft General (Aeroplanes)

44	B	PPL4 Technical; Safety Equipment; Fire Extinguishers
45	C	PPL4 Technical; Airworthiness; Aircraft Documents
46	A	PPL4 Technical; The Electrical System; Aircraft Batteries
47	B	PPL4 Technical; Airworthiness; Aircraft Documents
48	C	PPL4 Technical; Loading and Performance; Take-off Performance
49	B	PPL4 Technical; The Heating and Ventilation Systems; The Heating and Ventilation System
50	A	PPL4 Technical; The Electrical System; Electrical Systems

Answers and Reference — Aircraft General (Aeroplanes)

Paper 4

1	A	PPL4 Technical; The Atmosphere and Properties of Air; The Atmosphere
2	B	PPL4 Technical; The Atmosphere and Properties of Air; The Atmosphere
3	B	PPL4 Technical; The Atmosphere and Properties of Air; The Atmosphere
4	C	PPL4 Technical; Stability and Control; The Three Planes of Movement *also* Stability in Yaw
5	B	PPL4 Technical; Descending; Gliding Performance
6	A	PPL4 Technical; Loading and Performance; Take-off Performance
7	B	PPL4 Technical; The Flying Controls; Slats, Slots and Airbrakes
8	A	PPL4 Technical; Stability and Control; The Three Planes of Movement
9	C	PPL4 Technical; The Flying Controls; Slats, Slots and Airbrakes
10	B	PPL4 Technical; The Aero Engine and Propeller; Carburettor Icing
11	B	PPL4 Technical; The Flying Controls; The Rudder
12	A	PPL4 Technical; The Aero Engine and Propeller; Propellers
13	C	PPL4 Technical; The Aero Engine and Propeller; Propellers
14	B	PPL4 Technical; Stability and Control; Control in Roll
15	B	PPL4 Technical; Engine Handling; Starting
16	C	PPL4 Technical; Stalling; Factors Effecting Stalling Airspeed
17	C	PPL4 Technical; Descending; Gliding Performance
18	A	PPL4 Technical; The Atmosphere and Properties of Air; The Atmosphere
19	B	PPL4 Technical; The Flying Controls; The Elevator
20	C	PPL4 Technical; The Electrical System; Aircraft Batteries
21	B	PPL4 Technical; The Aero Engine and Propeller; Fuel System Serviceability Checks and Handling
22	C	PPL4 Technical; The Aero Engine and Propeller; The Ignition System
23	A	PPL4 Technical; Engine Handling; In the Cruise
24	A	PPL4 Technical; The Aircraft Instruments; The Altimeter
25	B	PPL4 Technical; The Aircraft Instruments; The Airspeed Indicator (ASI)
26	B	PPL4 Technical; The Aircraft Instruments; The Vertical Speed Indicator (VSI)
27	A	PPL4 Technical; The Electrical System; Electrical Systems
28	B	PPL4 Technical; Airworthiness; Aircraft Documents
29	A	PPL4 Technical; The Aero Engine and Propeller; Propellers
30	B	PPL4 Technical; The Aircraft Instruments; The Heading Indicator
31	A	PPL4 Technical; The Aircraft Instruments; The Altimeter
32	C	PPL4 Technical; The Flying Controls; Control Locks
33	B	PPL4 Technical; Loading and Performance; Centre of Gravity
34	A	PPL4 Technical; Climbing; Climb Performance
35	C	PPL4 Technical; Stalling; The Basics
36	C	PPL4 Technical; Stalling; Factors Effecting Stalling Airspeed *and* Stall Accident Scenarios
37	C	PPL4 Technical; The Aircraft Instruments; The Pitot-Static System
38	C	PPL4 Technical; Stability and Control; Stability in Pitch
39	A	PPL4 Technical; Take-off and Initial Climb; Forces in the Take-off Run
40	C	PPL4 Technical; Safety Equipment; Fire Extinguishers
41	C	PPL4 Technical; Climbing; The Basics
42	B	PPL4 Technical; Loading and Performance; Centre of Gravity
43	B	PPL4 Technical; Loading and Performance; Weight Limits
44	C	PPL4 Technical; Climbing; Climb Performance

Answers and Reference Aircraft General (Aeroplanes)

45 A PPL4 Technical; Loading and Performance; Take-off Performance *and* Landing Performance
46 C PPL4 Technical; Airworthiness; Pilot Maintenance
47 B PPL4 Technical; Loading and Performance; Take-off Performance
48 A PPL4 Technical; The Electrical System; Electrical Systems
49 B PPL4 Technical; Airworthiness; Pilot Maintenance
50 B PPL4 Technical; Airworthiness; Aircraft Documents

Human Performance and Limitations

Paper 1

1	B	PPL5 Human Factors; The Functions of the Body (Basic Physiology); The breathing machine
2	C	PPL5 Human Factors; The Functions of the Body (Basic Physiology); Breathing problems and flight at high altitude
3	B	PPL5 Human Factors; The Functions of the Body (Basic Physiology); Breathing problems and flight at high altitude
4	C	PPL5 Human Factors; The Functions of the Body (Basic Physiology); The Ears
5	B	PPL5 Human Factors; The Functions of the Body (Basic Physiology); Breathing problems and flight at high altitude
6	A	PPL5 Human Factors; The Functions of the Body (Basic Physiology); Breathing problems and flight at high altitude
7	C	PPL5 Human Factors; The Functions of the Body (Basic Physiology); The eyes
8	C	PPL5 Human Factors; The Functions of the Body (Basic Physiology); Breathing problems and flight at high altitude
9	C	PPL5 Human Factors; Health and Flying; Toxic hazards
10	A	PPL5 Human Factors; The Functions of the Body (Basic Physiology); The Ears
11	A	PPL5 Human Factors; Cockpit Design and Procedures; Eye datum
12	A	PPL5 Human Factors; The Functions of the Mind (Basic Psychology); Lookout
13	C	PPL5 Human Factors; Safety and Survival Equipment; Passenger briefing and the pilot's responsibilities
14	A	PPL5 Human Factors; The Functions of the Mind (Basic Psychology); Lookout
15	C	PPL5 Human Factors; The Functions of the Mind (Basic Psychology); Lookout
16	B	PPL5 Human Factors; Safety and Survival Equipment; Motion Sickness
17	C	PPL5 Human Factors; Health and Flying; Common ailments and medication
18	C	PPL5 Human Factors; The Functions of the Mind (Basic Psychology); Spatial disorientation, visual illusions
19	B	PPL5 Human Factors; Health and Flying; Incapacitation
20	A	PPL5 Human Factors; The Functions of the Body (Basic Physiology); 'G' Effects

Answers and Reference Human Performance and Limitations

Paper 2

1	C	PPL5 Human Factors; The Functions of the Body (Basic Physiology); Composition of the atmosphere
2	B	PPL5 Human Factors; The Functions of the Body (Basic Physiology); Breathing problems and flight at high altitude
3	A	PPL5 Human Factors; The Functions of the Body (Basic Physiology); Breathing problems and flight at high altitude
4	B	PPL5 Human Factors; The Functions of the Body (Basic Physiology); Breathing problems and flight at high altitude
5	C	PPL5 Human Factors; The Functions of the Body (Basic Physiology); Breathing problems and flight at high altitude
6	B	PPL5 Human Factors; The Functions of the Mind (Basic Psychology); Spatial disorientation, visual illusions
7	B	PPL5 Human Factors; Health and Flying; Toxic hazards
8	A	PPL5 Human Factors; The Functions of the Mind (Basic Psychology); Lookout
9	C	PPL5 Human Factors; The Functions of the Body (Basic Physiology); The breathing machine
10	B	PPL5 Human Factors; The Functions of the Body (Basic Physiology); Breathing problems and flight at high altitude
11	A	PPL5 Human Factors; The Functions of the Mind (Basic Psychology); Lookout
12	C	PPL5 Human Factors; The Functions of the Mind (Basic Psychology); Lookout
13	A	PPL5 Human Factors; The Functions of the Body (Basic Physiology); The eyes
14	C	PPL5 Human Factors; Stress and Managing Stress; Stress, arousal and performance
15	A	PPL5 Human Factors; Health and Flying; Incapacitation
16	A	PPL5 Human Factors; Health and Flying; Common ailments and medication
17	A	PPL5 Human Factors; Health and Flying; Common ailments and medication
18	B	PPL5 Human Factors; Personalities and Cockpit Resource Management; Group decision making
19	A	PPL5 Human Factors; The Functions of the Mind (Basic Psychology); Spatial disorientation, visual illusions
20	A	PPL5 Human Factors; Health and Flying; Common ailments and medication

Answers and Reference   Human Performance and Limitations

Paper 3

#	Ans	Reference
1	A	PPL5 Human Factors; The Functions of the Body (Basic Physiology); Composition of the atmosphere
2	B	PPL5 Human Factors; The Functions of the Body (Basic Physiology); Composition of the atmosphere
3	A	PPL5 Human Factors; The Functions of the Body (Basic Physiology); The breathing machine
4	C	PPL5 Human Factors; The Functions of the Body (Basic Physiology); The breathing machine
5	B	PPL5 Human Factors; The Functions of the Body (Basic Physiology); The breathing machine
6	B	PPL5 Human Factors; The Functions of the Body (Basic Physiology); Composition of the atmosphere
7	A	PPL5 Human Factors; The Functions of the Body (Basic Physiology); The breathing machine
8	C	PPL5 Human Factors; The Functions of the Body (Basic Physiology); The breathing machine
9	C	PPL5 Human Factors; Cockpit Design and Procedures; Flight instrument displays
10	A	PPL5 Human Factors; The Functions of the Body (Basic Physiology); The eyes
11	C	PPL5 Human Factors; The Functions of the Mind (Basic Psychology); Situational awareness, confirmation bias
12	A	PPL5 Human Factors; Health and Flying; Diet and Health
13	B	PPL5 Human Factors; Health and Flying; Diet and Health
14	A	PPL5 Human Factors; Health and Flying; Alcohol and Drugs
15	C	PPL5 Human Factors; Health and Flying; Common ailments and medication
16	B	PPL5 Human Factors; The Functions of the Body (Basic Physiology); Breathing problems and flight at high altitude
17	B	PPL5 Human Factors; Personalities and Cockpit Resource Management; Hazardous attitudes
18	A	PPL5 Human Factors; Health and Flying; Alcohol and Drugs
19	C	PPL5 Human Factors; The Functions of the Mind (Basic Psychology); Lookout
20	C	PPL5 Human Factors; Cockpit Design and Procedures; Flight instrument displays

Paper 4

#	Ans	Reference
1	B	PPL5 Human Factors; The Functions of the Body (Basic Physiology); Breathing problems and flight at high altitude
2	A	PPL5 Human Factors; The Functions of the Body (Basic Physiology); Breathing problems and flight at high altitude
3	A	PPL5 Human Factors; Cockpit Design and Procedures; Controls
4	C	PPL5 Human Factors; The Functions of the Body (Basic Physiology); The eyes
5	B	PPL5 Human Factors; The Functions of the Body (Basic Physiology); Composition of the atmosphere
6	A	PPL5 Human Factors; Health and Flying; Common ailments and medication
7	A	PPL5 Human Factors; Safety and Survival Equipment; Head protection
8	A	PPL5 Human Factors; Cockpit Design and Procedures; Eye datum
9	C	PPL5 Human Factors; Health and Flying; Common ailments and medication
10	B	PPL5 Human Factors; The Functions of the Mind (Basic Psychology); Situational awareness, confirmation bias
11	B	PPL5 Human Factors; The Functions of the Mind (Basic Psychology); Lookout
12	A	PPL5 Human Factors; The Functions of the Body (Basic Physiology); Breathing problems and flight at high altitude
13	A	PPL5 Human Factors; Stress and Managing Stress; Stress, arousal and performance
14	B	PPL5 Human Factors; Stress and Managing Stress; Stress, arousal and performance
15	C	PPL5 Human Factors; Cockpit Design and Procedures; Eye datum
16	A	PPL5 Human Factors; Safety and Survival Equipment; Motion Sickness
17	B	PPL5 Human Factors; The Functions of the Body (Basic Physiology); The Ears
18	A	PPL5 Human Factors; Health and Flying; Alcohol and Drugs
19	B	PPL5 Human Factors; The Functions of the Body (Basic Physiology); Breathing problems and flight at high altitude
20	C	PPL5 Human Factors; Cockpit Design and Procedures; Flight instrument displays

Answers and Reference Human Performance and Limitations

Paper 5

1	B	PPL5 Human Factors; The Functions of the Body (Basic Physiology); Breathing problems and flight at high altitude
2	C	PPL5 Human Factors; Health and Flying; Alcohol and Drugs
3	A	PPL5 Human Factors; The Functions of the Body (Basic Physiology); Breathing problems and flight at high altitude
4	C	PPL5 Human Factors; The Functions of the Mind (Basic Psychology); Spatial disorientation, visual illusions
5	C	PPL5 Human Factors; Cockpit Design and Procedures; Flight instrument displays
6	C	PPL5 Human Factors; The Functions of the Body (Basic Physiology); Breathing problems and flight at high altitude
7	B	PPL5 Human Factors; Safety and Survival Equipment; Passenger briefing and the pilot's responsibilities
8	A	PPL5 Human Factors; Safety and Survival Equipment; Seat belts and harnesses
9	B	PPL5 Human Factors; The Functions of the Mind (Basic Psychology); Lookout
10	C	PPL5 Human Factors; Safety and Survival Equipment; Motion Sickness
11	A	PPL5 Human Factors; Safety and Survival Equipment; Passenger briefing and the pilot's responsibilities
12	B	PPL5 Human Factors; The Functions of the Mind (Basic Psychology); Spatial disorientation, visual illusions
13	C	PPL5 Human Factors; Cockpit Design and Procedures; Eye datum
14	C	PPL5 Human Factors; The Functions of the Mind (Basic Psychology); Lookout
15	C	PPL5 Human Factors; The Functions of the Mind (Basic Psychology); Lookout
16	C	PPL5 Human Factors; Personalities and Cockpit Resource Management; Group decision making
17	C	PPL5 Human Factors; Personalities and Cockpit Resource Management; Group decision making
18	B	PPL5 Human Factors; The Functions of the Body (Basic Physiology); The eyes
19	B	PPL5 Human Factors; The Functions of the Mind (Basic Psychology); Lookout
20	A	PPL5 Human Factors; The Functions of the Mind (Basic Psychology); Spatial disorientation, visual illusions

Answers and Reference　　　　　　　　　　　　　　　　　　Human Performance and Limitations

Paper 6

1	C	PPL5 Human Factors; The Functions of the Body (Basic Physiology); Breathing problems and flight at high altitude
2	B	PPL5 Human Factors; The Functions of the Body (Basic Physiology); Breathing problems and flight at high altitude
3	B	PPL5 Human Factors; Health and Flying; Alcohol and Drugs
4	A	PPL5 Human Factors; Health and Flying; Toxic hazards
5	A	PPL5 Human Factors; The Functions of the Body (Basic Physiology); Breathing problems and flight at high altitude
6	B	PPL5 Human Factors; The Functions of the Body (Basic Physiology); The Ears
7	A	PPL5 Human Factors; The Functions of the Body (Basic Physiology); Breathing problems and flight at high altitude
8	C	PPL5 Human Factors; The Functions of the Mind (Basic Psychology); Spatial disorientation, visual illusions
9	C	PPL5 Human Factors; The Functions of the Body (Basic Physiology); The breathing machine
10	C	PPL5 Human Factors; Health and Flying; Incapacitation
11	B	PPL5 Human Factors; The Functions of the Body (Basic Physiology); Breathing problems and flight at high altitude
12	A	PPL5 Human Factors; The Functions of the Mind (Basic Psychology); Spatial disorientation, visual illusions
13	A	PPL5 Human Factors; The Functions of the Mind (Basic Psychology); Lookout
14	B	PPL5 Human Factors; Personalities and Cockpit Resource Management; Group decision making
15	C	PPL5 Human Factors; Personalities and Cockpit Resource Management; Group decision making
16	C	PPL5 Human Factors; Health and Flying; Alcohol and Drugs
17	A	PPL5 Human Factors; The Functions of the Body (Basic Physiology); The eyes
18	C	PPL5 Human Factors; Cockpit Design and Procedures; Flight instrument displays
19	B	PPL5 Human Factors; The Functions of the Mind (Basic Psychology); Lookout
20	A	PPL5 Human Factors; The Functions of the Mind (Basic Psychology); Spatial disorientation, visual illusions

Answers and Reference   Human Performance and Limitations

Paper 7

#	Ans	Reference
1	C	PPL5 Human Factors; The Functions of the Body (Basic Physiology); Breathing problems and flight at high altitude
2	C	PPL5 Human Factors; The Functions of the Mind (Basic Psychology); Spatial disorientation, visual illusions
3	B	PPL5 Human Factors; The Functions of the Body (Basic Physiology); Light aircraft oxygen systems
4	A	PPL5 Human Factors; The Functions of the Body (Basic Physiology); The ears
5	C	PPL5 Human Factors; The Functions of the Body (Basic Physiology); The breathing machine
6	A	PPL5 Human Factors; The Functions of the Body (Basic Physiology); The eyes
7	A	PPL5 Human Factors; Health and Flying; Alcohol and Drugs
8	B	PPL5 Human Factors; The Functions of the Body (Basic Physiology); Breathing problems and flight at high altitude
9	B	PPL5 Human Factors; The Functions of the Body (Basic Physiology); Breathing problems and flight at high altitude
10	C	PPL5 Human Factors; Cockpit Design and Procedures; Eye datum
11	A	PPL5 Human Factors; The Functions of the Mind (Basic Psychology); Situational awareness, confirmation bias
12	C	PPL5 Human Factors; The Functions of the Body (Basic Physiology); The ears
13	A	PPL5 Human Factors; The Functions of the Body (Basic Physiology); Breathing problems and flight at high altitude
14	C	PPL5 Human Factors; The Functions of the Mind (Basic Psychology); Situational awareness, confirmation bias
15	B	PPL5 Human Factors; Stress and Managing Stress; Stress, arousal and performance
16	A	PPL5 Human Factors; Safety and Survival Equipment; Motion Sickness
17	C	PPL5 Human Factors; The Functions of the Body (Basic Physiology); Breathing problems and flight at high altitude
18	C	PPL5 Human Factors; The Functions of the Mind (Basic Psychology); Spatial disorientation, visual illusions
19	B	PPL5 Human Factors; Cockpit Design and Procedures; Controls
20	A	PPL5 Human Factors; Cockpit Design and Procedures; Flight instrument displays

Answers and Reference Human Performance and Limitations

Paper 8

1	C	PPL5 Human Factors; The Functions of the Body (Basic Physiology); Breathing problems and flight at high altitude
2	B	PPL5 Human Factors; The Functions of the Mind (Basic Psychology); Spatial disorientation, visual illusions
3	B	PPL5 Human Factors; The Functions of the Mind (Basic Psychology); Lookout
4	C	PPL5 Human Factors; The Functions of the Body (Basic Physiology); Breathing problems and flight at high altitude
5	B	PPL5 Human Factors; The Functions of the Body (Basic Physiology); 'G' Effects
6	C	PPL5 Human Factors; The Functions of the Body (Basic Physiology); Breathing problems and flight at high altitude
7	A	PPL5 Human Factors; Health and Flying; Alcohol and Drugs
8	C	PPL5 Human Factors; Health and Flying; Toxic hazards
9	A	PPL5 Human Factors; The Functions of the Body (Basic Physiology); The eyes
10	C	PPL5 Human Factors; Personalities and Cockpit Resource Management; Hazardous attitudes
11	C	PPL5 Human Factors; Health and Flying; Alcohol and Drugs
12	C	PPL5 Human Factors; Stress and Managing Stress; Stress, arousal and performance
13	C	PPL5 Human Factors; Health and Flying; Alcohol and Drugs
14	C	PPL5 Human Factors; Health and Flying; Alcohol and Drugs
15	C	PPL5 Human Factors; Personalities and Cockpit Resource Management; Hazardous attitudes
16	C	PPL5 Human Factors; The Functions of the Mind (Basic Psychology); Spatial disorientation, visual illusions
17	B	PPL5 Human Factors; Health and Flying; Alcohol and Drugs
18	B	PPL5 Human Factors; The Functions of the Body (Basic Physiology); Light aircraft oxygen systems
19	C	PPL5 Human Factors; The Functions of the Mind (Basic Psychology); Spatial disorientation, visual illusions
20	A	PPL5 Human Factors; Cockpit Design and Procedures; Warnings

Answers and Reference — Human Performance and Limitations

Paper 9

#	Ans	Reference
1	C	PPL5 Human Factors; The Functions of the Body (Basic Physiology); Composition of the atmosphere
2	A	PPL5 Human Factors; The Functions of the Body (Basic Physiology); The eyes
3	B	PPL5 Human Factors; The Functions of the Mind (Basic Psychology); Lookout
4	B	PPL5 Human Factors; The Functions of the Body (Basic Physiology); 'G' Effects
5	A	PPL5 Human Factors; The Functions of the Body (Basic Physiology); The ears
6	C	PPL5 Human Factors; Health and Flying; Toxic hazards
7	B	PPL5 Human Factors; Health and Flying; Toxic hazards
8	A	PPL5 Human Factors; Health and Flying; Common ailments and medication
9	A	PPL5 Human Factors; The Functions of the Body (Basic Physiology); Breathing problems and flight at high altitude
10	B	PPL5 Human Factors; The Functions of the Mind (Basic Psychology); Lookout
11	C	PPL5 Human Factors; Health and Flying; Incapacitation
12	C	PPL5 Human Factors; Personalities and Cockpit Resource Management; Group decision making
13	A	PPL5 Human Factors; Health and Flying; Common ailments and medication
14	A	PPL5 Human Factors; Health and Flying; Alcohol and Drugs
15	A	PPL5 Human Factors; The Functions of the Body (Basic Physiology); The eyes
16	A	PPL5 Human Factors; The Functions of the Mind (Basic Psychology); Spatial disorientation, visual illusions
17	B	PPL5 Human Factors; Personalities and Cockpit Resource Management; Group decision making
18	A	PPL5 Human Factors; Stress and Managing Stress; Stress, arousal and performance
19	A	PPL5 Human Factors; Cockpit Design and Procedures; Flight instrument displays
20	C	PPL5 Human Factors; Health and Flying; Common ailments and medication

Answers and Reference Human Performance and Limitations

Paper 10

1	C	PPL5 Human Factors; Safety and Survival Equipment; Basics of survival
2	A	PPL5 Human Factors; Safety and Survival Equipment; Common survival equipment
3	B	PPL5 Human Factors; The Functions of the Body (Basic Physiology); Breathing problems and flight at high altitude
4	C	PPL5 Human Factors; The Functions of the Body (Basic Physiology); Breathing problems and flight at high altitude
5	C	PPL5 Human Factors; The Functions of the Body (Basic Physiology); The breathing machine
6	C	PPL5 Human Factors; The Functions of the Body (Basic Physiology); Breathing problems and flight at high altitude
7	B	PPL5 Human Factors; Cockpit Design and Procedures; Controls
8	C	PPL5 Human Factors; The Functions of the Body (Basic Physiology); The eyes
9	A	PPL5 Human Factors; The Functions of the Body (Basic Physiology); The eyes
10	B	PPL5 Human Factors; Health and Flying; Toxic hazards
11	A	PPL5 Human Factors; Personalities and Cockpit Resource Management; Group decision making
12	A	PPL5 Human Factors; Personalities and Cockpit Resource Management; Hazardous attitudes
13	B	PPL5 Human Factors; The Functions of the Mind (Basic Psychology); Spatial disorientation, visual illusions
14	A	PPL5 Human Factors; Personalities and Cockpit Resource Management; Hazardous attitudes
15	C	PPL5 Human Factors; Stress and Managing Stress; Stress, arousal and performance
16	C	PPL5 Human Factors; Stress and Managing Stress; Environmental stresses
17	A	PPL5 Human Factors; Health and Flying; Alcohol and Drugs
18	C	PPL5 Human Factors; Health and Flying; Incapacitation
19	A	PPL5 Human Factors; Personalities and Cockpit Resource Management; Group decision making
20	C	PPL5 Human Factors; Cockpit Design and Procedures; Flight instrument displays

Radiotelephony (RTF)

Paper 1

1	C	PPL2 Radiotelephony; Pre-flight; Use of the AIP
2	B	PPL2 Radiotelephony; En-route Procedures; VHF Direction Finding
3	C	PPL2 Radiotelephony; Pre-flight; Introduction to VHF Radio
4	A	PPL2 Radiotelephony; Departure Procedures; Standard Phraseology; *also* Glossary
5	C	PPL2 Radiotelephony; En-route Procedures; Level and Position Reporting
6	A	PPL2 Radiotelephony; En-route Procedures; Avoiding confusion; *also* Glossary
7	B	PPL2 Radiotelephony; En-route Procedures; Use of Transponder
8	C	PPL2 Radiotelephony; General Operating Procedures; Transmission of Numbers and Transmission of Time
9	C	PPL2 Radiotelephony; General Operating Procedures; Transmission of Numbers and Transmission of Time
10	A	PPL2 Radiotelephony; Departure Procedures; Items Requiring Read Back; *and* En-route Procedures; Items Requiring Read Back
11	C	PPL2 Radiotelephony; Callsigns, Abbreviations, General Procedures; Callsigns
12	A	PPL2 Radiotelephony; Emergency Procedures; Emergency Frequencies
13	B	PPL2 Radiotelephony; En-route Procedures; MATZs
14	C	PPL2 Radiotelephony; Departure Procedures; Items Requiring Read Back; *and* En-route Procedures; Items Requiring Read Back
15	C	PPL2 Radiotelephony; General Operating Procedures; Transmission of Numbers and Transmission of Time
16	B	PPL2 Radiotelephony; General Operating Procedures; Transmission of Numbers and Transmission of Time
17	C	PPL2 Radiotelephony; Departure Procedures; Departure Clearance/Departure Instructions
18	C	PPL2 Radiotelephony; En-route Procedures; Frequency Changing

19 **"Mayday, Mayday, Mayday**…

Name of Station Addressed	…Nottingham Radio…
Aircraft Callsign	…G-DINA…
Aircraft Type	…AA-5…
Nature of Emergency	…Engine failure…
Intentions of Pilot	immediate forced landing 27…
Position/level/heading	position 2 miles north of airfield, 2500ft QNH, heading 090…
Pilot qualifications	student (tyro) pilot …
Any other information	… one person on board"

Answers and Reference — Radiotelephony

Paper 2

#	Ans	Reference
1	A	PPL2 Radiotelephony; En-route Procedures; Use of Transponder
2	A	PPL2 Radiotelephony; Departure Procedures; Radio Check
3	A	PPL2 Radiotelephony; En-route Procedures; Frequency Changing
4	A	PPL2 Radiotelephony; Callsigns, Abbreviations, General Procedures; Callsigns
5	A	PPL2 Radiotelephony; En-route Procedures; Level and Position Reporting
6	C	PPL2 Radiotelephony; En-route Procedures; Use of Transponder
7	C	PPL2 Radiotelephony; General Operating Procedures; Transmission of Numbers and Transmission of Time
8	A	PPL2 Radiotelephony; Departure Procedures; Taxying Instructions, Holding Instructions, Take-off Instructions
9	B	PPL2 Radiotelephony; Departure Procedures; Items Requiring Read Back; *and* En-route Procedures; Items Requiring Read
10	C	PPL2 Radiotelephony; En-route Procedures; Standard Phraseology; *also* Establishing Contact – Passing Details
11	A	PPL2 Radiotelephony; Arrival/Traffic Pattern Procedures; Standard Circuit Procedures
12	C	PPL2 Radiotelephony; Emergency Procedures; Priority Messages
13	A	PPL2 Radiotelephony; En-route Procedures; Use of Transponder
14	C	PPL2 Radiotelephony; Departure Procedures; Conditional Clearances
15	B	PPL2 Radiotelephony; En-route Procedures; VOLMET and ATIS
16	B	PPL2 Radiotelephony; En-route Procedures; Airspace Classifications
17	C	PPL2 Radiotelephony; Emergency Procedures; Distress/Urgency Calls
18	B	PPL2 Radiotelephony; Emergency Procedures; Priority Messages

19   121.5 MHz

"**Pan Pan, Pan Pan, Pan Pan**...
Name of Station Addressed   ...London Centre...
Aircraft Callsign   ...G-BNHK...
Aircraft Type   ...C-152...
Nature of Emergency   ...Lost on a flight from Luton to Shobdon...
Intentions of Pilot   ...request position fix...
Position/level/heading   ... last known position Banbury at time 15, presently at 3000ft otswold QNH 1020, heading 260...
Pilot qualifications   ... student [tyro] pilot...
Any other information   ... flying solo [or one person on board]. One hour fuel emaining, transponder equipped"

Answers and Reference   Radiotelephony

Paper 3

1	A	PPL2 Radiotelephony; En-route Procedures; VHF Direction Finding
2	C	PPL2 Radiotelephony; En-route Procedures; Standard Phraseology; *also* Glossary
3	A	PPL2 Radiotelephony; Callsigns, Abbreviations, General Procedures; Callsigns
4	C	PPL2 Radiotelephony; Arrival/Traffic Pattern Procedures; Landing Clearance
5	C	PPL2 Radiotelephony; En-route Procedures; Level and Position Reporting
6	C	PPL2 Radiotelephony; En-route Procedures; Level and Position Reporting
7	A	PPL2 Radiotelephony; Departure Procedures; Items Requiring Read Back; *and* En-route Procedures; Items Requiring Read
8	B	PPL2 Radiotelephony; Departure Procedures; Taxying Instructions, Holding Instructions, Take-off Instructions
9	A	PPL2 Radiotelephony; Arrival/Traffic Pattern Procedures; Standard Circuit Procedures
10	C	PPL2 Radiotelephony; En-route Procedures; Frequency Changing
11	B	PPL2 Radiotelephony; Emergency Procedures; Priority Messages
12	C	PPL2 Radiotelephony; Callsigns, Abbreviations, General Procedures; Callsigns
13	A	PPL2 Radiotelephony; En-route Procedures; Radar and Non-Radar Services
14	A	PPL2 Radiotelephony; En-route Procedures; Establishing Contact – Passing Details
15	B	PPL2 Radiotelephony; Callsigns, Abbreviations, General Procedures; Spoken Abbreviations
16	C	PPL2 Radiotelephony; En-route Procedures; Radar and Non-Radar Services
17	C	PPL2 Radiotelephony; Arrival/Traffic Pattern Procedures; Landing Clearance
18	B	PPL2 Radiotelephony; Arrival/Traffic Pattern Procedures; Wake Turbulence

19   "**Pan Pan, Pan Pan, Pan Pan**…

Name of Station Addressed	…Sheffield Approach…
Aircraft Callsign	…G-BNSP…
Aircraft Type	…Slingsby…
Nature of Emergency	…rough running engine…
Intentions of Pilot	…routing to Finningley disused airfield for landing…
Position/level/heading	… 5 miles west of Finningley, Flight Level 55, heading 110…
Pilot qualifications	… PPL…
Any other information	… one person on board"

Answers and Reference — Radiotelephony

Paper 4

1	B	PPL2 Radiotelephony; En-route Procedures; Avoiding Confusion; *and* Glossary
2	C	PPL2 Radiotelephony; En-route Procedures; Level and Position Reporting
3	C	PPL2 Radiotelephony; En-route Procedures; Standard Phraseology; *and* Glossary
4	A	PPL2 Radiotelephony; Callsigns, Abbreviations, General Procedures; Callsigns
5	C	PPL2 Radiotelephony; General Operating Procedures; Transmission of Numbers and Transmission of Time
6	C	PPL2 Radiotelephony; Emergency Procedures; Priority Messages
7	C	PPL2 Radiotelephony; General Operating Procedures; Transmission of Numbers and Transmission of Time
8	B	PPL2 Radiotelephony; Arrival/Traffic Pattern Procedures; Go-around
9	C	PPL2 Radiotelephony; En-route Procedures; VHF Direction Finding
10	B	PPL2 Radiotelephony; Departure Procedures; Items Requiring Read Back; *and* Airfield Data and Taxy Instructions
11	A	PPL2 Radiotelephony; Departure Procedures; Departure Clearance/Departure Instructions
12	C	PPL2 Radiotelephony; En-route Procedures; Standard Phraseology; *also* Establishing Contact – Passing Details
13	C	PPL2 Radiotelephony; En-route Procedures; Use of Transponder
14	A	PPL2 Radiotelephony; Emergency Procedures; Emergency Facilities
15	A	PPL2 Radiotelephony; Emergency Procedures; Practice Emergencies
16	C	PPL2 Radiotelephony; En-route Procedures; Standard Phraseology; *also* Establishing Contact – Passing Details
17	A	PPL2 Radiotelephony; En-route Procedures; Airspace Classifications
18	C	PPL2 Radiotelephony; Departure Procedures; Items Requiring Read Back; *and* En-route Procedures; Items Requiring Read Back

19 **"Mayday, Mayday, Mayday**…

Name of Station Addressed	…Biggin Tower…
Aircraft Callsign	…G-BPZP…
Aircraft Type	…Robin DR400…
Nature of Emergency	…bird strike and canopy damage, some handling problems…
Intentions of Pilot	…immediate landing 03…
Position/level/heading	…downwind, 1000ft QFE, heading 200…
Pilot qualifications	… PPL …
Any other information	… two persons on board"

Answers and Reference — Radiotelephony

Paper 5

1	C	PPL2 Radiotelephony; Arrival/Traffic Pattern Procedures; Circuit Joining and Overhead Joins
2	A	PPL2 Radiotelephony; Callsigns, Abbreviations, General Procedures; Callsigns
3	A	PPL2 Radiotelephony; En-route Procedures; MATZs
4	B	PPL2 Radiotelephony; Emergency Procedures; Distress/Urgency Calls
5	C	PPL2 Radiotelephony; En-route Procedures; Use of Transponder
6	A	PPL2 Radiotelephony; Departure Procedures; Items Requiring Read Back; *and* En-route Procedures; Items Requiring Read Back
7	C	PPL2 Radiotelephony; En-route Procedures; Use of Transponder
8	C	PPL2 Radiotelephony; Emergency Procedures; Priority Messages
9	B	PPL2 Radiotelephony; Emergency Procedures; Maintenance of Silence
10	A	PPL2 Radiotelephony; Departure Procedures; Radio Check
11	B	PPL2 Radiotelephony; Departure Procedures; Roger
12	B	PPL2 Radiotelephony; Callsigns, Abbreviations, General Procedures; Spoken Abbreviations
13	B	PPL2 Radiotelephony; En-route Procedures; Radar and Non-Radar Services
14	C	PPL2 Radiotelephony; Emergency Procedures; Priority Messages
15	A	PPL2 Radiotelephony; Arrival/Traffic Pattern Procedures; Go-around
16	C	PPL2 Radiotelephony; Emergency Procedures; Distress/Urgency Calls
17	B	PPL2 Radiotelephony; En-route Procedures; Level and Position Reporting
18	B	PPL2 Radiotelephony; En-route Procedures; VOLMET and ATIS

19   "**Mayday, Mayday, Mayday**…

Name of Station Addressed	…Southampton Approach…
Aircraft Callsign	…Autoair 03…
Aircraft Type	…Piper Malibu…
Nature of Emergency	…complete engine failure…
Intentions of Pilot	…immediate forced landing Beaulieu disused airfield…
Position/level/heading	…1 mile north of Lymington, altitude 1500ft QFE, heading 40…
Pilot qualifications	… PPL …
Any other information	… two persons on board"

Answers and Reference   Radiotelephony

Paper 6

1. C   PPL2 Radiotelephony; Emergency Procedures; Practice Emergencies
2. B   PPL2 Radiotelephony; Departure Procedures; Radio Check
3. A   PPL2 Radiotelephony; En-route Procedures; Frequency Changing
4. B   PPL2 Radiotelephony; Callsigns, Abbreviations, General Procedures; Callsigns
5. B   PPL2 Radiotelephony; Arrival/Traffic Pattern Procedures; Go-around
6. C   PPL2 Radiotelephony; General Operating Procedures; Transmission of Numbers and Transmission of Time
7. A   PPL2 Radiotelephony; Departure Procedures; Departure Clearance/Departure Instructions
8. C   PPL2 Radiotelephony; Departure Procedures; Items Requiring Read Back; *and* En-route Procedures; Items Requiring Read Back
9. B   PPL2 Radiotelephony; Emergency Procedures; Priority Messages *and* Emergency Frequencies
10. C   PPL2 Radiotelephony; En-route Procedures; Level and Position Reporting
11. A   PPL2 Radiotelephony; En-route Procedures; Use of Transponder
12. A   PPL2 Radiotelephony; Departure Procedures; Conditional Clearances
13. C   PPL2 Radiotelephony; En-route Procedures; MATZs
14. C   PPL2 Radiotelephony; Callsigns, Abbreviations, General Procedures; Spoken Abbreviations
15. A   PPL2 Radiotelephony; En-route Procedures; Radar and Non-Radar Services
16. B   PPL2 Radiotelephony; Arrival/Traffic Pattern Procedures; Landing Clearance
17. C   PPL2 Radiotelephony; Emergency Procedures; Relay of Emergency Messages
18. C   PPL2 Radiotelephony; Air Traffic Service Units; Types of ATSU
19.   **"Pan Pan, Pan Pan, Pan Pan**…

Name of Station Addressed	…London Information…
Aircraft Callsign	…G-BNZG…
Aircraft Type	…Piper Arrow…
Nature of Emergency	…have in sight small boat in difficulties…
Intentions of Pilot	… I will keep the boat in sight until assistance arrives…
Position/level/heading	… position 10 miles south of Isle of Wight, at 3000ft altitude in right-hand orbit…
Pilot qualifications	… PPL IMC…
Any other information	… request that you notify the coastguard, will pass on exact position fix shortly"

Answers and Reference   Radiotelephony

Paper 7

1	B	PPL2 Radiotelephony; Departure Procedures; Radio Check
2	A	PPL2 Radiotelephony; En-route Procedures; Avoiding confusion; *also* Glossary
3	A	PPL2 Radiotelephony; En-route Procedures; Avoiding confusion; *also* Glossary
4	C	PPL2 Radiotelephony; En-route Procedures; Radar and Non-Radar Services
5	C	PPL2 Radiotelephony; General Operating Procedures; Transmission of Numbers and Transmission of Time
6	A	PPL2 Radiotelephony; Departure Procedures; Items Requiring Read Back; *and* En-route Procedures; Items Requiring Read Back
7	B	PPL2 Radiotelephony; Departure Procedures; Items Requiring Read Back; *and* En-route Procedures; Items Requiring Read Back
8	C	PPL2 Radiotelephony; General Operating Procedures; Transmission of Numbers and Transmission of Time
9	C	PPL2 Radiotelephony; Emergency Procedures; Priority Messages
10	A	PPL2 Radiotelephony; Departure Procedures; Immediate Take-off
11	B	PPL2 Radiotelephony; Emergency Procedures; Emergency Frequencies
12	C	PPL2 Radiotelephony; En-route Procedures; Radar and Non-Radar Services
13	B	PPL2 Radiotelephony; Arrival/Traffic Pattern Procedures; Landing Clearance
14	C	PPL2 Radiotelephony; En-route Procedures; Frequency Changing
15	A	PPL2 Radiotelephony; En-route Procedures; Radar and Non-Radar Services
16	B	PPL2 Radiotelephony; Air Traffic Service Units; Types of ATSU
17	A	PPL2 Radiotelephony; Callsigns, Abbreviations, General Procedures; Spoken Abbreviations
18	B	PPL2 Radiotelephony; Emergency Procedures; Practice Emergencies

19   "**Mayday, Mayday, Mayday**…

Name of Station Addressed	…Wycombe Tower…
Aircraft Callsign	…G-BXPS…
	…I have intercepted a **Mayday** from G-BNCR, I say again G-BNCR…
Aircraft Type	…Piper Warrior…
Nature of Emergency	…Engine fire…
Intentions of Pilot	…immediate forced landing…
Position/level/heading	…position 4 miles south of Thame, altitude 2000ft, heading 270…
Pilot qualifications	… CPL …
Any other information	… one person on board"

Answers and Reference   Radiotelephony

Paper 8

1	C	PPL2 Radiotelephony; General Operating Procedures; Transmission of Numbers and Transmission of Time
2	B	PPL2 Radiotelephony; En-route Procedures; VHF Direction Finding
3	A	PPL2 Radiotelephony; Departure Procedures; Standard Phraseology; *also* Over and Out
4	B	PPL2 Radiotelephony; En-route Procedures; Standard Phraseology; *also* Establishing Contact – Passing Details
5	C	PPL2 Radiotelephony; Departure Procedures; Conditional Clearances
6	B	PPL2 Radiotelephony; Arrival/Traffic Pattern Procedures; Landing Clearance
7	C	PPL2 Radiotelephony; Arrival/Traffic Pattern Procedures; Go-around
8	A	PPL2 Radiotelephony; Arrival/Traffic Pattern Procedures; Circuit Joining and Overhead Joins
9	B	PPL2 Radiotelephony; Emergency Procedures; Distress/Urgency Calls
10	C	PPL2 Radiotelephony; Arrival/Traffic Pattern Procedures; Touch and Go
11	C	PPL2 Radiotelephony; Emergency Procedures; Distress/Urgency Calls
12	A	PPL2 Radiotelephony; En-route Procedures; Use of Transponder
13	C	PPL2 Radiotelephony; Departure Procedures; Items Requiring Read Back;
14	A	PPL2 Radiotelephony; En-route Procedures; Use of Transponder
15	C	PPL2 Radiotelephony; En-route Procedures; Use of Transponder
16	A	PPL2 Radiotelephony; En-route Procedures; Radar and Non-Radar Services
17	A	PPL2 Radiotelephony; En-route Procedures; Use of Transponder
18	B	PPL2 Radiotelephony; Callsigns, Abbreviations, General Procedures; Callsigns

19   "**Pan Pan, Pan Pan, Pan Pan**…

Name of Station Addressed	…Bristol Approach…
Aircraft Callsign	…G-DASH…
Aircraft Type	…Rockwell Commander…
Nature of Emergency	…rough running engine…
Intentions of Pilot	…diverting to Bristol airfield for landing…
Position/level/heading	… 1 mile west of Clevedon, Flight Level 50, heading 160…
Pilot qualifications	… PPL…
Any other information	… three persons on board"

Answers and Reference Radiotelephony

Paper 9

1	C	PPL2 Radiotelephony; General Operating Procedures; Transmission of Numbers and Transmission of Time
2	C	PPL2 Radiotelephony; Departure Procedures; Radio Check
3	B	PPL2 Radiotelephony; Departure Procedures; Standard Phraseology; *also* Glossary
4	C	PPL2 Radiotelephony; Callsigns, Abbreviations, General Procedures; Callsigns
5	C	PPL2 Radiotelephony; En-route Procedures; Standard Phraseology; *also* Establishing Contact – Passing Details
6	A	PPL2 Radiotelephony; En-route Procedures; Standard Phraseology *also* Frequency Changing
7	C	PPL2 Radiotelephony; General Operating Procedures; Transmission of Numbers and Transmission of Time
8	C	PPL2 Radiotelephony; Departure Procedures; Taxying Instructions, Holding Instructions, Take-off Instructions
9	C	PPL2 Radiotelephony; Air Traffic Service Units; Types of ATSU
10	B	PPL2 Radiotelephony; En-route Procedures; Use of Transponder
11	A	PPL2 Radiotelephony; Emergency Procedures; Priority Messages
12	A	PPL2 Radiotelephony; En-route Procedures; Radar and Non-Radar Services
13	B	PPL2 Radiotelephony; Arrival/Traffic Pattern Procedures; Landing Clearance
14	A	PPL2 Radiotelephony; Arrival/Traffic Pattern Procedures; Standard Circuit Procedures
15	C	PPL2 Radiotelephony; En-route Procedures; ATZs; *also* MATZs
16	B	PPL2 Radiotelephony; Departure Procedures; Items Requiring Read Back; *and* En-route Procedures; Items Requiring Read Back
17	C	PPL2 Radiotelephony; En-route Procedures; Frequency Changing
18	A	PPL2 Radiotelephony; Emergency Procedures; Relay of Emergency Messages
19		"**Pan Pan, Pan Pan, Pan Pan**" **N**ame of Station Addressed **A**ircraft Callsign **A**ircraft Type **N**ature of Emergency **I**ntentions of Pilot **P**osition/level/heading **P**ilot qualifications **A**ny other information

Answers and Reference Radiotelephony

Paper 10

1	C	PPL2 Radiotelephony; En-route Procedures; MATZs
2	B	PPL2 Radiotelephony; General Operating Procedures; Transmission of Numbers and Transmission of Time
3	C	PPL2 Radiotelephony; Arrival/Traffic Pattern Procedures; Vacating the Runway and Taxy Instructions
4	A	PPL2 Radiotelephony; En-route Procedures; Radar and Non-Radar Services
5	B	PPL2 Radiotelephony; General Operating Procedures; Transmission of Numbers and Transmission of Time
6	C	PPL2 Radiotelephony; En-route Procedures; Standard Phraseology; *also* Establishing Contact – Passing Details
7	A	PPL2 Radiotelephony; Arrival/Traffic Pattern Procedures; Landing Clearance
8	C	PPL2 Radiotelephony; En-route Procedures; Use of Transponder
9	C	PPL2 Radiotelephony; Emergency Procedures; Maintenance of Silence
10	A	PPL2 Radiotelephony; Emergency Procedures; Priority Messages
11	B	PPL2 Radiotelephony; Emergency Procedures; Practice Emergencies
12	B	PPL2 Radiotelephony; Air Traffic Service Units; Types of ATSU
13	A	PPL2 Radiotelephony; Departure Procedures; Items Requiring Read Back; *and* En-route Procedures; Items Requiring Read Back
14	C	PPL2 Radiotelephony; En-route Procedures; Radar and Non-Radar Services
15	B	PPL2 Radiotelephony; En-route Procedures; Avoiding confusion
16	C	PPL2 Radiotelephony; Arrival/Traffic Pattern Procedures; Landing Clearance
17	A	PPL2 Radiotelephony; Arrival/Traffic Pattern Procedures; Landing Clearance
18	C	PPL2 Radiotelephony; Callsigns, Abbreviations, General Procedures; Callsigns
19		**"Mayday, Mayday, Mayday"**
		Name of Station Addressed
		Aircraft Callsign
		Aircraft Type
		Nature of Emergency
		Intentions of Pilot
		Position/level/heading
		Pilot qualifications
		Any other information

Student Answer Sheets

Answers Sheet   Aviation Law

	Paper 1				Paper 2		
	A	B	C		A	B	C
1	☐	☐	☐	1	☐	☐	☐
2	☐	☐	☐	2	☐	☐	☐
3	☐	☐	☐	3	☐	☐	☐
4	☐	☐	☐	4	☐	☐	☐
5	☐	☐	☐	5	☐	☐	☐
6	☐	☐	☐	6	☐	☐	☐
7	☐	☐	☐	7	☐	☐	☐
8	☐	☐	☐	8	☐	☐	☐
9	☐	☐	☐	9	☐	☐	☐
10	☐	☐	☐	10	☐	☐	☐
11	☐	☐	☐	11	☐	☐	☐
12	☐	☐	☐	12	☐	☐	☐
13	☐	☐	☐	13	☐	☐	☐
14	☐	☐	☐	14	☐	☐	☐
15	☐	☐	☐	15	☐	☐	☐
16	☐	☐	☐	16	☐	☐	☐
17	☐	☐	☐	17	☐	☐	☐
18	☐	☐	☐	18	☐	☐	☐
19	☐	☐	☐	19	☐	☐	☐
20	☐	☐	☐	20	☐	☐	☐
21	☐	☐	☐	21	☐	☐	☐
22	☐	☐	☐	22	☐	☐	☐
23	☐	☐	☐	23	☐	☐	☐
24	☐	☐	☐	24	☐	☐	☐
25	☐	☐	☐	25	☐	☐	☐

Answers Sheet Aviation Law

	Paper 3				Paper 4		
	A	B	C		A	B	C
1	☐	☐	☐	1	☐	☐	☐
2	☐	☐	☐	2	☐	☐	☐
3	☐	☐	☐	3	☐	☐	☐
4	☐	☐	☐	4	☐	☐	☐
5	☐	☐	☐	5	☐	☐	☐
6	☐	☐	☐	6	☐	☐	☐
7	☐	☐	☐	7	☐	☐	☐
8	☐	☐	☐	8	☐	☐	☐
9	☐	☐	☐	9	☐	☐	☐
10	☐	☐	☐	10	☐	☐	☐
11	☐	☐	☐	11	☐	☐	☐
12	☐	☐	☐	12	☐	☐	☐
13	☐	☐	☐	13	☐	☐	☐
14	☐	☐	☐	14	☐	☐	☐
15	☐	☐	☐	15	☐	☐	☐
16	☐	☐	☐	16	☐	☐	☐
17	☐	☐	☐	17	☐	☐	☐
18	☐	☐	☐	18	☐	☐	☐
19	☐	☐	☐	19	☐	☐	☐
20	☐	☐	☐	20	☐	☐	☐
21	☐	☐	☐	21	☐	☐	☐
22	☐	☐	☐	22	☐	☐	☐
23	☐	☐	☐	23	☐	☐	☐
24	☐	☐	☐	24	☐	☐	☐
25	☐	☐	☐	25	☐	☐	☐

Answers Sheet Meteorology

Paper 5

Paper 4

Paper 3

Paper 2

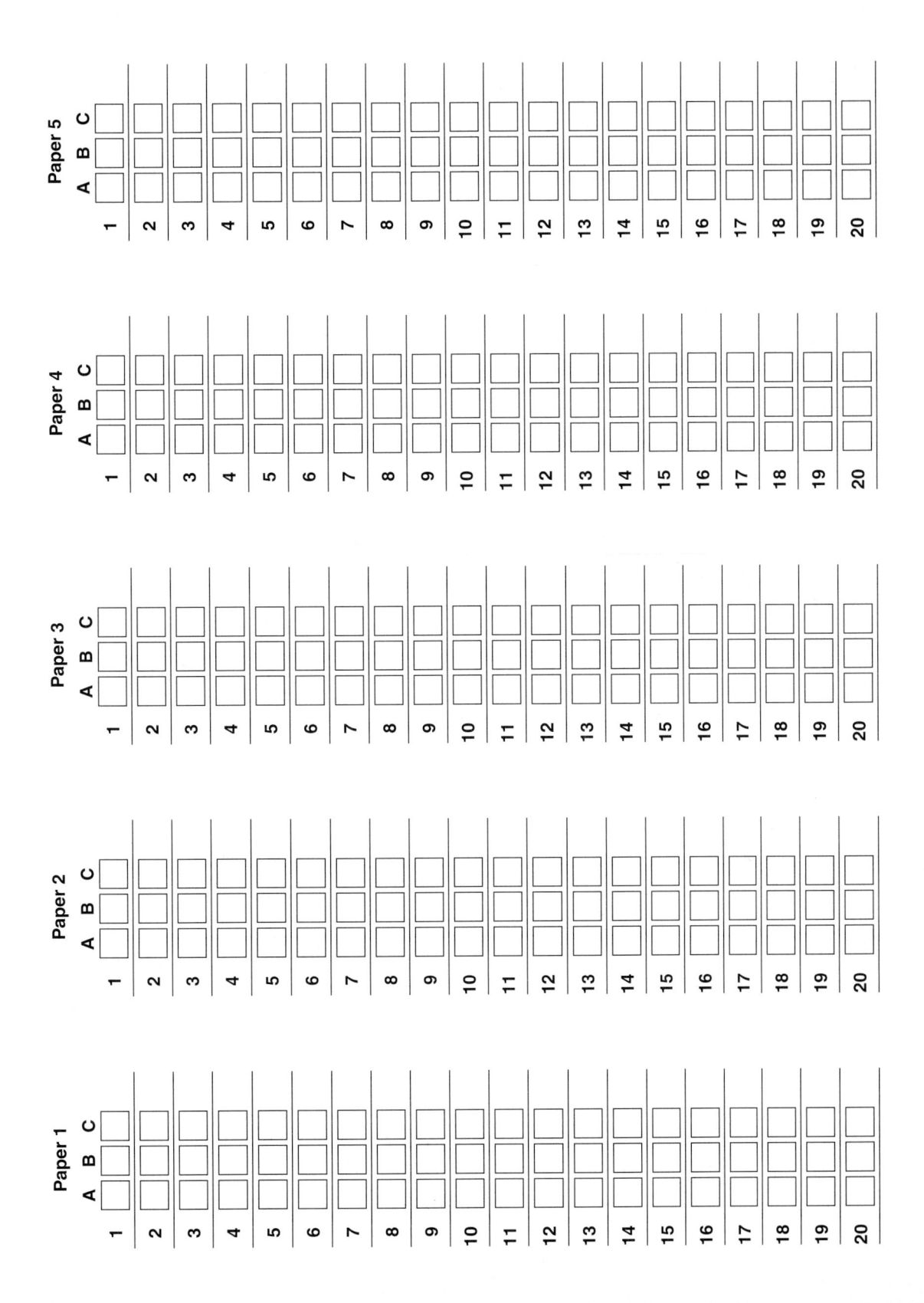

Paper 1

Answers Sheet

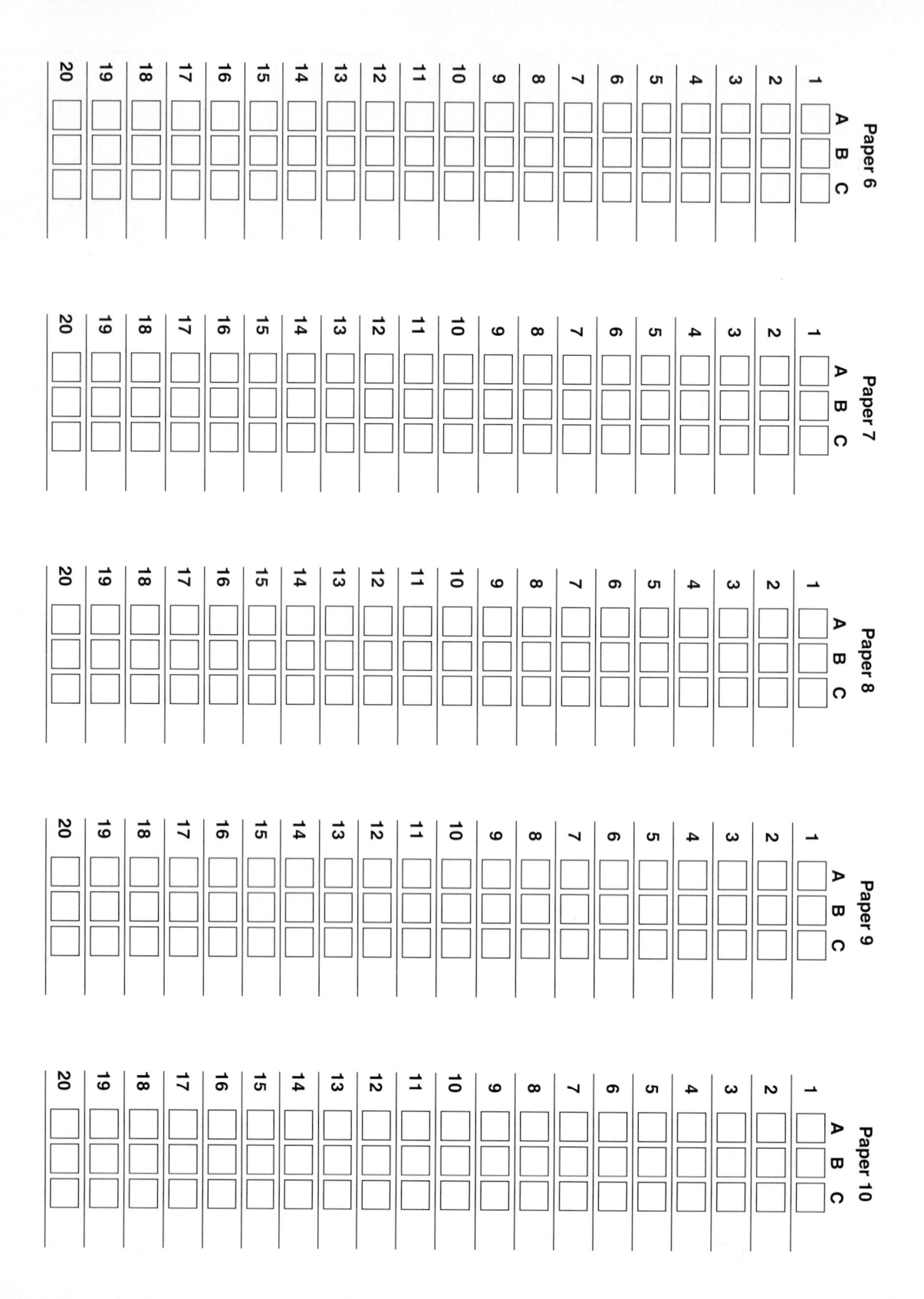

Meteorology

Paper 6

Paper 7

Paper 8

Paper 9

Paper 10

Answers Sheet Navigation

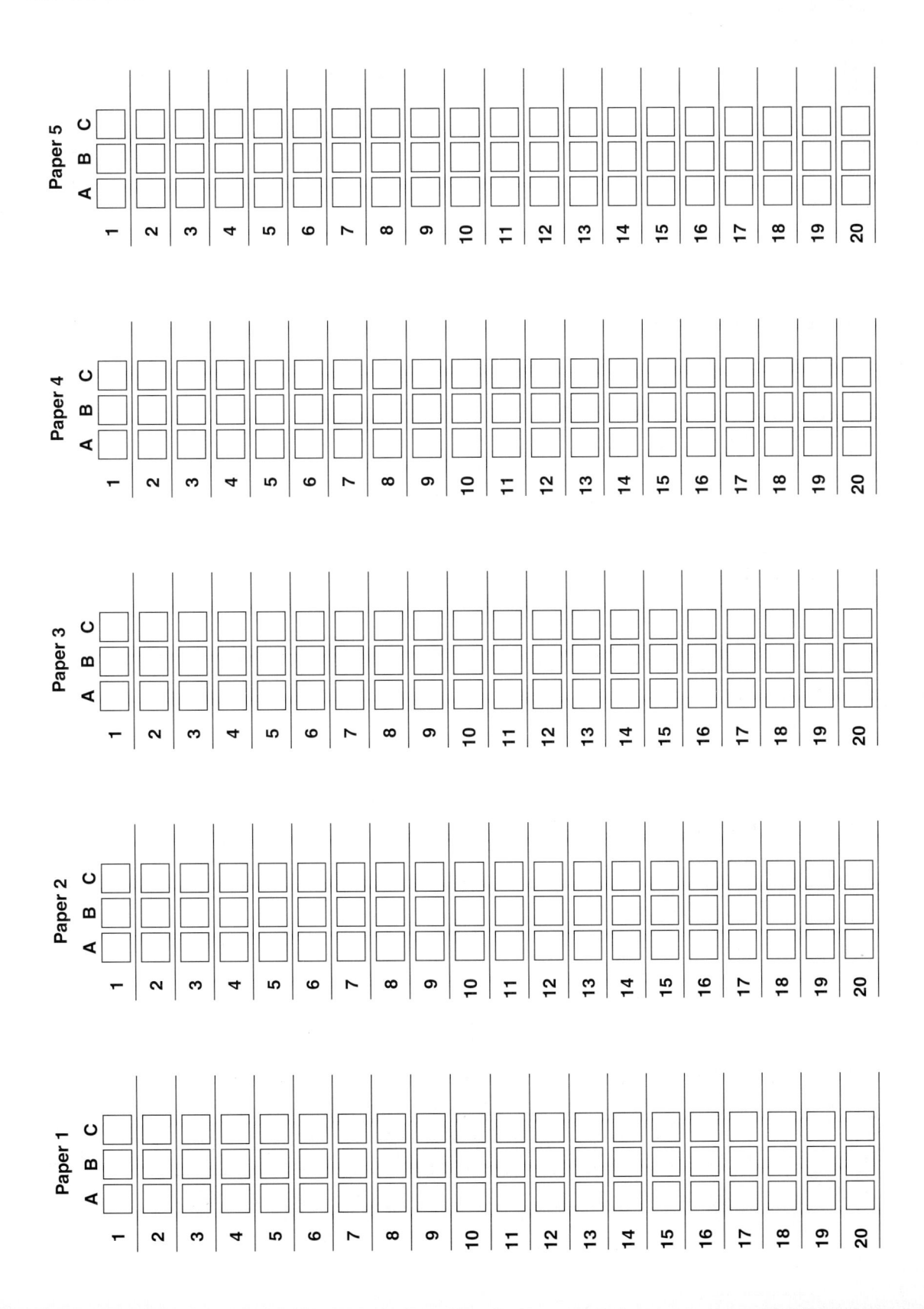

Paper 5
	1	2	3	4	5	6	7	8	9	10	11	12	13	14	15	16	17	18	19	20
A	☐	☐	☐	☐	☐	☐	☐	☐	☐	☐	☐	☐	☐	☐	☐	☐	☐	☐	☐	☐
B	☐	☐	☐	☐	☐	☐	☐	☐	☐	☐	☐	☐	☐	☐	☐	☐	☐	☐	☐	☐
C	☐	☐	☐	☐	☐	☐	☐	☐	☐	☐	☐	☐	☐	☐	☐	☐	☐	☐	☐	☐

Paper 4
	1	2	3	4	5	6	7	8	9	10	11	12	13	14	15	16	17	18	19	20
A	☐	☐	☐	☐	☐	☐	☐	☐	☐	☐	☐	☐	☐	☐	☐	☐	☐	☐	☐	☐
B	☐	☐	☐	☐	☐	☐	☐	☐	☐	☐	☐	☐	☐	☐	☐	☐	☐	☐	☐	☐
C	☐	☐	☐	☐	☐	☐	☐	☐	☐	☐	☐	☐	☐	☐	☐	☐	☐	☐	☐	☐

Paper 3
	1	2	3	4	5	6	7	8	9	10	11	12	13	14	15	16	17	18	19	20
A	☐	☐	☐	☐	☐	☐	☐	☐	☐	☐	☐	☐	☐	☐	☐	☐	☐	☐	☐	☐
B	☐	☐	☐	☐	☐	☐	☐	☐	☐	☐	☐	☐	☐	☐	☐	☐	☐	☐	☐	☐
C	☐	☐	☐	☐	☐	☐	☐	☐	☐	☐	☐	☐	☐	☐	☐	☐	☐	☐	☐	☐

Paper 2
	1	2	3	4	5	6	7	8	9	10	11	12	13	14	15	16	17	18	19	20
A	☐	☐	☐	☐	☐	☐	☐	☐	☐	☐	☐	☐	☐	☐	☐	☐	☐	☐	☐	☐
B	☐	☐	☐	☐	☐	☐	☐	☐	☐	☐	☐	☐	☐	☐	☐	☐	☐	☐	☐	☐
C	☐	☐	☐	☐	☐	☐	☐	☐	☐	☐	☐	☐	☐	☐	☐	☐	☐	☐	☐	☐

Paper 1
	1	2	3	4	5	6	7	8	9	10	11	12	13	14	15	16	17	18	19	20
A	☐	☐	☐	☐	☐	☐	☐	☐	☐	☐	☐	☐	☐	☐	☐	☐	☐	☐	☐	☐
B	☐	☐	☐	☐	☐	☐	☐	☐	☐	☐	☐	☐	☐	☐	☐	☐	☐	☐	☐	☐
C	☐	☐	☐	☐	☐	☐	☐	☐	☐	☐	☐	☐	☐	☐	☐	☐	☐	☐	☐	☐

Answers Sheet Navigation

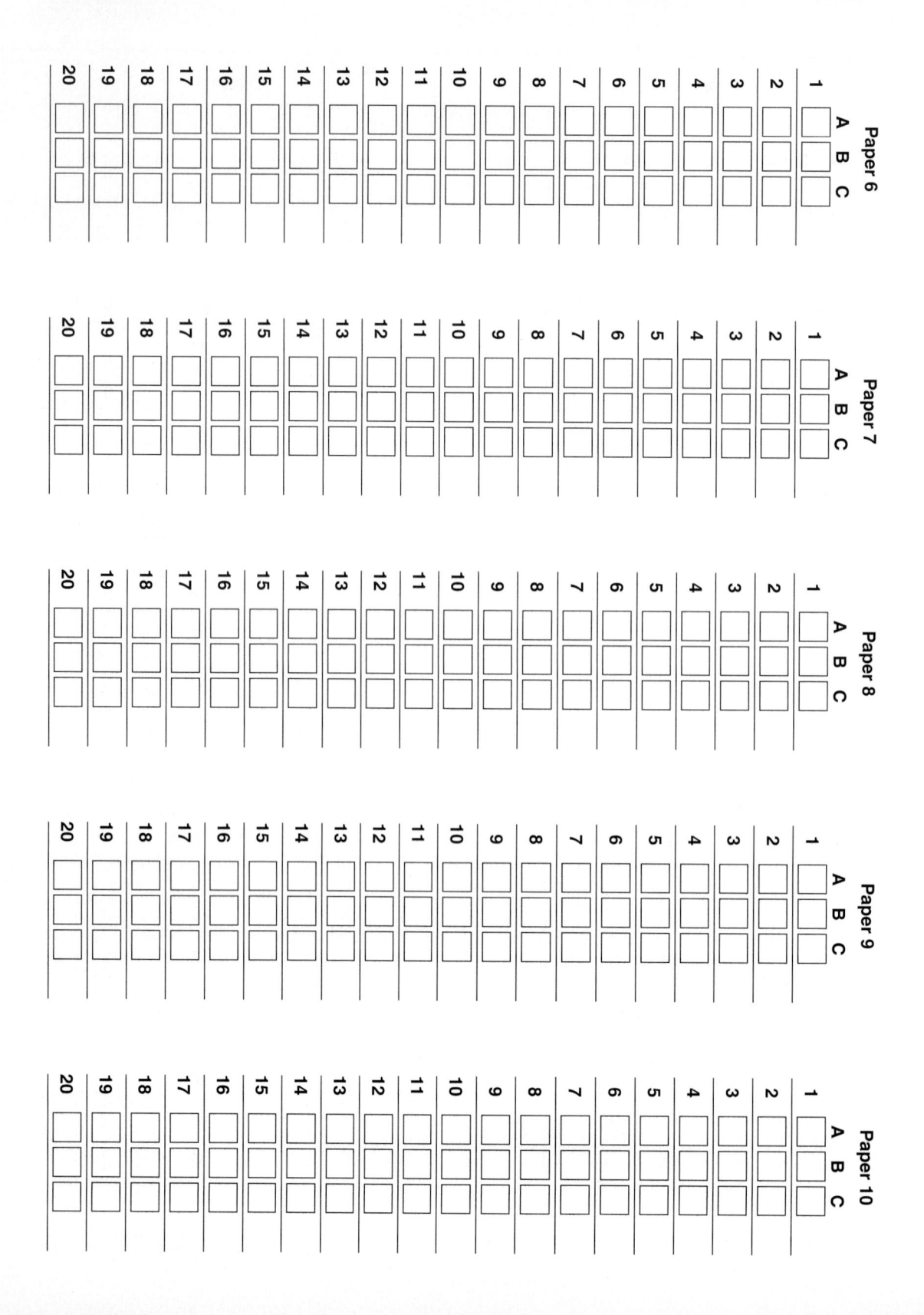

Paper 6 | A B C | 1–20
Paper 7 | A B C | 1–20
Paper 8 | A B C | 1–20
Paper 9 | A B C | 1–20
Paper 10 | A B C | 1–20

Answers Sheet Aircraft General (Aeroplanes)

Paper 1

	A	B	C		A	B	C
1				26			
2				27			
3				28			
4				29			
5				30			
6				31			
7				32			
8				33			
9				34			
10				35			
11				36			
12				37			
13				38			
14				39			
15				40			
16				41			
17				42			
18				43			
19				44			
20				45			
21				46			
22				47			
23				48			
24				49			
25				50			

Paper 2

	A	B	C		A	B	C
1				26			
2				27			
3				28			
4				29			
5				30			
6				31			
7				32			
8				33			
9				34			
10				35			
11				36			
12				37			
13				38			
14				39			
15				40			
16				41			
17				42			
18				43			
19				44			
20				45			
21				46			
22				47			
23				48			
24				49			
25				50			

Answers Sheet

Aircraft General (Aeroplanes)

Paper 3

	A	B	C		A	B	C
1	☐	☐	☐	26	☐	☐	☐
2	☐	☐	☐	27	☐	☐	☐
3	☐	☐	☐	28	☐	☐	☐
4	☐	☐	☐	29	☐	☐	☐
5	☐	☐	☐	30	☐	☐	☐
6	☐	☐	☐	31	☐	☐	☐
7	☐	☐	☐	32	☐	☐	☐
8	☐	☐	☐	33	☐	☐	☐
9	☐	☐	☐	34	☐	☐	☐
10	☐	☐	☐	35	☐	☐	☐
11	☐	☐	☐	36	☐	☐	☐
12	☐	☐	☐	37	☐	☐	☐
13	☐	☐	☐	38	☐	☐	☐
14	☐	☐	☐	39	☐	☐	☐
15	☐	☐	☐	40	☐	☐	☐
16	☐	☐	☐	41	☐	☐	☐
17	☐	☐	☐	42	☐	☐	☐
18	☐	☐	☐	43	☐	☐	☐
19	☐	☐	☐	44	☐	☐	☐
20	☐	☐	☐	45	☐	☐	☐
21	☐	☐	☐	46	☐	☐	☐
22	☐	☐	☐	47	☐	☐	☐
23	☐	☐	☐	48	☐	☐	☐
24	☐	☐	☐	49	☐	☐	☐
25	☐	☐	☐	50	☐	☐	☐

Paper 4

	A	B	C		A	B	C
1	☐	☐	☐	26	☐	☐	☐
2	☐	☐	☐	27	☐	☐	☐
3	☐	☐	☐	28	☐	☐	☐
4	☐	☐	☐	29	☐	☐	☐
5	☐	☐	☐	30	☐	☐	☐
6	☐	☐	☐	31	☐	☐	☐
7	☐	☐	☐	32	☐	☐	☐
8	☐	☐	☐	33	☐	☐	☐
9	☐	☐	☐	34	☐	☐	☐
10	☐	☐	☐	35	☐	☐	☐
11	☐	☐	☐	36	☐	☐	☐
12	☐	☐	☐	37	☐	☐	☐
13	☐	☐	☐	38	☐	☐	☐
14	☐	☐	☐	39	☐	☐	☐
15	☐	☐	☐	40	☐	☐	☐
16	☐	☐	☐	41	☐	☐	☐
17	☐	☐	☐	42	☐	☐	☐
18	☐	☐	☐	43	☐	☐	☐
19	☐	☐	☐	44	☐	☐	☐
20	☐	☐	☐	45	☐	☐	☐
21	☐	☐	☐	46	☐	☐	☐
22	☐	☐	☐	47	☐	☐	☐
23	☐	☐	☐	48	☐	☐	☐
24	☐	☐	☐	49	☐	☐	☐
25	☐	☐	☐	50	☐	☐	☐

Answers Sheet

Human Performance and Limitations

Paper 5

	1	2	3	4	5	6	7	8	9	10	11	12	13	14	15	16	17	18	19	20
A	☐	☐	☐	☐	☐	☐	☐	☐	☐	☐	☐	☐	☐	☐	☐	☐	☐	☐	☐	☐
B	☐	☐	☐	☐	☐	☐	☐	☐	☐	☐	☐	☐	☐	☐	☐	☐	☐	☐	☐	☐
C	☐	☐	☐	☐	☐	☐	☐	☐	☐	☐	☐	☐	☐	☐	☐	☐	☐	☐	☐	☐

Paper 4

	1	2	3	4	5	6	7	8	9	10	11	12	13	14	15	16	17	18	19	20
A	☐	☐	☐	☐	☐	☐	☐	☐	☐	☐	☐	☐	☐	☐	☐	☐	☐	☐	☐	☐
B	☐	☐	☐	☐	☐	☐	☐	☐	☐	☐	☐	☐	☐	☐	☐	☐	☐	☐	☐	☐
C	☐	☐	☐	☐	☐	☐	☐	☐	☐	☐	☐	☐	☐	☐	☐	☐	☐	☐	☐	☐

Paper 3

	1	2	3	4	5	6	7	8	9	10	11	12	13	14	15	16	17	18	19	20
A	☐	☐	☐	☐	☐	☐	☐	☐	☐	☐	☐	☐	☐	☐	☐	☐	☐	☐	☐	☐
B	☐	☐	☐	☐	☐	☐	☐	☐	☐	☐	☐	☐	☐	☐	☐	☐	☐	☐	☐	☐
C	☐	☐	☐	☐	☐	☐	☐	☐	☐	☐	☐	☐	☐	☐	☐	☐	☐	☐	☐	☐

Paper 2

	1	2	3	4	5	6	7	8	9	10	11	12	13	14	15	16	17	18	19	20
A	☐	☐	☐	☐	☐	☐	☐	☐	☐	☐	☐	☐	☐	☐	☐	☐	☐	☐	☐	☐
B	☐	☐	☐	☐	☐	☐	☐	☐	☐	☐	☐	☐	☐	☐	☐	☐	☐	☐	☐	☐
C	☐	☐	☐	☐	☐	☐	☐	☐	☐	☐	☐	☐	☐	☐	☐	☐	☐	☐	☐	☐

Paper 1

	1	2	3	4	5	6	7	8	9	10	11	12	13	14	15	16	17	18	19	20
A	☐	☐	☐	☐	☐	☐	☐	☐	☐	☐	☐	☐	☐	☐	☐	☐	☐	☐	☐	☐
B	☐	☐	☐	☐	☐	☐	☐	☐	☐	☐	☐	☐	☐	☐	☐	☐	☐	☐	☐	☐
C	☐	☐	☐	☐	☐	☐	☐	☐	☐	☐	☐	☐	☐	☐	☐	☐	☐	☐	☐	☐

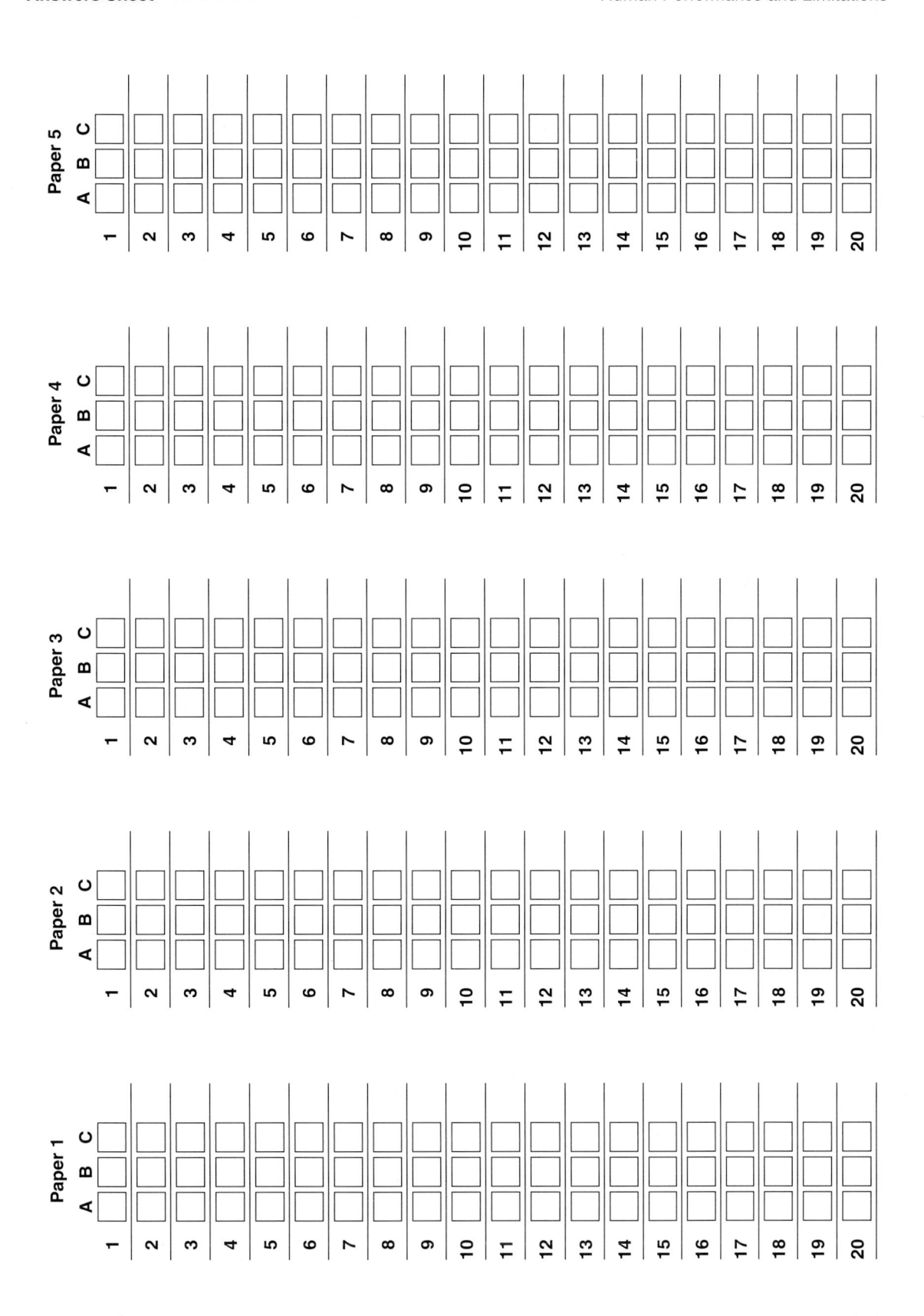

Answers Sheet

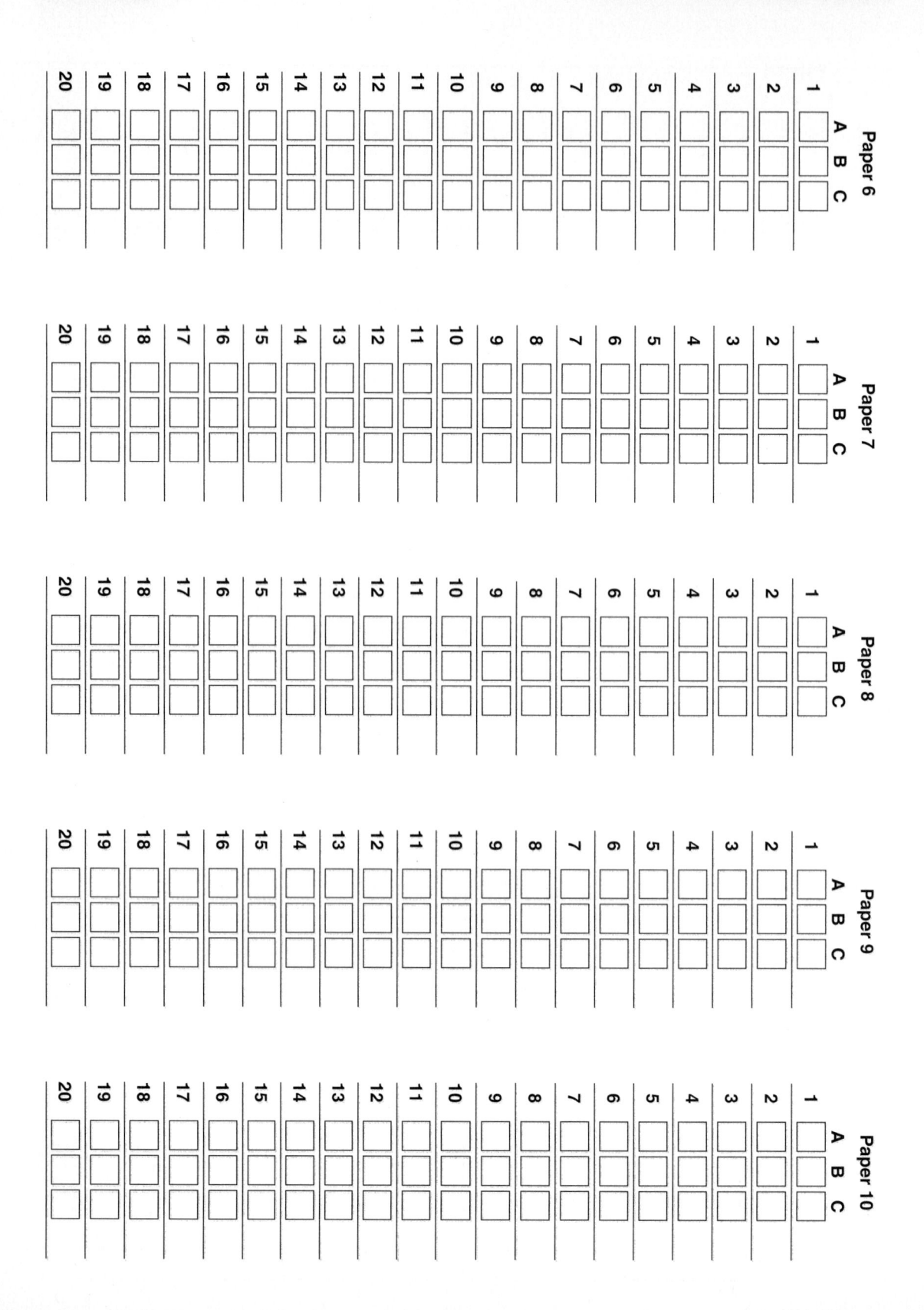

Human Performance and Limitations

Paper 6

Paper 7

Paper 8

Paper 9

Paper 10

Answers Sheet Radiotelephony

Paper 1

	A	B	C
1	☐	☐	☐
2	☐	☐	☐
3	☐	☐	☐
4	☐	☐	☐
5	☐	☐	☐
6	☐	☐	☐
7	☐	☐	☐
8	☐	☐	☐
9	☐	☐	☐
10	☐	☐	☐
11	☐	☐	☐
12	☐	☐	☐
13	☐	☐	☐
14	☐	☐	☐
15	☐	☐	☐
16	☐	☐	☐
17	☐	☐	☐
18	☐	☐	☐

19.

Paper 2

	A	B	C
1	☐	☐	☐
2	☐	☐	☐
3	☐	☐	☐
4	☐	☐	☐
5	☐	☐	☐
6	☐	☐	☐
7	☐	☐	☐
8	☐	☐	☐
9	☐	☐	☐
10	☐	☐	☐
11	☐	☐	☐
12	☐	☐	☐
13	☐	☐	☐
14	☐	☐	☐
15	☐	☐	☐
16	☐	☐	☐
17	☐	☐	☐
18	☐	☐	☐

19.

Answers Sheet Radiotelephony

Paper 3

	A	B	C
1	☐	☐	☐
2	☐	☐	☐
3	☐	☐	☐
4	☐	☐	☐
5	☐	☐	☐
6	☐	☐	☐
7	☐	☐	☐
8	☐	☐	☐
9	☐	☐	☐
10	☐	☐	☐
11	☐	☐	☐
12	☐	☐	☐
13	☐	☐	☐
14	☐	☐	☐
15	☐	☐	☐
16	☐	☐	☐
17	☐	☐	☐
18	☐	☐	☐

19.

Paper 4

	A	B	C
1	☐	☐	☐
2	☐	☐	☐
3	☐	☐	☐
4	☐	☐	☐
5	☐	☐	☐
6	☐	☐	☐
7	☐	☐	☐
8	☐	☐	☐
9	☐	☐	☐
10	☐	☐	☐
11	☐	☐	☐
12	☐	☐	☐
13	☐	☐	☐
14	☐	☐	☐
15	☐	☐	☐
16	☐	☐	☐
17	☐	☐	☐
18	☐	☐	☐

19.

Answers Sheet Radiotelephony

	Paper 5					Paper 6		
	A	B	C			A	B	C
1	☐	☐	☐		1	☐	☐	☐
2	☐	☐	☐		2	☐	☐	☐
3	☐	☐	☐		3	☐	☐	☐
4	☐	☐	☐		4	☐	☐	☐
5	☐	☐	☐		5	☐	☐	☐
6	☐	☐	☐		6	☐	☐	☐
7	☐	☐	☐		7	☐	☐	☐
8	☐	☐	☐		8	☐	☐	☐
9	☐	☐	☐		9	☐	☐	☐
10	☐	☐	☐		10	☐	☐	☐
11	☐	☐	☐		11	☐	☐	☐
12	☐	☐	☐		12	☐	☐	☐
13	☐	☐	☐		13	☐	☐	☐
14	☐	☐	☐		14	☐	☐	☐
15	☐	☐	☐		15	☐	☐	☐
16	☐	☐	☐		16	☐	☐	☐
17	☐	☐	☐		17	☐	☐	☐
18	☐	☐	☐		18	☐	☐	☐

19

19

Answers Sheet

Radiotelephony

Paper 7

	A	B	C
1	☐	☐	☐
2	☐	☐	☐
3	☐	☐	☐
4	☐	☐	☐
5	☐	☐	☐
6	☐	☐	☐
7	☐	☐	☐
8	☐	☐	☐
9	☐	☐	☐
10	☐	☐	☐
11	☐	☐	☐
12	☐	☐	☐
13	☐	☐	☐
14	☐	☐	☐
15	☐	☐	☐
16	☐	☐	☐
17	☐	☐	☐
18	☐	☐	☐

19.

Paper 8

	A	B	C
1	☐	☐	☐
2	☐	☐	☐
3	☐	☐	☐
4	☐	☐	☐
5	☐	☐	☐
6	☐	☐	☐
7	☐	☐	☐
8	☐	☐	☐
9	☐	☐	☐
10	☐	☐	☐
11	☐	☐	☐
12	☐	☐	☐
13	☐	☐	☐
14	☐	☐	☐
15	☐	☐	☐
16	☐	☐	☐
17	☐	☐	☐
18	☐	☐	☐

19.

Answers Sheet Radiotelephony

	Paper 9					Paper 10		
	A	B	C			A	B	C
1	☐	☐	☐		1	☐	☐	☐
2	☐	☐	☐		2	☐	☐	☐
3	☐	☐	☐		3	☐	☐	☐
4	☐	☐	☐		4	☐	☐	☐
5	☐	☐	☐		5	☐	☐	☐
6	☐	☐	☐		6	☐	☐	☐
7	☐	☐	☐		7	☐	☐	☐
8	☐	☐	☐		8	☐	☐	☐
9	☐	☐	☐		9	☐	☐	☐
10	☐	☐	☐		10	☐	☐	☐
11	☐	☐	☐		11	☐	☐	☐
12	☐	☐	☐		12	☐	☐	☐
13	☐	☐	☐		13	☐	☐	☐
14	☐	☐	☐		14	☐	☐	☐
15	☐	☐	☐		15	☐	☐	☐
16	☐	☐	☐		16	☐	☐	☐
17	☐	☐	☐		17	☐	☐	☐
18	☐	☐	☐		18	☐	☐	☐

19

19